DATE DUE

FEB 1 6 1999	
NOV 1 6 1999	
Gibsons & District	
due June 30/00	
MAR 1 2 2001	
OCT 1 9 2004	

BRODART   Cat. No. 23-221

Prenatal Testing

Prenatal Testing

A SOCIOLOGICAL PERSPECTIVE

Aliza Kolker & B. Meredith Burke

Foreword by
ARTHUR L. CAPLAN

BERGIN & GARVEY
Westport, Connecticut • London

Library of Congress Cataloging-in-Publication Data

Kolker, Aliza.
 Prenatal testing : a sociological perspective / Aliza Kolker and
B. Meredith Burke ; foreword by Arthur L. Caplan.
  p. cm.
 Includes bibliographical references and index.
 ISBN 0–89789–337–9 (alk. paper)
 1. Prenatal diagnosis—Social aspects. 2. Genetic counseling—
Social aspects. 3. Prenatal diagnosis—Psychological aspects.
4. Genetic counseling—Psychological aspects. I. Burke, B.
Meredith. II. Title.
RG628.K65 1994
618.2'2—dc20   93–43731

British Library Cataloguing in Publication Data is available.

Library of Congress Catalog Card Number: 93–43731
ISBN: 0–89789–337–9

First published in 1994

Bergin & Garvey, 88 Post Road West, Westport, CT 06881
An imprint of Greenwood Publishing Group, Inc.

Printed in the United States of America

The paper used in this book complies with the
Permanent Paper Standard issued by the National
Information Standards Organization (Z39.48–1984).

10 9 8 7 6 5 4 3 2 1

Copyright Acknowledgments

Contents

Tables

Foreword

Few medical technologies promise to deliver as much benefit as prenatal testing. From its earliest days, in the late 1960s, when amniocentesis provided the first glimpse into the genetic and biochemical status of the living fetus, to the staggering present-day achievements such as the utilization of embryo biopsy to detect genetic diseases or gender in one-week-old embryos conceived in Petri dishes and the administration of bone marrow transplants in utero to fetuses identified through prenatal testing as suffering from various immunological disorders, prenatal testing has provided a great deal of useful information and insight to prospective parents. Yet, prenatal testing has also been at the center of a great deal of moral, legal, and social controversy.

For example, former Surgeon General C. Everett Koop, in the heat of the controversy in the early 1980s over the role the federal government should play in regulating the treatment of infants born prematurely or with severe congenital defects, once dismissed some forms of prenatal testing as nothing more than ''search and destroy'' missions. He was deeply concerned, as were many disability rights advocacy groups, about any technology that might be used to eliminate anything less than perfect fetuses.

The controversial nature of prenatal testing is a function of many factors. The ability of various prenatal tests such as amniocentesis or ultrasound to reveal information about the developing fetus and provide for the first time in human history a ''window'' into the womb also means that women must now face unprecedented choices about the continuation of their pregnancies. Prenatal testing and diagnosis has raced ahead of the ability of modern medicine to attempt therapeutic interventions for many of the conditions and disorders that testing revels. More often than not, prenatal tests are only capable of revealing problems or risks for which no cures or treatments exist. The history of misuse and abuse of information about genetics in this century and the social context in which prenatal testing has evolved provide further reasons for concern about prenatal testing and the directions it might take in the future.

Americans are strongly committed to the belief that self-determination ought to be the controlling value that guides the course of any health care relationship. They also believe just as strongly, as is reflected in both federal and state law, that individuals ought be free to make choices about their reproductive and procreative behavior. These beliefs have led Americans to generally favor public policies which they believe will enhance the availability of information. Few would dispute the premise that the more information available, the greater the chances for self-determination.

Prenatal testing, through the provision of information on the health, development, and well-being of the fetus, can greatly enhance parental self-determination. Yet, with few options available for ameliorating the problems or diseases that prenatal testing sometimes reveals, many parents are left with only the choice of terminating a pregnancy or deciding not to have other children. For some the price of greater self-determination afforded by more information seems too high given the limited, morally contentious options available for acting on the information.

The paradox of a technology which can increase the information available to those who are having babies but for which there are, in most cases, very limited ways of responding to that information is not the only source of moral and social uncertainty about prenatal testing. Prenatal testing may be used not only to detect disorder and disease but also to identify conditions, traits, and behaviors which parents, for various reasons, might find simply undesirable. It is not at all clear what the dividing line is between normality and disorder. Nor is it clear whether medicine should take as part of its mandate fulfilling all the dreams and desires of parents about their future children.

What are prospective parents to make of the disclosure that their fetus has an extra Y chromosome, or that the fetus appears to have a much larger head than is normal for its stage of development? And what are doctors to do when a family requests information on the gender of their fetus for no reason other than they have strong feelings about the desirability of boys or girls? As new genetic knowledge expands the number of conditions that can be detected to include predispositions toward such conditions as breast or colon cancer, schizophrenia, allergy, asthma or depression, what sorts of assessments are parents to make of this information?

Just as the line between health and disease is often blurry, so is the line dividing self-determination from the indulgence of preferences, whims, fancies, or biases. When parents seek prenatal testing to establish the gender of their fetus, saying perhaps they would like to have a boy as their first-born child, is such a choice nothing more than the reflection of whim or bias, or does it fall within the scope of legitimate self-determination over one's procreative behavior? To the extent to which the lines between choice and whim remain vague, the potential exists for prenatal testing to become enmeshed in the pursuit of the frivolous or to be put in the service of ignorance, prejudice, and bigotry.

Talk of misuse or misapplicaton with reference to prenatal testing is not merely the handwringing of those who seem unable to look at any new medical advance without finding three or four reasons why it ought not be embraced. Rather, it is born of the stark reality of the misuse of genetic information by medicine, science, and government in this century in Germany in the form of the public health policies pursued by Adolph Hitler and his Nazi regime.

Before the Nazi party came to power in Germany in January of 1933, there were many distinguished German scientists and physicians who championed a theory they called racial hygiene. Alfred Ploetz, who first used this term in 1895, warned that a sound understanding of Darwinism and genetics led to the inexorable conclusion that the German people were at risk of suffering racial degeneration as a result of war, revolution, the rapid population growth of "inferior" peoples, and the survival of increasing numbers of the sick and disabled. Ploetz cautioned against the consequences of providing medical care to the "weak" and the poor who were still in their reproductive years, for such care allowed individuals to survive who otherwise would have been removed through the process of the natural selection of the unfit. The practice of medicine, Ploetz warned, while often good for the individual, could well prove to be the undoing of the race.

By the 1920 the German race hygiene movement had grown quite influential. It was by this time very concerned about declining birth rates and the "degeneration" of the German people as a result of insufficient reproduction among the elite members of society. German race hygienists, as well as their American, British, Canadian, and Australian counterparts, saw the health of the race as being jeopardized by the external threat of growing numbers of people of Slavic and Southern European descent in Europe and internally by the falling birthrates of the educated and economically advantaged.

By the early 1930s the race hygiene movement was laying the scientific foundation for the racist public health and euthanasia policies that the Nazis would implement with terrible results throughout the reign of the Third Reich from 1939 to 1945. Institutes of human genetics and eugenics sprang up all over universities in Germany. Scholars studied the inheritance of such traits as mental retardation, muscular dystrophy, mental illness, and crime. Others were concerned about the impact of interbreeding between Germans and different "races" such as Gypsies or Jews on the health of offspring.

The genetically inspired racism prevalent in German medicine and science proved to be a fertile source of ideas for Hitler and his minions. As one distinguished historian of German medicine has written, by the time Hitler took power "the Nazis found biology and medicine a suitable language in which to articulate their goals; scientists found the Nazis willing to support many of their endeavors. . . . Racial hygiene was not imposed on the German medical community; physicians eagerly embraced the racial ideal and the racial state'' (Proctor, 1988).

What is the connection between a woman in the United States today who is newly pregnant and in her early forties who decides to seek prenatal testing to allay her worries about having a child with a severe birth defect and the now decades-old racism of Nazi ideology? Oddly enough, a connection exists.

The woman who seeks information by means of prenatal testing today will find that those who offer testing, as well as those counselors who help interpret the information that prenatal tests provide, do so in a manner that is noticeably different from nearly every other testing and counseling situation in health care. If a person visits the doctor and reveals that she smokes three packs of cigarettes a day, the doctor will not simply present a mortality table concerning the health risks associated with smoking and leave matters at that. The heavy smoker, drug abuser, or person who fails to exercise or maintain a healthy diet can expect a very strongly worded, prescriptive speech about the importance and necessity of changing their behavior. But prescriptivism—telling patients what they ought and ought not do—is not in evidence in the realm of prenatal testing.

Those involved in prenatal testing and counseling have adopted a strict norm or ethic of nondirectiveness in carrying out the work they do with their clients. They do not see their role as extending beyond the provision of actual information and offering emotional support for whatever choices, decisions, or nondecisions their clients make. Unlike those in other areas of medicine or public health, who see their role as being one of promoting healthy lifestyles for their patients, and who might actually go so far as to discontinue caring for those who do not mend their ways in accordance with the recommendations that are offered, health care professionals involved with prenatal testing tread very softly around the question of what is best or desirable for their clients.

All counselors are taught from the beginning of their training that they must strive to remain value-neutral about the information they find and in its presentation to those in their care. They are also taught that their counseling ought be nondirective. They should not try to push or cajole clients into making particular decisions based upon the findings of prenatal testing.

The ethos of value neutrality and nondirectiveness has its roots in the horrible abuses of the Nazis in the name of public health during the first half of this century. The only way prenatal testing could flourish in light of the horrible crimes that had been carried out in the name of eugenics and racial hygiene by the Nazis was to draw as clear a line as possible between the normative, racist, and eugenic goals that had been embraced by the Nazis and the practice of prenatal testing and counseling. Value neutrality and nondirectiveness were critical to making prenatal testing and counseling morally acceptable.

Early American pioneers in the field of genetics counseling, such as the University of Minnesota's Sheldon Reed, were quick to disavow any connection between testing for disease or disorders in adults or fetuses and the old Nazi race hygiene theories or some of the more racist pronouncements of earlier generations of American social planners. Later leaders in the field, such as Joan Marks who created the first genetic counseling program at Sarah Lawrence University in Bronxville, New York, felt not only the influence of the crimes of the Second World War but also of a psychodynamic view of doctor-patient relationships that saw nondirectiveness as crucial for successful counseling.

The emphasis on nondirectiveness was only further reinforced by the fact that for many conditions detected by prenatal counseling clients would need to be told about the option of ending their pregnancies. The morally contentious nature of abortion only served to reinforce the value-neutral and nondirective stance so much in evidence in prenatal testing and counseling today. Thus, the key ethical linchpins for the practice of prenatal testing, value neutrality and nondirectiveness are as much a product of history as they are of any general consensus that these are the values most appropriate to the sphere of reproductive decision-making or procreative choice.

As prenatal testing evolves, it will find itself continually having to grapple both with its historical origins and with the moral ambiguity that surrounds the availability of more and more information earlier and earlier in pregnancy. Improvements in the ability to create embryos outside the human body and to bring younger and younger fetuses to term outside the womb may raise more opportunities for utilizing prenatal testing. It is not likely that the ethos of nondirectiveness and value neutrality so much in evidence as ideals for prenatal practice will long endure in the face of further technological and scientific advances. But it is also not at all clear which values ought take their place. Only through further study of the interactions between the clients of prenatal testing and those who provide it will an appropriate foundation be laid for constructing this new ethos.

Arthur L. Caplan

Preface

Fittingly enough, only the collegial kindness of two women helped me to retain a tenuous link to academic research. In my first graduate school I was the only woman in my department at the course-taking stage; at my doctoral institution I encountered overt sex discrimination from the department head. Small wonder that I remained an outsider and neither sought nor was offered academic employment upon receiving my degree.

After I had spent a few years carving out a nontraditional career, the late Leila Rosen Young invited me to participate in a panel at the Eastern Sociological Society meetings on building a career outside of academia. It was a novelty for me to be invited rather than rejected by a research social scientist. Then in 1982, Aliza Kolker called to invite my participation in a study she wanted to conduct of women who had used the then innovative technique of amniocentesis. Aliza, who had just had the test herself, knew of my interest in reproductive health, and she thought that my demographic and medical sociological training under Dr. Renee Fox would complement her sociological skills.

I welcomed the chance to be nosy about intimate matters, never thinking I was adding a permanent branch to my career. Soon advancing technology—the coming of CVS—raised additional research topics, and then we expanded our scope to include the viewpoint of counselors. I had primary responsibility for the counselor study and Aliza for the client survey; we were jointly responsible for the client in-depth interviews. Our contributions remained amazingly equal.

This book is a true collaboration, certainly stronger than either of us could have achieved alone. Only now, 11 years later, are we bringing our work on the psychosocial aspects of prenatal testing to a close.

The procedures described in our study are transitional. Invasive diagnosis, restricted to women who are at higher-than-average risk of abnormalities and largely to those who are from the middle or upper class, may soon be extinct. Within five years we expect routine prenatal care to include the culturing of fetal cells from a maternal blood sample. However, the issues we examine in this book will not be outdated. Indeed, as the pool of women eligible for prenatal diagnosis increases, still more women—many of them even less knowledgeable about heredity and genetics than those currently being counseled—will grapple with the decisions and the conflicting emotions we have chronicled.

Our research has been distinctive in more than one way. Except for the small university grant and research assistantships, Aliza acknowledges we had no formal funding. I was what is charitably known as an unaffiliated scholar for most of this period. My sole informal funding source was Tee L. Guidotti, M.D., Faculty of Medicine, University of Alberta, Edmonton—and a friend of very long standing. Believing in the worth of this research he would write me an occasional small check just as my photocopying, postage, and long-distance phone bills were mounting up. I hope he feels he has received adequate return on his investment!

Richard J. Kemmer housed and fed me while I conducted the Chicago interviews and has offered moral support throughout the years of our friendship. Appreciation is also due to Nicholas Whyte, a computer maven whose e-mail account permitted Aliza and me to thrash out many drafts of the concluding chapter despite the distance between us.

Aliza's husband, Dr. Ken Heitner, who greatly values his privacy, has suffered me as a house guest (with late hours yet!) on increasingly numerous occasions. Aliza's two sons, Ariel and Ethan Heitner, also tolerated disruptions of their routines. I promise them a batch of my finest chocolate chip cookies when the book formally appears!

Finally, I wish to thank my many respondents, counselors and clients alike, for the social pleasure and intellectual stimulation I derived from my interviews with them. The one difficulty I had as a researcher was how to maintain a scholarly distance with people with whom I would ordinarily delight in forging a friendship. I hope you too will feel the results reported in this book are a worthy return for the time you gave us.

B. Meredith Burke

Acknowledgments

This book would not have been possible without the help of many persons and institutions. Graduate research assistants Tobin Demsko, Kimberly O'Toole, and Jane U. Phillips helped with different phases of the research and writing. Other George Mason University students who helped without pay, just for the joy of learning, are Uma Balasurbrammanian, Jen Owens, Gala Radich, and Veronica Robello. Librarian Maureen Connors helped us navigate through electronic databases and locate a vast number of references. Martha Kubovchic, R.N.C., M.S.N., read the manuscript for technical accuracy.

The following people generously helped with information, advice, and more: Laird Jackson of Thomas Jefferson University; Oliver W. Jones of the University of California at San Diego Medical School; Seymour Kessler of the University of California at San Francisco; Herschel Lawson of the Centers for Disease Control; Beatrice Leopold of the National Society of Genetic Counselors; Rayna Rapp of the New School for Social Research; Barbara Katz Rothman of the City University of New York; Dorothy Wertz of the Shriver Center and Boston University School of Public Health; and all the counselors and mothers (expectant or "actual") who must remain anonymous.

The graduate school at George Mason University, in addition to providing three research assistants over several years, gave a small research grant that enabled us to start our study. The Department of Sociology and Anthropology at GMU footed many of the expenses incurred by the study.

We thank our editors at Greenwood Publishers, Lynn Flint and Bridget Austiguy, for their help and confidence in us.

Finally, I wish to thank my husband, Ken Heitner, for his unfailing support and encouragement, and my sons, Ariel and Ethan Heitner, who not only put up with my encroachments on their time but became actively interested in clinical genetics and sociology.

Aliza Kolker

Prenatal Testing

1

Prenatal Testing and the Social Construction of Pregnancy

Whether through astrology, motherly intuition, or prenatal diagnosis, the cartoon character Andrea (see next page), trendy woman that she is, believes that she knows all there is to know about her unborn child. With modern medicine making possible ever more detailed observation of babies in utero, she is not far wrong.

In the fourteenth century, for the first time since the Hellenistic period, European physicians began to dissect human cadavers. In the centuries that followed, scientists, freed from the prohibitions of the Church against autopsies, were able to penetrate a hitherto impermeable barrier, the skin, to peer into the *terra incognita* of the human body. The knowledge they gained revolutionized art, science, and medicine. As physicians' knowledge of human anatomy and physiology grew, so did their ability and desire to tinker with the body—to fix some problems through surgery (Siraisi, 1990).

Since the late 1960s a similar revolution has taken place in the remaining "black box," human gestation. Prenatal testing has created a window into the womb, which was previously a mysterious, sealed entity that could not be probed or opened without destroying its contents. Today, with the help of medical instruments, much can be learned about the fetus—its physiological condition, its chromosomal and genetic composition, its "life-style" including eye movements and breathing habits, and its sex. Some even claim that the fetal *personality* may be gauged by trained scientists with the proper instruments (Piontelli, 1992). The uses to which this knowledge may be put are controversial.

Pioneer sociologists W. I. Thomas and Dorothy S. Thomas (1928, p. 572) pointed out that reality is largely subjective: "If [people] define situations as real, they are real in their consequences." It is a tenet of sociology that we construct our reality. Although we perceive our physical and social environment as external to ourselves, it is in fact shaped or constructed by our own experiences and expectations (Berger and Luckmann, 1967). The implications of medical technology are not "given"; they are constructed by individuals on the basis of their own experiences and perceptions. The significance and consequences of prenatal technologies are shaped by the cultural context in which they were developed, by the medical profession that controls their use, and by the changing roles of women who use them. This book is about how prenatal diagnosis has been shaped by social forces and, in turn, has profoundly influenced the social construction of pregnancy, childbirth, and parenthood.

THE RISE AND EXPANSION OF PRENATAL TESTING

Until the 1960s genetic counseling consisted almost entirely of advising couples who already had a child with an abnormality about their chances of having another affected child. Geneticists could calculate these odds from the pattern of the occurrence of the disease in a family over several generations. There was no way to tell before a baby was born whether she or he carried the condition.

Prenatal diagnosis of abnormalities became possible with the discovery of the structure of DNA, the building blocks of genes. This finding, which earned scientists James D. Watson and Francis H. C. Crick a Nobel Prize in medicine in 1962, ushered in a revolution in biology by revealing the mechanism of heredity. Dr. Watson later went on to head the Human Genome Project at the National Institutes of Health. Within a few years scientists broke the genetic code and learned to read the messages encoded in the DNA. These messages, the genes, govern the chemistry of life.

CATHY copyright Cathy Guisewite. Reprinted with permission of UNIVERSAL PRESS SYNDI-CATE. All rights reserved.

In the human organism each cell carries complete genetic materials in the shape of 23 pairs of rod-shaped bodies called chromosomes. Chromosomes are comprised of thousands of individual genes. Genetic diseases are caused either by abnormalities in a chromosome or by gaps or "spelling errors" in a gene. The number of known conditions has grown steadily. A list published in 1990 by geneticist Victor A. McKusick contains about five thousand such conditions. Prenatal tests screen for a small fraction of these. They include hereditary disorders, such as muscular dystrophy, where there is a family history of the abnormality or a parent is a known carrier. They also include chromosomal aberrations that occur in the process of embryonic cell division.

The most common chromosomal abnormality is Down's syndrome, which is caused by the presence of an extra chromosome 21 in the cells. This condition, characterized by varying degrees of mental retardation and multiple physical defects, occurs in 1 in 650 to 1 in 1,000 of all live births (Cohen, 1984, p. 34). The combined incidence of all chromosomal abnormalities is about twice that of Down's syndrome. According to geneticist Margaret Thompson (Thompson, McInnes, and Willard, 1991, p. 7), "As a group chromosome disorders are quite common, affecting about 7 of 1,000 liveborn infants and accounting for about half of all spontaneous abortions."

The odds of such abnormalities rise with maternal age. A woman aged 30 has approximately a 1 in 885 chance of having a liveborn child with Down's syndrome and about twice that risk of having a child with *any* chromosomal abnormality. At 35 the incidence of all chromosomal abnormalities is 1 in 180 (approximately 0.5 percent). At 40 the risk is 1 in 65 or about 1.5 percent, and five years later it rises to 1 in 20 or 5 percent. (Hook, 1981).

Prenatal technology was originally designated for pregnancies judged by medical norms to be at high risk of fetal abnormality, whether because of a family history of hereditary disorders or because of maternal age. Yet the use of these tests is spreading as more and more women have sought, or have been persuaded, to undergo screening. Many millions of pregnant women have had so-called noninvasive procedures, MSAFP (maternal serum alpha-fetoprotein) screening and ultrasound. Even invasive procedures like amniocentesis and CVS (chorionic villus sampling) are used widely as the definition of "at-risk pregnancy" expands. Not only the woman's age, but also her "anxiety" about abnormality—a socially constructed artifact of the procedure's availability itself—is now regarded as an appropriate indication for having the procedures. Some physicians have argued that since the risks of amniocentesis and CVS are now quite low, the maternal age limit should be lowered from 35 to 30. Others have argued that no age limit at all should be set; any woman who wants amniocentesis or CVS should be given it (Golbus, 1992; Kaffe and Hsu, 1992).

What has driven this expansion? Partly it is the sheer availability of the technology. High-profile genetic research and new methods of prenatal detection have highlighted genetic disorders, including those that most women had never heard of, and fueled new anxieties.

In some cases genetic screening has been spectacularly successful. As a result of a well-targeted and publicized screening campaign, a fatal disease, Tay-Sachs, has been nearly wiped out in the population most likely to inherit it—Jews of Ashkenazic (Eastern and Central European) backgrounds. However, this "victory" has been achieved at a painful, though little-known, cost—the suffering of parents who have aborted an affected fetus, perhaps as late as five months into the pregnancy (see Chapter 9).

Moreover, the public health campaign against Tay-Sachs has not brought an end to this genetic disease. As cases of Tay-Sachs among Jews have decreased, the disease has shown up disproprotionately among non-Jews, who are not screened routinely. Meanwhile, new and devastating diseases to which Jews are particularly (although not exclusively) susceptible have been discovered— Gaucher's disease and Canavan's disease.

Other screening programs, such as those for sickle-cell anemia, a condition that disproportionately affects people of African descent, have been less successful. Debate is now raging about the effectiveness and ethics of a massive screening program for cystic fibrosis, the most serious genetic disorder in the United States. The drive to expand genetic testing aims at wiping out certain genetic disorders. Whether this goal is reachable—and at what psychic, social, and moral costs—is less certain.

The changes in women's roles have also fueled the expansion of prenatal testing. Many women who have come of age since the beginning of the women's movement have devoted their young adulthood to pursuing training and careers, postponing childbearing until their 30s or 40s. Other women must postpone childbearing until they find suitable mates, which occurs later in an era of later marriages and more frequent divorces. Others are forced to wait until infertility problems can be resolved. At the same time, the surge in women's careers has raised the cost and difficulty of rearing a handicapped child (Breslau, 1983). Improved medical care, which has prolonged the life expectancy of children with many genetic conditions, also contributes to the financial and emotional costs of care. The legalization of abortion—a right now increasingly under attack—has given women the option to abort legally a fetus found to be abnormal. As sociologist Dorothy C. Wertz and historian Richard W. Wertz (1989, p. 241) put it, "In the age of choice, the wanted fetus as potentially perfect child and as object of affection has a higher value than in earlier times."

The women's movement has led women to demand control over their bodies. Unmedicated, "natural" childbirth has become the norm. Yet the search for a "perfect" baby has contributed to an unprecedented medicalization of pregnancy and childbirth. Concerned about the health of their unborn children, women have eagerly subjected themselves to invasive prenatal and obstetric technologies. As Wertz and Wertz (1989, p. 244) point out, "When it comes to the health of their children, most are not risk-takers. This is why every fetus is becoming subject to quality control and why tests originally indicated for a few are applied to so many."

Other pressures to expand testing come from the medical profession. In several high-profile "wrongful birth" lawsuits, obstetricians were sued for failure to counsel women in their mid-30s to have amniocentesis or other tests and held responsible for the birth of a child with disabilities. While many obstetricians oppose what they see an unnecessary testing, others recommend such tests to protect themselves from malpractice suits (Elias and Simpson, 1992). Cost-benefit studies comparing the price to society of prenatal screening with that of caring for children with disabilities have also encouraged testing (Goldstein and Philip, 1990). Critics of these studies have pointed out that since births to women under age 35 far outnumber those to older women, most babies with chromosomal abnormalities are born to younger women. From a societal point of view, prenatal diagnosis for maternal age does not "prevent" abnormalities in sufficient numbers to justify the added risks. Furthermore, analysis of the economic benefits of screening invariably overlooks its psychological costs to women (Farrant, 1985).

Until the mid-1980s prenatal diagnosis was confined to a small group of women. These were disproportionately middle- or upper-class women who had voluntarily postponed childbirth, had insurance coverage to pay for the procedures, lived near urban centers where facilities were available, and were knowledgeable and sophisticated enough to seek the most advanced medical care. Many poor and minority women had amniocentesis too, especially in states where Medicaid paid for it. Yet amniocentesis became a rite of passage, a symbolic badge of the "designer pregnancy" (Rapp, 1988; Rothman, 1986). Today prenatal diagnosis affects pregnant women of all social classes, ethnic groups, and, increasingly, ages. In coming years, as the tests' accuracy improves and their risks decline, there will undoubtedly be a further "democratization" of the client population.

Many women experience prenatal testing not as an option but as a requirement. Even those who refuse testing—for example, women who would not consider aborting a defective fetus and those who would rather not subject their pregnancies to what they deem hazardous and unnecessary interventions—must confront the decision. They must make their reasons for declining explicit and convincing to themselves, their partners, their health care givers, and sometimes to strangers. *New York Times* columnist Anna Quindlen describes why, pregnant at age 36 with her third child, she resisted pressures to have amniocentesis or CVS:

Perhaps if this child were unwanted, I could think of it as a fetus. But my children...have all been wanted; they were babies from the moment I knew they were coming. I do not know what it would take for me to stop their lives. . . . In some sense, the future's already writ. This child is already something: boy, girl, healthy, ill. . . . I know only one thing now. This child is ours, for better or worse, in sickness and in health. (*The New York Times*, May 12, 1988)

Many readers criticized Ms. Quindlen's decision as selfish (although others supported her). One reader wrote,

If I knowingly brought a handicapped child into this less-than-compassionate world . . . my conscience would plague me with that, not the more merciful abortion. And if the child knew, would it not be justified in saying, 'You did *this* to me?' Ms. Quindlen should stop dwelling on herself and her feelings and think of the child, and have the amnio. (Marie Klein, letter to the editor, June 9, 1988)

Another reader, congratulating herself on having prenatal diagnosis in her own pregnancy, asked, "Does she really believe that not having tests after the age of 35 . . . shows that she wants her baby more than I want mine?" (Susan Battles, letter to the editor, June 9, 1988).

Clearly, for women over 35, and increasingly for younger women, prenatal testing—with all its consequences—has become a norm. Societal norms, as sociologists know, exercise their own pressures for compliance. In one way or another, then, the use of prenatal testing affects all pregnancies. It is also challenging society's values about human life, autonomy, and motherhood.

BETWEEN SCYLLA AND CHARYBDIS: PSYCHOLOGICAL AND ETHICAL DILEMMAS OF PRENATAL TESTING

Every technological advance produces a host of unintended and, for the most part, unforeseen consequences (Merton, 1968). Prenatal testing has transformed pregnancy and parenthood and given rise to ethical and personal dilemmas that would-be parents, the medical profession, and society are only beginning to confront.

When the mythical Greek hero Ulysses sailed home from the Trojan wars, he had to pass through narrow straits flanked by two mortal dangers. On one side, in a cave high up on a cliff, dwelled Scylla, a six-headed monster who preyed on sailors passing through the straits. On the other side was Charybdis, a frightful whirlpool that would engulf any vessel coming through at high tide. To reach safe havens Ulysses had to choose between losing his entire ship and crew to Charybdis and sacrificing "only" six sailors to Scylla. He chose Scylla, convincing himself that she was the lesser evil.

Ulysses' dreadful choice, one of the many travails he encountered on the journey home, has become a metaphor for those who must make a deliberate and cruel choice between two potentially tragic alternatives. Invasive prenatal diagnosis presents women with a similar dilemma. On one hand, there are the numerical odds of having a baby with a serious abnormality; on the other, women face the risk of fetal loss arising from the procedure itself.

The two events—Scylla and Charybdis, an abnormal diagnosis versus damage to the fetus caused by the procedure—are not equivalent or even reducible to the same scale. Nevertheless, the weighing of these risks has produced a calculus that is expected to govern decision making about reproduction. On the basis of genetic information and numerical data about the procedures' dangers, women are supposed to decide whether or not to have prenatal diagnosis, which test to have, whether or not to terminate the pregnancy if an abnormality is found, and whether or not to have another child (or any child).

Prior to the DNA revolution, providing this information was the province of pediatricians and Ph.D-level geneticists. Today, in the United States the providers are genetic counselors, most often holders of master's degrees, whose training combines science, social work, and counseling techniques. Like their clients, genetic counselors are typically female. As anthropologist Rayna Rapp (1988, p. 107) points out, these are the gatekeepers "between science and social experience." They regulate "the information on which decisions will be made. In their work, genetic counselors identify with and serve pregnant women, while representing the universal claims of science. At stake in their profession is the technological transformation of pregnancy and maternal 'choice'."

The objective of prenatal diagnosis is the detection of major abnormalities in utero. However, for most chromosomal and genetic disorders there is no treatment. In the case of a serious abnormality, the only alternative to bearing a sick, untreatable child is to terminate the pregnancy. Thus, in the words of historian Ruth Schwartz Cowan (1992, p. 246), "for the foreseeable future, the ethical and social implications of [prenatal genetic testing] are going to be inextricable from the ethical and social implications of abortion."

Abortions are morally unacceptable to some and, in the wake of political and legal challenges and attacks on clinics and providers, increasingly unavailable. Even for those who support abortion rights and have access to these services, terminating a wanted pregnancy is a personal tragedy. When the abortion must take place in midpregnancy, it is even more traumatic. Prenatal testing makes the consideration of abortion an integral part of the route to motherhood; the creation of life becomes possible only if the parents are willing to accept the prospect of terminating that life. The ethical implications of abortion for abnormality are the subject of a heated public debate, yet the psychological implications—the personal tragedy of terminating a wanted pregnancy—have received scant attention from researchers, health care providers, and society.

A diagnosis of serious fetal abnormality is statistically rare: over 98 percent of all women who are tested ultimately will receive good news. Yet, the experience scars them too. The test's focus on abnormality heightens women's fears for their babies' health. The late gestational age at which some prenatal procedures take place makes the experience even more disturbing. Some women try to avoid bonding with the baby or telling others about the pregnancy until they receive the test results, although as the pregnancy progresses this becomes very difficult (Hodge, 1989). The stress imposed by what sociologist Barbara Katz Rothman (1986) has termed "the tentative pregnancy" is an unanticipated consequence, or byproduct, of prenatal testing.

The other side of the prenatal diagnosis equation is the small but determinate risk to the fetus from the procedure itself. Perhaps 1 in 200 women who have amniocentesis or CVS (higher proportions in less experienced clinics) will suffer a miscarriage as a result of the procedure. Sometimes it is impossible to tell whether the miscarriage was caused by the intervention or occurred spontaneously. There are also unconfirmed reports of serious birth defects resulting, ironically, from the very tests designed to prevent genetic disorders. Thus, while prenatal diagnosis has benefited countless women by helping them to control their reproductive lives and to avoid tragedy, the price—the major unintended, tragic consequence—has been the hazard of fetal loss or malformation as a result of the procedure.

Prenatal diagnosis has fueled a growing challenge to the rights and autonomy of pregnant women. The technology has focused attention on the fetus, making the mother's body physically and, for some, morally transparent. Obstetrical medicine has come to regard the fetus as the patient; the "rights" of the fetus are seen as separate from those of the mother and possibly as superseding them.

In Washington, D.C., a 27-year-old cancer patient named Angela Carder, 26 weeks pregnant, lay dying in a hospital bed. A judge ordered the hospital to deliver the fetus by a caesarian section, although physicians knew that the surgery would hasten the woman's death. The severely premature baby lived less than three hours; the mother died two days later. The judge's decision in Angela Carder's case was based on a Georgia court case five years earlier. In that case a pregnant woman named Jessie Mae Jefferson, in labor and fully conscious, had refused a doctor-ordered caesarian section. The State Supreme Court gave temporary custody of the fetus to the State Human Resources Department. Those officials, the court said, could take whatever action they deemed best for the fetus, including cutting through the mother's body to get it out (Gorney, 1988). Three years after Angela Carder's death, an appeals court ruled against the hospital's decision to deliver the baby.

The "rights" of the fetus are presumed to exist at an ever-earlier gestational age, an age when there is no chance of survival outside the womb. In 1992, in Erlangen, Germany, the 12-week-old fetus of a dead woman was kept alive inside the mother's corpse. For a month nurses washed the corpse, machines kept the heart and lungs going, tubes delivered nutrition, and background tapes played Mozart symphonies to the fetus inside the dead woman's body in the hospital's intensive care unit. The Catholic Church decried the violation of the sanctity of the dead, and many Germans were appalled by the turning of a dead woman into "an inert childbearing system," with echoes of Nazi policy (Fisher, 1992). Eventually, the fetus died and the dead woman's corpse could be buried.

In most cases, of course, the mother is alive. The issue is not respect for the dead but the rights of the living. Some writers argue that "the pregnant woman has taken on a unique responsibility for the well being of the fetus, and that her cooperation in diagnosing and treating life-threatening problems is morally required. From a legal perspective, rights of bodily integrity are generally protected, but they are not absolute" (Johnson and Elkins, 1988, p. 415). Others contend that it is never permissible to force a pregnant woman to undergo surgery in order to save the life of the fetus and that any coercive medical treatment is "brutish and horrible" (Elias and Annas, 1983, p. 811). At issue, then, is protecting the dignity and autonomy of pregnant women in the face of medicine's growing attention to the fetus—made possible by prenatal technology—and the courts' tendency to endow the fetus with personhood and "rights."

At the other end of the spectrum, some writers warn about the possible abuse of prenatal testing by parents who try to achieve perfect children. With ever more sophisticated diagnostic tools, parents may choose the characteristics of their children by aborting fetuses with minor disabilities or even those of the "wrong" sex. The potential for such practices has raised the specter of eugenics. As Harvard biologist Ruth Hubbard (1988, p. 232) points out, the link between eugenics and prenatal diagnosis is "the belief that disability is an unmitigated disaster, that we would be better off if people with disabilities did not exist."

The problem arises from the ability of prenatal testing to detect conditions that cause only mild handicaps or will manifest themselves only after several decades of a normal life. Among the milder chromosomal abnormalities are Turner's syndrome, the absence in a girl of one of the two X chromosomes. This causes short stature, sterility, and underdeveloped sex organs, yet the girl is of normal intelligence. Or the fetus may be diagnosed with cystic fibrosis, an inherited condition that affects the pancreas and the lungs. These children, who develop normally at first, will become very sick and die in adolescence or early adulthood.

Which fetuses should be aborted? And who is to decide? Many parents of children with disabilities would not abort another child with the same disorder (Breslau, 1987; Wertz et al., 1991). At the same time, in a society that does not provide adequate resources for the disabled, parents may feel pressured to abort a less than perfect fetus. In Los Angeles, television anchorwoman Bree Walker became the unwilling subject of a public controversy when she decided to have a second child. Ms. Walker has a rare genetic disorder called ectrodactyly: the bones of her fingers and toes are partially fused. The baby stood a 50 percent chance of inheriting this condition. (He did, as did his older sister.) A radio talk show host, making clear her own disapproval, invited listeners to comment on Ms. Walker's decision to have a second child without prenatal diagnosis. Many listeners pronounced her decision "irresponsible." Advocates for disability rights, including Ms. Walker and her husband, filed a complaint against the radio station with the Federal Communications Commission (*Newsweek*, October 28, 1991, p. 73). The fundamental question—parents' right to make their own reproductive decisions without interference or coercion—was not addressed in the media controversy that ensued.

As genetic testing makes possible the detection of more conditions, pressures on the parents will grow. Yet anomalies occur more often than most people realize; no prenatal intervention can guarantee a perfect child. By one recent estimate, 1 in every 30 babies has a defect that varies in medical, cosmetic, or surgical significance (Thompson, McInnes, and Willard, 1991, p. 8).

How far do we expect prenatal diagnosis to go in assuring us of a perfect child? What about a child of the "right" sex? Where did we—as parents, health care givers, and society—draw the line? What is the value of life itself, the value of parenthood, regardless of disabilities or imperfections in our children? At the same time, how can parents' autonomy—the right to make their own decisions about prenatal testing and abortion for whatever reasons—be preserved in the face of pressures for restricting those options?

To be sure, most diseases and disabilities in young children are not caused by chromosomes or genes. Many debilitating conditions arise from complications in the birth process, sometimes as a consequence of obstetrical interventions. Other disorders—particularly low birth weight, the leading cause of infant mortality—are caused by social and economic conditions. The availability of prenatal diagnosis has focused attention on a small fraction of all handicaps. Ruth Hubbard (1988, p. 233) speaks for many medical and social researchers when she points out that "if we, as a society, are concerned to produce as healthy babies as we can, we should be putting our energies into meeting women's needs for education, healthful home and work environments, good nutrition and prenatal care."

THE RESEARCH QUESTIONS

The dilemmas outlined above are some of the questions we address in this book. We explore these questions primarily through the prism of our own study of genetic counselors and clients who have used two principal methods of prenatal diagnosis: amniocentesis and CVS. We have used the growing literature in this field to supplement our own findings.

A major purpose of our research was to compare the social constructions of pregnancy, abortion, risk, and parenthood involved in the two techniques. How much difference does the timing in the pregnancy make? Compared to amniocentesis clients, are CVS users less attached to the pregnancy and to impending motherhood and, hence, better able to cope with abortion? How do the users of the two techniques perceive the relative risk of the procedure to the fetus? What tradeoffs do they make between the avowedly greater risk of CVS and the earlier time at which it is available? And how do genetic counselors view the implications of the two procedures? Phrased differently, we were interested in finding out how the newer procedure, CVS, has changed the subjective experience and meaning of prenatal diagnosis.

This was the initial charge we set for ourselves. However, it soon became clear that the differences are not as great, and the tradeoffs are not as clear-cut as we initially expected. CVS and amniocentesis have many similarities: both are invasive medical procedures that hold great promise and have benefited countless parents, yet entail heavy (and often overlooked) costs. Perhaps it is more useful to distinguish between invasive methods, which are restricted to pregnancies judged to be at high risk, and noninvasive, presumably safe procedures whose use is more common. Imaging techniques (primarily ultrasound) form a third category. Many of the issues go beyond specific procedures: they involve genetic testing as a medical field and a phenomenon that has changed women's lives.

We are neither physicians nor authorities on ethics or genetics. As social scientists, we hope to offer insights into the social-psychological, ethical, and policy issues on the basis of our own research and that of others. Our findings represent the experiences and views of those on the "front line" of the new prenatal technologies—women who pass through the narrow straits of genetic testing on the way to motherhood and counselors who inform, guide, and comfort them through their passage.

THE RESEARCH METHODS

In 1982 we embarked on an exploratory study of the social-psychological ramifications of amniocentesis. At that time amniocentesis was relatively new, used by only 2 percent of all women aged 35 and over in the United States. For social science research it was uncharted territory. We used snowball sampling: that is, we contacted women we knew who referred us to other women of their acquaintances. We interviewed a total of twenty-four women, all white, mostly upper-middle-class. All had normal pregnancies and healthy babies. They told us about their concerns and, most importantly, about their dismay at having to undergo the diagnostic procedure and confront the possibility of abortion in the second trimester of the pregnancy. The results of this, our pilot study, are reported in Chapter 5.

Before this first study could be published, prenatal diagnosis was revolutionized by a first-trimester technique, CVS. CVS seemed to provide a solution to the problems with amniocentesis, the answer to women's prayers—if only its safety could be established. We were interested in finding out whether, indeed, CVS could fulfill that promise and what additional issues—unanticipated consequences—it might raise. We enlisted the cooperation of two clinics, one in suburban Washington, D.C., and the other in San Diego, California. These were among the first centers in the country that offered the procedure. Women who came to those clinics before the twelfth week of their pregnancy were given a choice of amniocentesis or CVS. Those who came after the twelfth week were offered amniocentesis.

In 1986 and 1987 survey questionnaires were handed out to clients who had either amniocentesis or CVS at the Washington clinic, with requests to fill them out and mail them back to us in preaddressed, postage-paid envelopes. In San Diego the survey questionnaires were mailed to clients shortly after they had the procedure. Altogether we received 120 completed survey questionnaires, 60 from each location. The response rate was 50 percent. Although this response rate is relatively low, it is not out of line with that reported by other surveys of reproductive behavior (Black, 1989; Metheny et al., 1988).

Although our sample was not scientifically chosen, it is representative of the clienteles of the two clinics: the demographic characteristics of our respondents matched those of the clinics' client population. Out of the 120 respondents who completed the survey questionnaires 72 had amniocentesis (28 in Washington and 44 in San Diego) and 48 had CVS (32 in Washington and 16 in San Diego). The characteristics of our sample are discussed in Chapter 6 and in Appendix D. The statistical analyses of clients' responses presented in this book are based on the survey returns.

The survey asked women, in addition to standard background questions, why they chose either procedure, how they estimated their risks of having a child with abnormality and of harm to the fetus or to themselves as a result of the procedure, their views about abortion, and their childbearing plans.

In addition to numerical responses, however, we wanted the kind of information that only open-ended questions can provide: the complexities of women's concerns and hopes about their pregnancies, the sharing of decisions about childbearing between husbands and wives, and feelings about parenthood. We therefore included open-ended questions in the survey and encouraged women to comment in their own words. The survey questionnaire is reprinted in Appendix A.

In addition, we conducted in-depth interviews with thirty-one women who had CVS or amniocentesis between 1986 and 1990. Some of these women were selected through snowball sampling from our own acquaintances, in a fashion similar to the first round. Others were clinic patients who responded to a letter requesting a personal interview or who indicated they would prefer a personal interview to a mailed questionnaire. Altogether, we interviewed twenty-three women who had CVS, four who had amniocentesis, three who had both in different pregnancies, and one who chose not to have any screening. Each interview lasted one to two hours.

To gain a better perspective on prenatal diagnosis we sought the views of professionals in the field. First, we conducted eight exploratory interviews in Washington and Baltimore, five of which are included in the analysis below. Using a standardized open-ended questionnaire, we then interviewed an additional twenty-five genetic counselors in New York City, Chicago, and San Diego. It was a convenience sample: in each city we asked clinics affiliated with teaching hospitals if any of their staff were willing to participate. No clinic and no counselor declined; we met with two to four counselors at each clinic. Interviews generally lasted an hour. An additional six counselors from Rochester and Long Island (New York State) mailed back answers to our open-ended questionnaire. The counselors' interview schedule is reprinted in Appendix B. The genetic counselors' perspective presented in this book is based on the thirty-six interviews and mailed-back questionnaires that provided information in a standardizable form.

The names of respondents and some biographical details have been changed to protect their privacy. Yet the people whose voices you will hear in this book are real people—users and providers of genetic testing who have given much thought to the implications of the tests of their own lives and for society. These are, overwhelmingly, women's voices. Although most geneticists and physicians who perform the procedures are men, there were only two males among the genetic counselors in our sample. In our interviews with clients, only two husbands were present with their wives. While we do not wish to downplay the importance of men's involvement in pregnancy and parenthood, this book is primarily about women and motherhood.

Given the small size and nonrepresentative nature of our sample, our findings are not generalizable. What we have to say is not conclusive but merely suggestive. Our intent is not to provide definitive answers, but to explore the complexities of the questions.

A NOTE ON TERMINOLOGY

Words are powerful; they shape reality. In a field as sensitive as the subject of this book, the choice of words and phrases is politically charged: pro-life or anti-abortion? Pro-choice or pro-abortion? When is a fetus an unborn child or, as some would have it, a pre-born child?

Women who use prenatal diagnosis are, in our view, users or clients rather than patients. Feminists have long decried the medicalization of pregnancy and childbirth: pregnant women are not sick. Yet in our culture the term *patient* refers not only to sick persons but also to anyone who seeks the services of health professionals, including those who see a dentist or buy medicines from a pharmacist. Sometimes, then, it makes sense to refer to users of prenatal medical services as patients.

Similarly, we prefer *pregnant woman* to *mother*, and *fetus* to *baby*. Yet the pregnant women in our study are in the process of becoming mothers and usually embrace motherhood eagerly. They are concerned about the health of their unborn babies, not abstract fetuses. To some extent, then, we use the words interchangeably to avoid repetition.

THE PLAN OF THIS BOOK

The next chapter describes the context of our study: the rapidly changing field of prenatal diagnosis. It presents an overview of the procedures, their promises and limitations, and the issues they raise for women's lives and for society. Although the technology changes rapidly, the issues transcend specific procedures.

Beginning with Chapter 3, we present the findings of our study. Chapters 3 and 4 briefly explore the profession of genetic counseling, its history, structure, and professional norms. These chapters also describe the counselors' perspective on the ethics of their profession and on their own role in the prenatal diagnosis process.

Chapter 5 analyzes the reactions of the "moral pioneers," women who had amniocentesis at the point when it was first becoming widespread—the early 1980s. The bulk of the book—chapters 6–10—analyzes the perceptions and concerns of today's amniocentesis and CVS users. These women, especially the users of the newer technology, CVS, are still in many ways pioneers. Without societal norms, they are constructing the array of meanings for motherhood— for their own lives—that arise from the technologies. To the views of clients we counterpose, where possible, counselors' perceptions of these issues.

Chapter 11 presents some conclusion. Mostly, however, it raises questions provoked by our research—questions that must be faced by parents, practitioners, and society.

Although some technical discussion of our data collection and analysis is unavoidable, most technical information is reserved for the appendixes. Appendixes A–C present our research instruments, whereas Appendix D discusses our measurements of clients' socioeconomic status.

2

The Procedures

Joanie, a middle-aged lawyer working on Capitol Hill, finds herself pregnant unexpectedly. After some soul searching, she and her husband Rick, a reporter, decide to have the baby. Joanie schedules amniocentesis. She lies awake at night worrying about the procedure, while her husband worries mainly about the family car.

The next day at breakfast, Joanie's distress is mounting. Aware that pregnancy after 40 is "risky," she is worried not only about the impending needle prick but also about the results. Rick, who tries to be supportive, is too busy at work to accompany his wife to the clinic.

At the clinic the staff tries to reassure Joanie about the procedure, telling her to relax. Joanie asks to see the needle but is refused; she is told jokingly that it is "wheeled in" only after the patient is blindfolded. After the tap Joanie comments about the size of the needle, which looked more like a weapon. She wonders whether it was developed by the Pentagon.

Back at home, Joanie and Rick anxiously await the results. Finally, the clinic gives them the good news that there is no finding of abnormality. Relieved, the couple ask about the baby's sex. The counselor says, "It's a boy." She continues in a dead-pan fashion that he will have sandy hair, freckles, and an aptitude for math, and that he will be a Red Sox fan (unlikely since they live in Washington, D.C.). Jeffrey, a healthy baby, is born some months later. (Based on the comic strip "Doonesbury" by Gary Trudeau)

Joanie and Rick are comic-strip characters, but their fictional predicament reflects a growing reality. By the 1980s amniocentesis had become a rite of passage of pregnancy in the upper middle class. Ten years later invasive procedures, amniocentesis and CVS, have spread to younger and less affluent women, while other procedures have become a routine aspect of prenatal care. How did prenatal testing become, first, a badge of the "designer pregnancy" and later, in one form or another, a part of nearly all pregnancies?

In this chapter we describe the major prenatal diagnostic procedures, their uses, and their consequences. Prenatal technologies change rapidly. New techniques become available and older techniques are improved. New data accumulate on accuracy, range of diagnosable disorders, and risk levels. Although some of the technical information in this chapter may be obsolete by the time you read this book, the social and ethical issues arising from prenatal testing will not go away. This chapter provides a brief and, we hope, not too technical overview of the field as it was in 1993. It sets the background for the issues discussed in the rest of the book.

There are three types of prenatal tests: invasive procedures that remove a sample of tissues from the fetus or its surroundings; procedures that measure chemicals or analyze fetal cells in the mother's blood to assess the fetal condition; and imaging techniques. Invasive procedures include amniocentesis, chronic villus sampling (CVS), and embryo biopsy. The most common maternal blood test is alpha-fetoprotein or AFP. Imaging the fetus is done primarily by ultrasound.

AMNIOCENTESIS

Amniocentesis was first used for prenatal diagnosis in 1968. When an early study sponsored by the National Institute of Child Health and Human Development (NICHD) found it both safe and accurate, a pediatrician on the NICHD staff enthused, "Few advances compare with amniocentesis in their capability for prevention of disability" (quoted in Culliton, 1975, p. 537).

Amniocentesis is usually performed between the fourteenth and eighteenth week of the pregnancy. With the woman lying down, a needle is passed through her abdomen and through the uterine wall to the amniotic sac that surrounds the fetus. A syringe is attached to the needle and several teaspoonfuls of amniotic fluid are drawn off. The amniotic fluid is analyzed in a laboratory, in a process that takes about two weeks (down from four or five weeks in the early years), for chromosomal or metabolic disorders. Among the disorders that may be diagnosed in this way are Down's syndrome and other trisomies (that is, occurrences of an extra chromosome), Tay-Sachs disease, and neural tube defects such as spina bifida (an opening in the spine).

There is a small chance that the procedure may result in miscarriage or damage to the fetus. The risk is cited as less than one-half of 1 percent; it is higher in multiple pregnancies (Pruggmayer et al., 1991). Because of its risk, this test is not offered to all pregnant women but only to those who have an elevated risk of fetal abnormality because of heredity or maternal age.

Beside the hazard of miscarriage, the major drawbacks of amniocentesis are the late gestational age at which it is performed and the long waiting time for the results. By the time the findings are in, the woman is 18 to 22 weeks along in her pregnancy, a time when she feels the fetal movements and is getting quite attached to the unborn baby. Abortion at this stage is physically and emotionally traumatic; it is experienced as the death of a child. Even when no abnormality is found, women find the uncertainty very stressful (Chervin et al., 1977; Kolker and Burke, 1987). This uncertainty—a baby or an abortion?—has created what might be termed "the tentative pregnancy" (Rothman, 1986).

Recent advances in ultrasound and in cell culturing techniques have made it possible in some centers to perform amniocentesis as early as the eleventh to fourteenth week of the pregnancy. The earlier procedure is controversial because the results are harder to interpret. Moreover, early amniocentesis may cause more miscarriages since the volume of fluid removed for testing constitutes a larger proportion of the total amniotic fluid (D'Alton and DeCherney, 1993). Some researchers, however, claim that the safety and accuracy of early amniocentesis are comparable to those of CVS or second-trimester amniocentesis (Penso et al., 1990).

CHORIONIC VILLUS SAMPLING (CVS)

CVS is performed in the ninth to twelfth week of the pregnancy. It involves obtaining cells from the hairlike projections (villi) of the chorion, the outer tissue of the sac that surrounds the embryo early in the pregnancy and later develops into the placenta. The composition of the chorion is similar to that of the fetus. In fact, the chorionic villi are the endpoints of fetal circulation, "the functional units of the fetal portion of the placenta. They permit transfer of metabolic products between the maternal and fetal circulations" (Jackson, 1985a, p. 39). Analysis of the villi yields information on chromosomal and biochemical abnormalities in the fetus, although not on neural tube defects. The tissue may be analyzed directly, without culturing. Early results may be obtained by direct observation of the cells within twenty-four to forty-eight hours, while final results from cultured cells take between ten and fourteen days.

The tissue for analysis is obtained with the guidance of ultrasound, by inserting a catheter either through the woman's vagina and cervix or through her abdomen under sterile conditions. Later in the pregnancy the placenta can be accessed more easily through the abdomen than through the cervix. Although physicians disagree about which CVS procedure—transcervical or transabdominal—is safer and easier, a randomized clinical trial sponsored by NICHD has shown the two methods to be equally safe (Jackson et al., 1992).

Given the advantages of early diagnosis, we might wonder why CVS was not developed earlier. In fact, research on CVS began approximately at the same time that amniocentesis was being tried out. Between 1968 and 1975 Swedish and Danish geneticists performed the transcervical procedure on ninety-five volunteers shortly before elective termination of the pregnancy. Unable to visualize the placenta, they managed to obtain only a few samples for analysis. Many of the volunteers experienced complications such as accidental rupture of the amniotic sac that would have led to miscarriage in a continuing pregnancy. In addition, where the fetal tissue could not be separated from maternal tissue, analysis of the fetus's condition was impossible.

Meanwhile, the relative safety and accuracy of amniocentesis had been established, and that technique was gaining rapid acceptance. In contrast to CVS, amniocentesis required simpler instruments and was easier for physicians to learn. Moreover, infection is less likely when the catheter passes through the abdominal skin than through the vagina. Amniocentesis rapidly became the technique of choice for prenatal diagnosis.

In 1975 a group of Chinese investigators, working without the guidance of ultrasound, were able to obtain fetal placental tissue. Their aim was not to diagnose fetal abnormalities but to identify the fetus's sex. The Chinese government at that time was aggressively pursuing a policy of two children per family (later reduced to one child). Since many couples were concerned about having a son, it soon became clear that CVS was being used for the selective abortion of female fetuses. In the absence of facilities for chemical analysis, CVS had no medical uses, and it was soon dropped (Jackson, 1985a and 1985b).

A few physicians continued to experiment with CVS. But the real breakthrough came in Moscow, where Hungarian obstetrician Zoltan Kazy and his Russian colleagues for the first time performed chorion sampling with real-time ultrasound guidance. They successfully tested 110 patients without serious complications (Kazy, Rozovsky, and Bakahrev, 1982). Dr. Kazy later wrote a letter to his Western counterparts describing his confidence in the procedure and his excitement about its potential:

Since I was trained in the [first-trimester diagnostic procedure] and was the first to work it out as being safe and harmless when done under ultrasound monitoring, I would be pleased if you took into consideration my experience. I think that they serve our common aim of the development and progress of medical science.

Believe me, after my first diagnostic chorion biopsy—preceded by long and thorough studies—I had many restless nights until the first healthy baby (girl) was born. After this I only had to worry about the next cases. I believed all the time in the correctness of the method and the necessity of developing it as a revolutionary method for the possibility of early prenatal genetic diagnosis. I know that its risk . . . is less than the risk of amniocentesis . . . . It is my belief that this method of obtaining a fetal sample is the earliest possible method of "today" and will serve as the test to precede the "gene surgery" of tomorrow. (Quoted in *CVS Newsletter*, July 26, 1985)

Meanwhile, in the West clients voiced increasing dissatisfaction with midtrimester testing. This led several British investigators to take another look at CVS. Like their Russian counterparts, they recognized that the key to success was the use of ultrasound guidance.

Other breakthroughs followed. In Milan, Italy, investigators developed a technique for direct biochemical and chromosomal studies of the villi, without first culturing the tissue in the lab. It now became possible to obtain the results only hours or days rather than weeks after the procedure (Simoni et al., 1984).

An American, Dr. Laird Jackson, after learning of the early successes of the British and Italian studies, initiated the first pilot project in the United States at Jefferson Medical College in Philadelphia. Dr. Jackson and his colleagues trained themselves by performing the procedure on volunteers scheduled for elective abortion. In 1984 they began to offer CVS to women whose pregnancies were at high risk of fetal abnormality. The first clients had particularly good reasons to reject amniocentesis. These were women who had previously suffered the anguish of losing a wanted pregnancy during the second trimester. For them, an earlier option was worth the still undetermined risks of the new procedure (Jackson, 1985a, 1985b). Soon other clinics began to offer CVS on an experimental basis.

Initial reports of CVS were hailed by physicians as a major advance, perhaps "the greatest thing since sliced bread" (Kolata, 1990, p. 57). Although all invasive procedures carry some risk, few doubted the superiority of a first-trimester procedure over a later one. Pregnant women, it was believed, would benefit from shortening the "tentative pregnancy." Should an abnormality be diagnosed, women would avoid the trauma of abortion in midpregnancy. First-trimester diagnosis might even make it possible to treat the fetus in utero. Eventually, many physicians and geneticists believed, CVS would replace amniocentesis altogether. They predicted that without the limitations of the older technique prenatal diagnosis would become more attractive, and its use would spread. Eventually, this would help to wipe out many genetic abnormalities.

The euphoria soon died down, however. Concerns about the safety and accuracy of CVS have limited its appeal. In Holland a study of two thousand pregnant women aged 36 or more showed that, while the acceptance of CVS grew after its comparative safety had been established, the total number of women who had prenatal diagnosis did not change. The newer procedure simply drew off some clients who would otherwise have had amniocentesis (Brandenburg et al., 1992).

Jefferson Medical College in Philadelphia, interested in accumulating enough data to determine the accuracy and safety of CVS, has been keeping an international registry of the procedure. This registry is based on voluntary reporting by physicians. By 1992 more than 150,000 CVS procedures performed in the United States had been reported to the Philadelphia center; the worldwide figure was approximately twice that (Dr. Laird Jackson, personal communication, March 10, 1993). The registry reveals a wide variation in the rate of pregnancy loss following CVS. The cumulative loss rates range from 20 percent in Stockholm and 13 percent in Glasgow to 2 percent or less in Los Angeles, Philadelphia, and Athens (*CVS Newsletter* No. 32, January 31, 1993). The pattern is clear: the more experienced the physician in performing the procedure, the lower the hazard (Williams et al., 1992).

The precise risk of miscarriage with CVS is hard to calculate. Miscarriage may occur as a result of accidental rupture of the amniotic sac, cervical infection, bleeding, or damage to the chorionic membrane. However, most *spontaneous* miscarriages occur in the first trimester of the pregnancy. Many fetal deaths occur in the first two months, but there is a delay of several weeks before the fetus is expelled and the miscarriage clinically recognized. Even when the pregnancy is viable at the time of the CVS, a spontaneous loss may occur later. The spontaneous loss rate is higher in older women, those who are candidates for prenatal diagnosis. In many cases there is no definitive way either to link it to the procedure or to rule out such causation (Green et al., 1988; Wilcox et al., 1988).

To determine the safety of CVS, a randomized clinical trial in Canada compared women who had CVS with those who had amniocentesis. Subtracting the "background loss," the investigators found out that the loss rate following CVS exceeded that of amniocentesis by less than 1 percent (Canadian Collaborative CVS-Amniocentesis Clinical Trial Group, 1989). Similar results were obtained in American studies, including a trial sponsored by NICHD (Goldberg et al., 1990; Green et al., 1988).

Maternal complications as a result of CVS are rare but not unknown. In San Francisco, a 34-year-old woman in the twelfth week of her pregnancy went into septic shock after the procedure and developed a high fever and kidney failure. When her condition did not improve after the fetus was removed in pieces, her uterus and ovaries were taken out. This woman, who had suffered two previous unsuccessful pregnancies, not only lost this hoped-for baby, but found her own life in danger and lost all chances of having biological children in the future (Barela et al., 1986).

Ironically, CVS, developed as an early and safe procedure to detect birth defects, has been implicated in causing such defects. Reports from Oxford, England, and from Chicago indicate that 1 to 2 percent of the babies born to women who had CVS were born with severe limb and jaw deformities. This condition occurs naturally in 1 in 175,000 live births. Possibly, removing villi from the chorion might have started tiny hemorrhages that disrupted the blood supply to the fetus and caused abnormalities in the limbs (Burton, Schulz, and Laurence, 1992; Firth et al., 1991). However, a panel of experts convened in 1992 by the National Institutes of Health concluded that the numbers involved are too small to link the deformity with the procedure. New data suggest that clusters of abnormalities may occur without apparent cause (van den Anker et al., 1993).

Other concerns have to do with the diagnostic accuracy of the procedure. Some abnormalities found in the placental cells are not present in the fetus. This is particularly true of mosaicisms, that is, abnormalities that affect some but not all of the cells. Tragically, such *false positive* results have led a few women to abort a fetus that was subsequently found to be normal (Rhoads et al., 1989).

It is now recognized that when a mosaicism or other unusual or ambiguous condition is diagnosed, a followup amniocentesis is required to confirm the diagnosis (Green et al., 1988; Miny et al., 1991).

The reports of possible complications and unresolved concerns resulting from CVS have tempered the rosy predictions of its pioneers. Moreover, the difference in timing between amniocentesis and CVS has narrowed. For reasons of safety and accuracy, CVS is now not recommended before the tenth to twelfth week of the pregnancy. At the same time, the gestational age for amniocentesis is dropping. The two procedures, though technically different, are not as divergent in their implications for women's lives as was once believed. Rather, they are variations on one theme: invasive procedures that have changed the stakes and the experience of pregnancy.

MATERNAL SERUM ALPHA-FETOPROTEIN (MSAFP)

In the early 1980s, when concerns about amniocentesis were becoming increasingly vocal, Rothman asked women whether they would find prenatal diagnosis more acceptable if they could have a simple blood test instead of an invasive, unpleasant, and hazardous procedure. The technology for AFP screening was already in place, but the possibility of a completely safe test still struck most people as science fiction. A small but definite risk had always been an integral part of the cost-benefit equation of prenatal diagnosis: women risked miscarriage in the hope of increasing their chances of having a healthy baby. Many believed that a noninvasive test would not only change that calculus but also revolutionize the meaning of motherhood by making screening universal and lowering society's tolerance for disabilities. As Rothman predicted,

I think that an early blood test will strip the problem down to its bare bones. I think it will take us past questions of risk, of date and of technique, to confront the essential moral and ethical issues. It will take us straight to the meaning of motherhood, the ethics of abortion, and the human ability to control nature. (1986, p. 79)

Today the AFP test is a routine part of prenatal care in many states and foreign countries. An estimated two million procedures had been performed in the United States by the end of 1990 (Elias and Simpson, 1992, p. 83). Yet this test continues to raise troublesome issues.

MSAFP is a simple, relatively inexpensive test performed in the sixteenth to eighteenth week of the pregnancy to measure the amount of alpha-fetoprotein, a substance produced by the fetus and excreted through the amniotic fluid to the pregnant woman's bloodstream. An abnormally high amount of AFP in the woman's blood indicates the possibility of a neural tube defect such as spina bifida or anencephaly. An abnormally low amount indicates that the fetus may have Down's syndrome. Since the test does not detect other chromosomal abnormalities, the total proportion of abnormalities excluded by a "normal" finding is very small. If the AFP count is outside the range regarded as normal, the woman is referred for further testing by amniocentesis or ultrasound to confirm the results.

The problem is that AFP testing is relatively inaccurate, with diagnostic errors occurring both in the *false negative* and *false positive* directions. The false negative refers to cases of abnormality missed by screening: about 10 percent of neural tube disorders and as many as two-thirds of Down's syndrome cases will escape detection. Recently, researchers have been able to improve the detection rate of fetuses with Down's syndrome by measuring additional chemicals in the mother's blood (Haddow et al., 1992).

False positives occur when the initial AFP results are abnormally high or low, yet the fetus turns out to be healthy. The vast majority of the abnormal readings are false positives. In only one out of forty or fifty cases does a followup amniocentesis or ultrasound confirm the presence of an abnormality.

The unreliability of AFP testing stems from variations in the quality of commercial kits available and in the rigor of the laboratory protocol. It also mirrors the naturally occurring differences in the level of chemicals produced by women of different ages, races, weights, and medical conditions at different points in the pregnancy. Since it is hard to establish exactly how much AFP and other chemicals each woman is supposed to have at each point in her pregnancy, it is not always clear what constitutes an abnormally high or low level and what such levels actually reveal about the fetus's condition (Blatt, 1988).

Concerned about the uneven quality of AFP screening, the American Society of Human Genetics (ASHG) has published policy statements for its appropriate use. The statements cover availability, staff training, standards of measurement, quality of laboratory work, interpretation of test results, counseling, and followup testing of positive findings. The policy statements recommend state licensing of laboratories and regulation of screening (ASHG, 1987; Garver, 1989). However, only a few states have followed these guidelines. Most states have little or no regulation, whether because of lack of funding, lack of interest, or lack of expertise at the state level (Cunningham and Kizer, 1990).

Economically, AFP screening is highly cost-effective. Health economists have calculated that the financial cost of detecting and "preventing" each case of neural tube defect or Down's syndrome is between one-eight and one-tenth that of caring for a disabled child over a lifetime. These savings assume the "replacement" of each aborted fetus with a normal child (Gill, Murday, and Slack, 1987; Milunsky and Alpert, 1984; Schwager and Weiss, 1987). Although babies are not replaceable to mothers, they are to society.

The American College of Obstetricians and Gynecologists (ACOG) and others recommend that AFP testing be offered to all pregnant women, including those younger than 35 and without reasons to fear an abnormality (ACOG, 1985; Elias and Simpson, 1992, p. 94). This recommendation is not explicitly motivated by concern for the parents' stake in the birth of healthy children. It is based, rather, on the potential costs of disability to physicians, who may be sued for practice over the birth of a child with a detectable abnormality, and to society, which must foot the medical and educational bills.

Both the cost-effectiveness studies and the ACOG recommendations ignore the emotional costs to pregnant women. The personal costs arise partly from the test's inaccuracy. For each fetus whose Down's syndrome or neural tube defect would not have been detected without AFP screening, forty or fifty women who initially had no reason for concern will suffer the dread of an abnormal finding. Unless they choose to accept the chances of a defective baby or to terminate the pregnancy right away, these women will have to undergo amniocentesis or ultrasound at eighteen or twenty weeks' gestational age. If they have amniocentesis, they must wait an additional several weeks for the results. By that time they will be in the fifth or sixth month of pregnancy.

By all accounts, the anxiety caused by bad news is very high. Genetic counselor Kathy Keenan and her colleagues in Albany, New York (1991), have found that on a standardized anxiety scale, women who receive an abnormal AFP result measure a whopping 56.5 compared to a mean of 36 for those who receive normal results. Expectant mothers score much higher than expectant fathers. (By contrast, the mean anxiety score for the average medical patient is 42 and for patients with acute anxiety, 48.) London psychologist Theresa Marteau and her colleagues (1992a, p. 211) report similar findings: "Receiving an abnormal AFP result on a routine screening test is associated with extremely high levels of maternal anxiety, as high as patients with a diagnosis of generalized anxiety disorder . . . and higher than patients the night before major surgery." Furthermore, women who have amniocentesis because of an abnormal AFP finding are so upset by the initial results that they view their pregnancies as substantially more vulnerable than those who choose amniocentesis for advanced maternal age alone. Their fears do not reflect the real dangers, since an equally high number—98 percent or more—eventually will receive good news (Evans et al., 1988).

Even when the initial abnormal finding turns out to be unfounded, the cloud cast over the pregnancy is not easily dispelled. Marteau and her colleagues (1992a, p. 208) have found that "three weeks following any possible subsequent tests, women who had received an abnormal result were still more anxious, more worried about their baby's health, and held more negative attitudes towards their pregnancy compared with women who had received a normal AFP test result on first testing." Fears persist because the pregnant woman believes that the initial bad results had to indicate some underlying problem, since "there is no smoke without fire." Or perhaps she is so upset that she simply cannot process any new information without distortion. The belief that something must be wrong is not entirely irrational. Several studies have found that regardless of any clinical finding of abnormality, an elevated AFP level in the mother's blood is associated with increased odds of subsequent fetal death from a variety of causes (Waller et al., 1991).

British researchers Helen Statham and Josephine Green report that the clinic staff is often unprepared to cope with fears caused by positive results from AFP testing. Staff "are lulled into a sense of security that the [followup] tests will give comfort . . . .[Clients] were told that something was sufficiently worrying to warrant an invasive procedure with a risk of miscarriage, and then told to go away and not worry" (1993, p. 175). The authors, acknowledging that many women want this screening, recommend better support services to help women cope with the distress of abnormal findings.

In principle, of course, pregnant women are free to reject any medical intervention. In practice, where MSAFP screening is routine, women are rarely given information in a way that encourages them to make an informed decision—or any decision. A woman coming for an appointment with her obstetrician might be told, along with a great deal of other information about prenatal care and blood tests:

- And we do another blood test for spina bifida.
- At about 16 or 17 weeks we do an AFP test to make sure the baby is normal. (See also Marteau et al., 1992b.)

UCLA researchers Nancy Ann Press and C. H. Browner (1993) charge that providers of AFP testing carefully construct a "collective fiction." They present the test to clients as a routine part of the standard prenatal care package, while avoiding details about the conditions for which it screens and omitting the fact that the only practical recourse for these conditions may be abortion. In the information booklet given to patients, not until the last page does one find "a small section entitled, 'What happens if the tests show that the fetus has a birth defect?' " The booklet then states that after further testing the patient will be given more information on the defect, that "different options will be discussed," and that services are available to "support whatever decision the woman makes." " 'Option' and 'decision', therefore, appear to be code words for abortion, while 'special services' and 'support' are the only indications that this decision may be painful or morally difficult" (p. 102). The authors charge that AFP providers deliberately obscure both the optional nature of the test and its potentially horrendous consequences because they must walk a political tightrope. On one hand, they are under pressure to offer the test to all pregnant women in order to forestall malpractice suits. On the other hand, they wish to avoid legislative and public scrutiny from anti-abortion forces.

Not surprisingly, clients surveyed by Press and Browner one to two months after the procedure remembered little about it. Most could not name the conditions for which it screened or describe their meaning. They interpreted the test primarily as a "ritual of reassurance" that the pregnancy was going well. Much was made of the importance of gaining as much knowledge as possible about the fetus; neither the value of this knowledge nor its implications for parental action were questioned. This is even more striking than it appears at first, for the clients in this study were all Catholic. Although most were opposed to abortion, they saw no inherent contradictions in the testing, perhaps because of the way they had been led through it.

In sum, AFP testing, despite its limits and ambiguities, is an increasingly routine part of prenatal care. Like other obstetrical interventions, this "choice" is in most cases neither presented nor perceived as a choice. It is something women have done to them and for which they have to pay the price. (Paradoxically, studies show that a "low-tech" intervention, multivitamins with folic acid, can lower the risk of malformations. Taken before conception or early in the pregnancy such nutritional supplements cut the risk of neural type defects.)

ULTRASOUND

Ultrasound originated as sonar, a technique developed in World War I for detecting submarines under water. By measuring the time it took pulses of high-frequency energy to be reflected back from a surface, scientists could measure an object hidden from view and produce its image on a monitor. Only in the 1960s did attention turn to visualizing fetuses as well as submarines (Wertz and Wertz, 1989 [1977], p. 246–247).

Ultrasound (or sonography) is used with other procedures to determine the gestational age and location of the fetus and to guide the instruments. It is also used by itself, to diagnose certain abnormalities of the fetus and the placenta, as well as to determine the gestational age and number of fetuses. The latest generation of high-resolution real-time scanners makes it possible for clinicians to observe an extensive range of fetal anatomy and physiology. At 18 to 20 weeks' gestational age, the central nervous system, facial anatomy, neck, thorax, heart, abdomen, kidneys, and limbs are visible to a skilled sonographer. Certain facial features may indicate the possibility of Down's syndrome. An obstruction of the small intestine by fetal stool suggests that the fetus may have cystic fibrosis. In some cases the ultrasound diagnosis is considered definitive; in others the woman is referred for more tests (Carlson and Platt, 1992; O'Brien, 1989).

Late in the pregnancy, ultrasound may be used to estimate the fetus's gestational age and assess its condition. A decreased volume of amniotic fluid or the absence of limb movements, eye movements, or breathing in the near-term fetus may indicate oxygen deficiency. This condition is associated with permanent neurological damage. In cases where the fetus appears threatened, labor may be induced or the baby delivered by a caesarian section (Manning, 1990).

Although few doubt the contributions of ultrasound to the diagnosis and management of specific problems, the medical community is divided over the merits of scanning all pregnancies. Randomized clinical studies have consistently failed to show that routine screening results in healthier babies overall (Ewigman et al., 1993). Moreover, although there are no observed immediate risks, the long-term effects of ultrasound in the fetus are not known.

Ultrasound, like MSAFP, is now used routinely in prenatal care, with most women subjected to multiple examinations during their pregnancy.[1] In several countries, including Britain, France, and Germany, obstetrical practice guidelines call for screening all pregnancies (D'Alton and DeCherney, 1993).

Ultrasound has revolutionized physicians' view of pregnancy, giving rise to a new specialty, maternal-fetal medicine. As the fetus has become a patient in its own right, obstetrical textbooks have devoted proportionately more pages to the fetus, and fewer to the mother (Gegor, 1992; Plauche, 1993). The results of fetal medicine, however, have been disappointing: most serious fetal disorders cannot be treated in utero.

Ultrasound has transformed the pregnancy experience for parents as well. Birth, once seen as the beginning of life, is now viewed almost as though it were merely a physical passage from one place to another. Imaging facilitates maternal bonding with the fetus before other signs of its life are present. During the second trimester it is often possible to determine the sex of the fetus by visualizing its genitals; this further humanizes it.

For parents-to-be, ultrasound, more than other prenatal tests, has gone a long way toward blurring the distinction between "expecting" and "having." A July 4, 1992, obituary in the *New York Times* for Rabbi Marc Tanenbaum, aged 66, lists among his many accomplishments "proud father-to-be of Joshua." Joshua, we learn, is not due to be born for three months after his father's death. Mr. Tanenbaum had grown children from his first marriage; Joshua was conceived in his second marriage. His family wanted him to know that even before birth he was much loved by his father. To his family he is real enough to be listed among the survivors of the deceased, although he is not yet a member of society.

Imaging the fetus is very enjoyable when all goes well. The ultrasound session may become a social event, with the couple's children and friends present. In Australia, physicians have found it necessary to warn that, "although ultrasound can be great fun" for the pregnant woman and her family, it should not be used for "entertainment" purposes alone, without medical reasons, because of its potential hazards and cost (Furness, 1990).

The enjoyment may turn into tragedy with little warning. Occasionally, the sonogram will show that the fetus is dead or that the pregnancy is nonviable. Unlike other tests, where the parents must wait for the lab report and bad news is mediated by the physician or genetic counselor, ultrasound takes place in "real time." The information is known to the technician and the patient at virtually the same time. This heightens the parents' shock and makes it harder for the staff to deal with the parents' grief (Green et al., 1988). When an untreatable abnormality is found and the woman terminates the pregnancy, a fetus that has been made more real by ultrasound is mourned more keenly.

PERCUTANEOUS UMBILICAL BLOOD SAMPLING (PUBS), FETAL BIOPSY, AND EMBRYOSCOPY

PUBS may be performed between the eighteenth and thirty-sixth week in the pregnancy. In this procedure physicians, while performing amniocentesis, insert a needle into the umbilical vein and draw a blood sample from it. Results are usually available within forty-eight to seventy-two hours. The sample may be tested for chromosomal defects as well as for AIDS, sickle-cell anemia, and other blood disorders. It may also be used for confirming ambiguous amniocentesis or CVS results. Unlike other techniques, where the only practical recourse for most anomalies is abortion, PUBS makes possible not only diagnosis but also, in some cases, therapy. Because it provides direct access to the fetus, PUBS may be used for interuterine blood transfusions and medications.

PUBS is difficult to perform because the umbilical cord is hard to reach and moves around. In addition, the blood sample may be contaminated with amniotic fluid. Infection, blood loss to the fetus, and accidental perforation of the uterine arteries may cause miscarriage. The rate of miscarriage is estimated at 1 to 2 percent more than the background risk to the fetus. The long-term effects of PUBS are not known (D'Alton and DeCherney, 1993; Hobbins et al., 1985).

Another procedure, fetal biopsy, may be used to obtain samples of the fetal skin, liver, or muscle. It is used to diagnose disorders that cannot be found by DNA analysis. Initially, such biopsies were performed by fetoscopy, which entails inserting a fetoscope through the woman's abdomen into the uterus. Today they are done with the guidance of ultrasound. The rate of fetal loss with both fetal biopsy and fetoscopy is relatively high (D'Alton and DeCherney, 1993).

A few physicians have used an experimental technique called embryoscopy. By inserting a tiny viewing scope into a woman's abdomen, they have been able to view, with remarkable clarity, an embryo just 6 weeks old. At this gestational age, the embryo is about half an inch long and shaped like a comma; an ultrasound would show only a blur. With this experimental technique physicians may be able to diagnose some defects that cannot be found with conventional methods, as well as those that normally cannot be detected until later in the pregnancy (Kolata, 1993).

EMBRYO DIAGNOSIS

In principle, the grief and trauma of abortion may be sidestepped if an embryo created through in vitro fertilization can be tested for abnormalities before implantation in the mother's womb. One cell from the embryo, which at this point consists of perhaps eight cells, can be extracted and tested for genetic disorders such as Tay-Sachs or cystic fibrosis. It can also be sexed. If the couple is at risk of passing to their sons a sex-linked disorder such as hemophilia, only female embryos will be implanted. The affected embryos (and, in cases where it is impossible to distinguish affected from normal male embryos, all male ones) are discarded. As of this writing, embryo diagnosis is limited to couples already undergoing IVF (in vitro fertilization).

As with older tests, however, medical researchers and practitioners have responded with enthusiasm. Some physicians believe that this technology will bring society closer to the elimination of genetic diseases by making it possible to discard defective embryos or, in the future, by treating the abnormal gene. Some writers foresee that if access to legal abortion is curtailed, embryo diagnosis will offer an alternative to prenatal testing and pregnancy termination. It is even possible that fertile couples who may be either morally opposed to termination or denied access to it will choose this route to have a healthy baby:

Embryo replacement would not raise any concern about "tentative pregnancies," since the embryos are created *in vitro* and any diseased ones are discarded . . . prior to being implanted in the woman's uterus and the establishment of a clinical pregnancy. Thus the detecting of abnormalities in the embryo would have the advantage of sparing some couples the emotional trauma of an abortion in the fifth month of pregnancy. (Steinbock, 1992, p. 205)

But embryo biopsy is fraught with ethical and pragmatic problems. The accuracy of results obtained from testing a single cell is of necessity limited; many false negatives and false positives occur. Furthermore, encouraging fertile couples to have IVF in order to avoid abortion is unconscionable. The rates of successful pregnancy with IVF are low, and the physical, psychological, and financial toll on the woman is very high. As political scientist Andrea Bonnicksen (1992, p. S6) points out, "Embryo diagnosis is a window to new technological tinkering with reproduction that, while holding promise, opens the door to stress, discomfort, and expense for women in the short run and pressures for assisted conception as a standard procedure in the long run." Rothman (1992, p. S11–S12) adds, "IVF and embryo retrieval procedures do not take place on a couple's body—it is a woman on the table, a woman who bears the costs of this treatment . . . .The 'gold' [embryos have been compared to gold nuggets] may be impressive, but it is mined, not without cost, from the bodies of women."

PRENATAL TESTS: A SYNTHESIS

The history of prenatal testing reveals the gap between the intended benefits of technological change and its unintended consequences. Each test, when first developed, is hailed with excitement in the medical community. In time, the diagnostic accuracy rises and the physical hazards decline. Use of the procedures spreads, prompting some writers to predict the eventual "eradication" of birth defects. Few in the medical community doubt that women will embrace the new technologies. The benefits seem obvious: for would-be parents, healthier babies, and not coincidentally, for society, a healthier population and a significant financial saving. The question of abortion—its continued availability and acceptability—is commonly sidestepped.

The psychological costs and ethical dilemmas raised by prenatal testing are explored less commonly. Clients' concerns about the trauma of terminating a wanted pregnancy, the agony of waiting for the results at a point in the pregnancy when abortion is unthinkable, and the stress arising from false positive results are often pushed aside as unimportant, if not as impediments to medical progress (Hodge, 1989).

In time there are new technological breakthroughs. The cycle begins again: initially, an unbounded optimism about the potential of the new procedure, later tempered by a realization of its limits, hazards, and costs. Meanwhile, the search goes on for a "perfect" procedure, one that is noninvasive and yet may be used early in the pregnancy, when (in the view of the medical community) abortion is not problematic. Yet for women, the dilemmas of prenatal testing do not vanish; they only change with the technology.

NOTE

1. In individual cases, however, ultrasound may be critical. Randomized studies carry little weight with physicians who have seen what can happen when ultrasound is not performed routinely. One of the counselors we interviewed for our study reported the following episode. A woman gave birth to a child with a holoproscencephaly (no division between the right and left hemisphere of the brain). This defect is usually lethal. The baby lived for a short time after birth. "The condition was discovered when an ultrasound was performed at 38 weeks to determine the delivery date. Then the father asked if this could not have been discovered earlier, which of course it could have been if a routine ultrasound had been done in the second trimester . . . .But a lot of doctors still themselves subscribe to the concept of 'natural pregnancy.' " An earlier ultrasound would have detected the anomaly in time for the woman to abort. The arguments in favor of routine screening, then, are genuine.

3

The Evolution of an Ethos:
Counselors and Nondirectiveness

CHANGING CHARACTERISTICS OF A CHANGING PROFESSION

As a profession, genetic counseling has changed notably in the past quarter-century. These changes reflect parallel shifts in the training and demographic characteristics of the typical counselor and in the risk factors of the typical client. In this chapter we summarize these changes in the counseling profession and examine whether counselors' self-reported behavior in several common scenarios is consistent with the ethos of nondirectiveness to which the profession subscribes. In the next chapter we examine individual variations in the conduct of a routine prenatal counseling session.

Until the advent of amniocentesis in the late 1960s, the typical counselor was an academically affiliated geneticist with or without an M.D. By the mid-1970s hospital-based pediatricians played an increasing role. Clients were typically parents who had already borne a child with a genetic disease or with a family history of genetic disease. They were referred to an M.D.–geneticist by the physician or hospital unit who was treating their sick child. Commonly, they faced recurrence risks of 10, 25, and even 50 percent, depending on their child's disorder (Bosk, 1992; Dicker and Dicker, 1978)

Medical sociologist James Sorenson has conducted one of the earliest large-scale studies of genetic counselors. In 1973 he obtained responses from nearly five hundred active U.S. counselors (three-quarters of the total identified). Eighty percent held M.D. degrees (including 10 percent with additional Ph.D.s); 11 percent held Ph.D.s solely; and 9 percent held other degrees. Seventy-four percent were male; respondents' mean age was 43. The understanding and prevention of genetic diseases dominated their professional goals, being rated as very important by 77 and 83 percent of respondents, respectively. However, nearly as many (74 percent) felt it very important to lessen the anxiety of clients. Only 10 percent felt that "improvement of the general health and vigor of the population" was "very important" (1973, p. 32).

The development of amniocentesis with its heretofore unavailable fetal information coincided with the liberalization of abortion laws. These events led to a surge of clients whose primary risk factor was advanced maternal age.

The mushrooming demand for genetic counseling strained existing facilities and personnel and sensitized practitioners to the need to address psychosocial as well as medical issues (Kenen, 1984). The staff shortage led first to an influx of psychologists, nurses, and social workers and then to the first master's level genetic counseling/associate program, at Sarah Lawrence College in 1969. Thus evolved a separate non-M.D. specialty grounded equally in medical science and in psychology. These new counselors shared a greater uniformity of training and a professional socialization stressing nondirective counseling.

By the late 1970s a research team led by Sorenson found that master's degree holders comprised 19 percent of the 205 counselors at nearly fifty clinics (Sorenson, Swazey, and Scotch, 1981). The proportion of M.D.s declined to 67 percent (8 percent with M.D.s/Ph.D.s), and of Ph.D.s alone to 6 percent. The sex composition of the counselors was not recorded in that study.

The first National Society of Genetic Counselors (NSGC) professional status survey, conducted in 1981, underscored the sea change that had occurred in the demographic characteristics of genetic counselors. Ninety percent of the 150 respondents (out of 238 full members) were female; 80 percent had a master's degree from a genetic counseling training program; and an additional 18 percent had a master's degree in a related area, including social work, nursing, public health, and counseling (Begleiter, Collins, and Greendale, 1981, p. 1).

By mid-1993 the NSGC had 1,061 members, of whom 464 were among the roughly 1,650 persons certified by the American Board of Medical Genetics (ABMG) (Bea Leopold of the NSGC, personal communication, June 22, 1993). NSGC members now receive their own professional certification from the American Board of Genetic Counseling; those already Board-certified retain their ABMG certification.

Demographically, today's NSGC members resemble their typical client more than they do the counselors surveyed in 1973. They have continued to be overwhelmingly female (93.3 percent) and youthful (78.3 percent of respondents to the 1990 NSGC members' survey were between the ages of 25 and 39; see Edwards, 1990, p. 7). More than 90 percent have a master's degree, and 57 percent had five or more years of experience.

COUNSELORS' TRAINING AND AN EVOLVING PROFESSIONAL ETHOS

Differences in training between M.S. and M.D./Ph.D. counselors were manifest in Sorenson's later study. While nearly all counselors reported having received both didactic courses and clinical training in human genetics, only among master's holders did a majority report having had didactic courses in counseling (89.5 percent of this group versus 27.7 percent of M.D.s and 12.5 percent of M.D./Ph.D.s: Sorenson, Swazey, and Scotch, 1981, pp. 39–40). The master's level counselors also shared a greater uniformity of training than did M.D. counselors.

Given the different professional codes subscribed to by these different disciplines, it is to be expected that their practitioners approach counseling goals differently. In 1973, 54 percent of all counselors supported total nondirectiveness, defined as "leaving all decisions to the parents." This group far outnumbered the 7 percent who would "always tell the parents what they would do in the same circumstances, or give outright advice on what parents 'ought' to do." But the large majority of counselors did not recoil from influencing clients' decisions indirectly, "not so much by direct advice as by the way they present information, emphasizing that which reflects their own experiences and attitudes. Fully 64 percent felt it was 'always appropriate' to inform counselees in a way that would 'guide them toward an appropriate decision' " (Sorenson, 1973, p. 32).

The changed ethos of the discipline is rooted partly in the shift in professional background, as sociologist Rose Weitz notes: "In the ideal [genetic counseling] situation, the client, not the physician, makes the final decision. This contrasts sharply with traditional medical norms, which stress that good medical practice consists of professionals making expert judgements based on their own clinical judgement" (1981, p. 208).

The counselor's sex also affects directiveness. Researchers who have conducted large-scale surveys of genetic counselors with various credentials agree that women counsel differently from men (Zare, Sorenson, and Heeren, 1984) and in particular, that women are less directive than men (Wertz and Fletcher, 1988). Therefore, the changing sex composition of counselors should also affect the counseling session's style and content.

The principle of "nondirectiveness" underlies several of the fourteen genetic counseling principles set forth in a casebook emanating from a workshop at Sarah Lawrence College (Marks et al., 1989). Under "respect the autonomy and decision-making capacity of the patient" are such items as "assume a nondirective stance," "refuse to answer the question, 'What would you do if you were in my shoes?'," and "support the patient's belief that he/she is the one best suited to make whatever decisions are appropriate." Related principles include "maintain surveillance over one's own biases and values" and "work consistently toward empowering patients to make autonomous decisions and to advocate on their own behalf."

How these principles are best honored in actual clinical practice is a matter of intense professional debate. Does directiveness encompass the counselors' professional judgment of the amount of information clients are able to absorb and their commitment to the view that clients should have as much information as possible themselves? Does directiveness signify solely the injection of someone else's opinions and values into the decision-making process, or does it include reassuring and supporting someone in following a clearly preferred path?

Rothman (1986) and Rapp (1988a) have discerned some directiveness in many routine management protocols that counselors believe are nondirective. Rothman and two research assistants interviewed twenty-five genetic counselors in the early to mid-1980s, in addition to spending a month observing three different counselors at work. They focused primarily on the ordinary counseling session for advanced maternal age. While honoring the nondirective ethos of the counselors and the profession, Rothman questions their ability to translate this ideal into practice. She concludes that counselors' private views and misgivings have to find their way into counselor-client interactions.

They are trying, if directing at all, to steer the woman in the direction they think she wants to go. . . . A number of counselors said that they tried to steer women with a history of infertility or repeated miscarriages away from amnio, or from doing anything that might disrupt the pregnancy; and some said they were most clearly directive when it comes to Tay-Sachs disease. (Rothman, 1986, p. 42)

Rapp, who observed more than two hundred genetic counseling sessions in New York City and interviewed some thirty counselors, shares Rothman's uneasiness. The counselors had been trained in a noninterventionist Rogerian therapy aimed at helping the patient make up her own mind through mutual counselor/patient participation in decision making. Yet in adapting the speech codes of scientific vocabulary and information-giving to the needs and worldviews of clients from diverse social classes and ethnic backgrounds, counselors experienced a tension between value-free and directive counseling.

CHALLENGES TO NONDIRECTIVENESS

In the clinics that participated in our study, genetic associates are the gatekeepers who conduct all preliminary interviews. Unless an anomaly is identified, clients never see an M.D. geneticist/counselor. Our respondents, all but two of whom were women, had characteristically been exposed to counseling-oriented training. Of a total of thirty-six counselors, half had been trained at Sarah Lawrence, another fourteen had masters in genetic counseling or other fields from other institutions, one (a pediatric geneticist) had an M.D., and three had only a bachelor's degree and on-the-job training (Table 3.1).

When they were interviewed, twenty-eight of our counselors were working at centers that offered both amnio and CVS, and eight were at centers that offered amnio only. (Some of these centers were preparing to offer CVS.)

Table 3.1
Counselor Training by Region of Employment (N=36[1])

| CITY/REGION | M.D. | ACADEMIC CREDENTIALS/BACKGROUND | | | | |
		M.S. GENETIC COUNSELING	M.S. GENETICS	NURSING	ON-THE-JOB TRAINING	TOTAL
NEW YORK CITY	-	14 (Sarah Lawrence)	1	-	-	15
NEW YORK STATE/CHICAGO	-	11	-	1 (pediatric spec.)	-	12
SAN DIEGO	-	-	1	1 (M.S.)	2 (one with B.A.)	4
WASHINGTON/ BALTIMORE	1	3	1	-	-	5
	1	28	3	2	2	36

[1] 34 women, 2 men

We anticipated that the shifts in the typical counselor's training and sex ought to be reflected in both a self-consciousness among counselors about behavior that might be considered "directive" and a reluctance to engage in directive behavior. Indeed, concerned that we would distort the intent behind their responses and mistrustful of our intentions, several counselors granted us interviews only after we reassured them that we had no preset agenda. On the other hand, we could make a contrary argument that the increased demographic resemblance between counselor and client might tempt a counselor to steer a client away from a decision that the counselor believes would be costly in all senses to the client and her family.

Commitment to nondirective counseling is tested in several contexts. The first decision a client has to make is whether to have prenatal testing; the second (if early enough) is whether to have CVS or amnio; a third decision is whether to have further testing after a high or low AFP result at week 16 of pregnancy; and the fourth is whether to have an abortion subsequent to an abnormal result. The first three decisions ultimately revolve around clients' perceptions of risk levels (see Chapter 7).

In the following sections, we examine whether the professional commitment to nondirective counseling is challenged by how a counselor perceives the genetic risk to an individual client or by the expected cost of the risked outcome (the probability of an adverse finding multiplied by the economic and parental/family burden of caring for an afflicted child). We also explore how counselors' nondirectiveness is tested in the more time-pressured context of counseling AFP-referred clients.

In addition to asking about specific counseling scenarios, we asked counselors where they put themselves on the directive–nondirective continuum and under what circumstances they might be more or less so. (See Appendix B for the genetic counselors' interview guide.) Counselors' reports on their own behavior were also embedded in several responses to risk interpretation questions.

To Test or Not to Test?

Question: Approximately what is the refusal rate here for both amnio and CVS; that is, how many clients decline any prenatal diagnosis after counseling? What reasons do they give? How do you feel about these reasons; that is, are there "good" and "bad" reasons for declining prenatal diagnosis?

All counselors surveyed believed that the decision whether or not to have prenatal diagnosis belonged solely and ultimately to the client (and her partner). Perhaps the strongest statement is the following (yet even this counselor can offer exceptions to this policy):

I never recommend. It's the core of our training: "reproductive freedom is reproductive freedom." I think nondirective counseling is hard on some clients. So I give examples: "Some couples may have tried very hard to achieve a pregnancy—they have used IVF [in vitro fertilization]—and won't risk for prenatal testing. Others don't have a problem [getting pregnant] and want to run the risk." Some people think having to make the decision is the hardest thing and decline the test.

This same counselor wondered whether informing the client of all options might itself seem directive: "Here we start off by stressing that testing is optional. If anything, I'm directive in letting them know it's not for everyone. If the [doctor] sends someone over with problems [i.e., a high-risk client], it's our first contact."

Counselors have become so sensitized to the insinuation of being directive that one could argue that they may be tempted to omit vital medical information. One counselor said, "I'm not sure this is directive: I'd suggest to a black [the option of] sickle-cell testing; to a Jew, Tay-Sachs."

Although the above counselors used the word "directive," no counselor viewed that kind of information and permission-giving as the sort of directiveness their training had warned against. Readers must judge for themselves if the following constitutes true directiveness:

I'm probably moderate—in the middle. I won't tell patients what to do. But I will say, "That sounds like a logical decision" or "that sounds good to me" and support them. . . . Once I had a patient who came for CVS and couldn't decide on that or amnio. She called the Friday before the Monday [of the test] and said, "I still can't make up my mind." I said, "Don't have it. There is no right decision. If this feels so bad, don't have it." She felt wonderful. I told her, "If you are this stuck, this is not the test for you. This [indecisiveness] has been going on for days." If you can hear they're not the average fence sitter, but really are uncomfortable, I'll support [whichever they're leaning toward].

The nondirective professional stance is clearly at variance with the counselors' personal preferences. Asked whether they would have prenatal testing themselves, all counselors without exception said yes. One counselor, however, an older woman past childbearing years, said without conviction, "I have normal children. I grew up in a time without it. I'd probably use it—why not." Repeatedly, counselors acknowledged they know too much about bad results, even if rare, to abide by even the recommended age guidelines, much less reject testing absolutely:

- For myself I'd have it at any age. I would try to be more objective, but I think anyone in mid-20s approaching 30 should have it. In this business, [there's] a total reversal [from denial] to feeling at risk for everything.
- I know a lot of counselors have amnio. At [mid-20s] I might not have anything, or might have amnio—probably have amnio. I'm at low risk, but at 16 weeks I'd worry enough to want to know for sure! I'm a worrier anyhow! It's based on the fact that I'm surrounded by abnormalities, not on objective risk. Otherwise, I'd be worried only at 35.

CVS or Amnio?

Question: If a client showed no preference, would you recommend CVS or amnio? Why?

For many women, avoiding a possible second-trimester abortion justifies taking the added procedural risk associated with CVS (see Chapter 7). All counselors believed the choice between CVS and amnio was ultimately the client's. Twenty-seven or three-fourth of our respondents stated this belief unequivocally:

- I would explore both options. I think it should be their decision. I actually have no preference.
- I don't recommend, just point out everything about both. A lot of people are terrified about chromosome abnormalities, and CVS won't show neural tube defects.
- I am *very* careful to correct misconceptions about the procedure: [No,] the needle doesn't go through the belly button, prick the baby, etc. Just so they can make an informed choice; after all, there are real procedural risks.

Community factors also affect practice. A respondent at a center with a low post-CVS complication rate nonetheless reported:

Our view has changed over the years. In the beginning, if they were early enough, we did recommend CVS. Now we discuss it only if they raise it . . . because we deal with a lot of community doctors' referrals who feel we might be overstepping our bounds; not all doctors are pro-CVS. The higher risk of miscarriage is hard to justify to anti-CVS doctors. . . . Even [patients] calling for CVS frequently don't realize this. . . . Once the patient sees the informed consent form, she frequently has second or third thoughts.

I sidestep the question of "Which would you choose?" I say, "I don't have your life, and I don't want to make decisions. I'm here to offer information."

Seven counselors who described themselves as nondirective cite medical considerations in their presentations to clients. The fact is, bleeding, a history of miscarriages, and fibroids do contraindicate invasive diagnostic procedures. Does venturing a clinical opinion render a medical expert "directive"?

- Nondirective: they have to live with it. There are some unique cases in which early diagnosis is necessary—such as sex for X-linked disorder—but otherwise I am neutral.
- Our policy is very strict: never to make any recommendations, only to provide relevant facts. If certain medical situations make one procedure better than another, that is pointed out.
- If the patient had a 25 percent risk or was over 40, I would recommend CVS. In either case I'd lay out the facts and let them choose.

Note that the last counselor has equated two quite different levels of risk. The risk of Down's syndrome is only 1 percent at age 40 and 3 percent at age 45 (with a total chromosomal risk approximately twice these).

Usually, no distinction is made between women whose high risk is due to familial history and those whose risk is due only to advanced maternal age. Yet these are two distinct populations confronting very different consequences of a procedure-associated miscarriage. A woman under 40 still has several years of childbearing left, whereas a woman in her 40s who loses a pregnancy may not be able to replace it. Ironically, when this possibility is taken into account, a woman of age 40+ (particularly a childless one) may well opt for amniocentesis, which carries a smaller chance of miscarriage than CVS. Yet this point is rarely raised in genetic counseling sessions.

Only one of our counselors pointed out that the tragic possibility of accidental miscarriage has to be weighed in:

I am concerned about the miscarriage rate [with CVS]. . . . We have seen several miscarriages following CVS with a normal diagnosis. . . . Parents who are at risk for Tay-Sachs, have a CVS with normal results and then miscarry see the miscarriage as self-induced, whether or not that's true. . . . They are on the floor! [i.e., mad with grief]. . . . I like CVS for many families but it's not the oasis it was once believed to be. Early testing will never replace amniocentesis because the issue of miscarriage will always be there: you will never, never, never be able to tell whether the miscarriage was self-induced or not. . . . That bothers me.

Counselors' ability to separate their subjective feelings from the disinterested stance they espouse in sessions with clients is put to a test by this issue. Thirty-two of our counselors mentioned their internal evaluations of the procedures. Half reported sufficiently strong misgivings about CVS that for themselves they would utilize amnio if possible. We include in this group those who sidestepped the issue by saying how relieved they were that in all probability they would have completed childbearing by age 35 and need not make the CVS versus amnio decision. Nearly all counselors would be comfortable with the procedural risks associated with amniocentesis, and two-thirds with those of CVS (see Chapter 7). Unlike clients, who tend to decide against CVS because of its heightened risk of miscarriage, counselors tend to subordinate such concerns to more technical objections. One problem with CVS is a possible diagnosis of mosaicism, which necessitates a followup amniocentesis. In addition, since CVS does not detect neural tube defects, those who have the procedure will need to have AFP testing (see Chapter 2).

• Maybe by the time I'm pregnant, the available procedures will change. . . . I'd choose early amnio against CVS because you still need follow-up AFP—and [there's] also the risk of mosaicism.

• It's hard to tell until I am actually pregnant, but I think I would go with an early amnio simply because I don't know that I would want to know that early. . . . I want to make sure the pregnancy is well-established before I do anything.

• I tell my clients the placental cells are the same as the fetus's—but I feel subjectively the amnio cells are more representative of the fetus. [Question: There's less maternal contamination?] Yes. Low-grade mosaicisms would require a follow-up amnio.

Fifteen counselors were neutral, defined as echoing the standard guidelines of utilizing amnio up to age 37, 38, or 40. (They wavered about the transition age.) They would switch to CVS for really advanced maternal age or for an autosomal recessive condition that carried a 1 in 4 risk. One counselor in each group suggested that only a risk as high as that merited CVS for herself.

We were surprised at the counselors' near-total silence about the chief benefit of CVS from the patient's viewpoint: the earlier knowledge and the shorter period of anxiety about the "tentative pregnancy" (see Chapters 7 and 9). Indeed, we encountered several women who declared they would not have gotten pregnant without the option of early genetic diagnosis. Only one genetic counselor, a physician, said she would opt for CVS because of the benefits of early diagnosis. Viewing the risks from CVS as not significantly higher than those from amniocentesis, she related the benefits of the earlier procedure to her own experience as a mother:

What does stand out is the [different] perception between a woman who has already had a baby and one who hasn't about the differences [between CVS and amnio]. . . . This is what they tell me: "I really don't wish to terminate a pregnancy in the second trimester because I know what it feels [like] to have a baby at that point." That is very striking to me. . . . Yes, I would go for CVS—but I have children, too.

The woman who hasn't had a baby will often choose amnio as the first option because of what [she perceives] as the difference in risk.

It appears, therefore, that in adopting a nondirective stance and avoiding recommendations of method unless there is a clear medical contraindication, counselors are working against their own subjective feelings that CVS should be used sparingly or not at all.

Counseling the AFP Client

Unlike invasive prenatal diagnostic techniques, AFP testing has spread far beyond the upper middle class. Although in theory women may refuse the test, in practice they may not realize this or understand the thicket of decisions an abnormal result may lead to (see Chapter 2).

Counselors who work with AFP clients note the distinctiveness of this group:

• [AFP referrals] are different because [unlike CVS or amnio patients] they have not thought about this testing for their whole pregnancy. In some ways they're different because they have gotten a laboratory result that to them seems very personal. It makes them more vulnerable than somebody who has known that she's 36 [and hence at an elevated risk] for the whole pregnancy. . . . But with the AFP result coming back high or low, it seems to make the patient more anxious. Certainly anecdotally, a higher percentage of these go on for additional testing and counseling. . . . They concentrate their anxiety in this brief period of time.

• Many come with misinformation. . . . A lot of time they've been informed that a low [reading] means Down's with 100 percent certainty, and they're a wreck when they come in two days later.

For counselors who are committed to the goal of patients' comprehension of the many complications in the reproductive process, counseling the AFP patient is both challenging and frustrating. Consider how this counselor must feel:

I definitely have patients who cannot understand, uneducated patients referred for low MSAFP. I have to cut it down to . . . what is the risk, we don't know the answer at this time, and what would you do if . . . [listing possible scenarios such as a bad test result or giving birth to a child with a defect]? If they say "I wouldn't terminate [anyway]," then this information may not be so important for them to know in advance.

This happens mainly with the lower socioeconomic group, the more uneducated public. They seem to run away from the information. I don't want to generalize; many were receptive [to counseling about fetal development and prenatal testing] at public clinics. Many didn't get individual counseling on AFP, why they had it done. . . . The O.B.s [at the county hospital] just include the test as part of routine care. . . . [The patient's] first visit may have been at 16 weeks, so there was no formal consent. I think patients must have a say in whether or not to be tested; they have to face the decisions afterwards.

Achieving the degree of patient knowledge that reassures a counselor that informed decisions are possible may require time that is not available by this stage of pregnancy:

AFP patients have more crisis counseling; they are forced into a decision in a very short period of time. In practice, we're very slow to bring up amnio. We wait to see. They could be off date. . . . Of those with correct [gestational] dates, 80 percent have amnio if they have low AFP. A lot of our highs may not elect amnio since we get so much from noninvasive procedures [that is, sonograms].

I may be a little more directive with AFP referrals. They're people under a lot of stress. I have to decipher what they're really saying or feeling, and therefore you try to help them see if they're leaning a certain way.

Counseling a client with an abnormal AFP result, then, presents a double challenge. Counselors must impart complex information to clients who may be emotionally unprepared or too wrought to absorb it. Although in most cases the abnormal results will prove a false alarm, in the interim decisions must be made and clients must be informed about the consequences of their decisions.

Counseling Clients with an Abnormal Diagnosis

Counseling the patient and couple whose fetus has an identified abnormality is the most rehearsed of all training scenarios. All our respondents perceived their role in post-procedural counseling as supplying requests for additional information (especially on the specifics of abortion procedures), fostering a balanced discussion about possible outcomes (including the possible psychological and financial costs to family members), referring to a clergyperson, psychologist, or support group as needed, and mediating in instances of disagreement between husband and wife. The issue of counselors' directiveness or involvement in decision making was raised in the most extreme situations:

- Nondirective in general. Directive towards termination if there's a severe abnormality and the baby wouldn't live.
- With mosaicism, I will be directive in stressing that they should wait for amnio if it's from CVS. But with amnio—a true mosaicism—I had a patient decide to abort, in my private opinion quite rightly.
- If I had to be directive, it would be in a situation where the woman was in danger to her health. If someone made it clear "I wouldn't terminate because I can't bear termination," and [the abnormality] is lethal, as in anencephaly, I can bear that. But with Trisomy 13 or 18—a lot of people think this is lethal, but I have heard or seen plenty of families with a living 10 year old [with this condition], where they complain, "The doctor told me he wouldn't live."

For both counselor and client the more ambiguous diagnoses, or syndromes without mental retardation, raise the most ambivalent emotions. Still, counselors respect clients' autonomy:

- You can't be directive because you don't know what's going on in their lives. I feel the most strongly about cases where they want to terminate for a condition like hemophilia. Personally, I would never terminate for that. But I am not they; I don't know their family situation; I don't have their fear of contracting AIDS through blood transfusions. I would never tell them what to do. I'd just tell them: This is what it is; this is what it's going to be like; these are your options.

- I don't think I am tempted to be directive with the abortion question per se. Certainly in some cases I would have an opinion as to what I would do or what I think might be better. If . . . I am afraid they don't have all the information we end up spending much more time with them. . . . For many people I think it could be worse to abort than to go ahead and have this baby, this child. . . . Everyone with a sex chromosome abnormality does come in for a counseling session because it seems to be a much more difficult decision as opposed to very quickly making a decision to abort [with more severe abnormalities]. It takes more discussion. Some of these people will continue the pregnancy.

An unresolved issue is the privacy of genetic information. If a chromosomal abnormality is detected, should the parents' relatives be told? Counselors may be torn between guarding their client's privacy and informing those relatives who are at risk of bearing an affected child. One counselor related,

I actually was directive in one case, but I still left it up to them. The parents had two children with Fragile X syndrome [an abnormality that may cause retardation and other problems]. The mother wouldn't inform her sisters of the diagnosis. I urged her to tell them. I don't know why she didn't want to tell—perhaps she didn't want the child labeled. But the child was already labeled as mentally retarded so why not tell about the diagnosis? There I was directive. I think I talked her into telling her sisters. I don't know what I would do if the sister gets pregnant.

What this counselor meant is, should she pick up the telephone and inform the sister—against the client's wishes—so the sister can have her fetus tested for this condition? Or should she uphold the sanctity of the client's genetic information? The counselor had no answer. As the number of diagnosable genetic conditions grows, this conflict is certain to loom larger.

Genetic counselors hate being the bearers of bad news; they often find it difficult not to get emotionally involved with clients' reproductive tragedies. Yet this situation—counseling the patient with an abnormal result—brings out the best in their training and socialization. Here, too, they see their major role as supplying information and supporting the parents, whatever their decision—that is, fostering the clients' autonomy.

Nondirectiveness in "Real Life"

Question: Some counselors try very hard to be nondirective, and others feel more directive counseling is appropriate under some circumstances. Where would you say you fall on this continuum? Under what circumstances do you find you are most directive in your counseling? Least directive?

Many of our respondents acknowledge quite openly that the ethos of nondirectiveness is tested by real situations.

- I try hardest to stay out of it when the couple has the greatest conflict. I feel I have greater impact when they're on the fence; I can let my guard down when they've pre-decided. For me, it's not the risk [that brings out directiveness], it's the clients' attitudes.

- I try to be nondirective. I work a little harder when I feel people are not understanding the information and are not perceiving the actual [genetic] risk. They don't have to have the test, but they must know the risk is there. If they're high risk and know that risk, [declining testing] is fine.

Just as Rothman reports (1986, p. 44), counselors consciously ''work harder'' when a patient's genetic risk is perceived as ''high'' or where a severe fetal anomaly has been identified. The tendency for counselors to ''work harder'' with such clients is consistent with the hypothesis that counselors vary their presentations according to their perception of clients' needs (see Chapter 4). Several counselors describe how they structure such an interview:

- If a person already has an affected child and is at high risk, I'd be more directive. I would try to make it absolutely clear that the recurrence risk is as high as it is; [we] can't deny the reality of the risk, so the test is recommended. I try to impress them with what it would take to rear two children with the exact same disorder, compare how their lives were without a child to their current life [with an affected child], and then imagine what it would be like [with more]. I'd be least directive if I think it makes little difference: a woman 31 or 32 years old [without a prior history of abnormality].

- I wouldn't be honest if I said I was equally nondirective with a very high versus a very low risk. I try to balance things out. For a 45-year-old woman, your risk is 1 in 18 or 19. . . . Risk of miscarriage is 1 in 200. . . . Putting things as they are takes the focus away from me and my feelings.

IS NONDIRECTIVENESS DESIRABLE, LET ALONE ATTAINABLE?

Sociologists have long acknowledged that no human behavior or speech, including scientific research, is free from value judgments. Both Rothman and Rapp have noted the subtle forms of directiveness that pervade genetic counseling. Yet, in everyday counseling practice ''directive'' is a dirty word: it has assumed the meaning of actively influencing if not outright making a client's decision.

Despite their disparate personal views, counselors believe that most of the time they employ a nondirective stance in counseling sessions. Their willingness to report subjective views that are at variance with their outward professional behavior suggests a high awareness of possible challenges to the ideal of non-directiveness. However, only taping counseling sessions and having the tapes analyzed by trained observers would answer the question of whether counselors accurately perceive and describe their own behavior.

Most counselors feel that a nondirective stance is most often tested by situations involving a client with high genetic risk. Like the counselors observed by Rothman, those in the current study admit to "working harder," that is, adducing extra information and reviewing all that has been presented, with clients whose genetic risk is perceived as "high" or whose fetus's abnormality is judged "severe." Counselors naturally vary their presentations in reaction to a client's "expected burden," defined as the probability of occurrence multiplied by the total costs imposed on the family unit.

Counselors assume that more (scientific) information is better than less and that all clients are better off with as much information as they can absorb. No counselor ever suggested to us that a client's resistance to information was a valid psychological defense mechanism except in the case of the middle-class pretest client who openly requests a postponement of the abortion description until relevant (see Chapter 4). Patients, many AFP-referred, who seem ill informed of the many possible reproductive complications, represent a challenge as well as a source of professional frustration. That it might be "directive" (but inescapable) for the counselor or the physician to decide how much information a client should receive was not considered.

Bioethicist Arthur Caplan (1993, p. 157) points out that in the psychotherapy fields that helped shape genetic counseling, the distinction between nondirective and directive therapeutic techniques has a different meaning. He suggests that genetic counseling should return to the older distinction. In psychotherapy, nondirectiveness does not imply the absence of value judgments. Rather, it simply "describes the stance that the counselor should adopt toward the counselee, one of openness and a willingness to listen. . . . [In contrast,] directive counseling would permit or require the counselor to be active, willing to engage in challenge, argument, and confrontation with clients." Nondirectiveness, he maintains, should not be confused with value neutrality (see Chapter 11).

Wertz and Fletcher, who have studied counselors' attitudes in eighteen countries, also question the extreme interpretation of nondirectiveness. They emphasize:

Nondirectiveness should not be nonsupportive neutrality . . . [which places] a heavy burden of decision making—and consequent guilt—on the patient. . . . We question whether [supporting any patient decision] is humanly possible, given the strength with which many geneticists hold moral convictions. . . . [It] implies total moral relativism. Those engaged in counseling should consider whether this is desirable. (1988, p. 593)

The principle that a counselor should never answer a client's query, "What would you do in my place?", however respectful of client autonomy, may accentuate the anxiety of an already anxious client. Since counselors' attitudes do vary so greatly, theoretically any individual answer would not signify a professional consensus on how to proceed. In practice, of course, in the client's eyes each counselor represents the profession at large.

Since this question arises so frequently, however, counselors might devise anxiety-reducing responses other than the now-standard one, "Some people will do this, and some will do that." The revealed preference theory so beloved by economists is tailor-made for this approach. A counselor need only ask the client to imagine that a friend with the exact values and preferences of the client were asking for advice. What "gut" reaction would the client have? Whatever the answer, this would be the "right" answer for this client. This additional mental distance might help clients to see their inner preferences more clearly.

Instead of condemning directiveness, it might be more productive to debate what is permissible directiveness and what is impermissible. The belief that medical authority knows better than the client is not necessarily "bad." Given the values of our society and health care system, of course it is permissible (more than that: desirable) to impart full risk information and to verify that the client has absorbed it as thoroughly as possible. To describe ethnically or racially linked syndromes to someone in the risk group is to impart objective and relevant information. Clients seek counseling precisely in order to acquire this information. Hereditary risk is not an "equal opportunity" condition, affecting all persons equally.

Counselors are also aware that they increasingly counsel clients from different cultures, some of whom neither expect nor are prepared for complete autonomy and informed consent. Counselors make their own judgments about clients' capacity for information and, in particular, how much information they can absorb about the odds of different abnormalities and the risk levels at different ages. Counselors must adapt the session's content to each client's unique situation. In the next chapter, we describe the variations in content that result from counselors' decisions about what material to include in the standard counseling sessions.

4

The Genetic Counseling Session

We were curious whether counselors followed a standard "script" when working with clients whose sole reason for testing is advanced maternal age, the most
common genetic counseling client today. As we shifted our focus from amniocentesis clients to CVS users and as the mass media accorded more attention
to prenatal diagnosis, we wondered if clients were presenting counselors with
changed information needs. Counselors might also have become self-conscious
about session content as a result of discussing Barbara Rothman's widely read
and reviewed book.

This chapter explores whether the advent of CVS and the more widespread
lay knowledge about prenatal diagnostic procedures have affected the content
of the pre-procedure counseling session. Given that session variability is a hall-
mark of client-centered counseling, which topics are standard and which expla-
nations discretionary? How do counselors account for differences in topic
selection? Do they believe that their own areas of comfort or concern play a
part in these along with adaptations to a specific client's situation? Are they
attuned to possible intercultural communication problems and biases?

An associated issue centers on what makes for professional satisfaction or
discomfort with the outcome of a session. Do these depend on the session's
content, the client's reaction, or clients' decisions that seem "rational" to the
counselor?

In analyzing genetic counseling sessions, researchers have paid less attention
to counselor than to client behavior. As physician Seymour Kessler observed,

"the genetic counseling session remains largely a mysterious black box" (1992, pp. 5–6). In part, the inviolability of the session may reflect the autonomy (within limits) that genetic counselors exhibit in deciding how to conduct and structure the session. In this they resemble other professionals who deal with privileged and semiprivileged client information. Uniformity of session content would not be expected given differences in clients' risk factors and in their background knowledge.

Rothman (1986) and Rapp (1988a, 1988b) have analyzed the counseling session for clients who come to a counselor because of advanced maternal age. Rothman focused on what was not said. She noted that only a few counselors routinely mentioned sex chromosomal abnormalities. As for abortion, some counselors always specify "what the choices are if Down's is found" and always raise the issue of termination without client prompting. Others do not raise these or other topics at all or only very briefly, unless a client requests more information. Rothman implies that this selectivity is due to the counselors' desire to avoid discussing the specifics of abortion or issues involving ambiguity.

Rapp concurs with Rothman about the informational goals of counseling sessions, adding that the counselor strives to communicate well enough with her client to address the client's questions and concerns. Rapp describes how social and ethnic differences between counselors and clients interfere with (and in her opinion, bias) the exchange of information on both sides. She stresses that the very concept of what constitutes a defect or handicap varies across class and ethnic lines.

Do variations in session content reflect the counselor's agenda or the client's? To answer this question, we need to know whether counselors can successfully identify the major topics clients wish to discuss and so adapt the session.

Wertz and her colleagues (1988) studied how often each party in a genetic counseling session knows what the other one wants to discuss. They found major misreadings by both parties. Wertz's team analyzed questionnaires completed after 880 counseling sessions by counselors and female clients. The data were collected between 1977 and 1979. At that time 60 percent of the counselors were physicians, with the rest primarily holding Ph.D.s in genetics; nearly half the clients were couples who already had borne a handicapped child. Clients and counselors were asked which of sixteen possible topics they had wanted to discuss.[1]

The researchers reported that in only 26 percent of the sessions were both counselor and client aware of the topic the other most wanted to discuss. In 48 percent, neither the counselor nor the client was aware of the other's desires. "The only client topic of which counselors were correctly aware more than half the time was the topic of risk. This was the topic that 46 percent of clients and 51 percent of counselors most wanted to discuss" (p. 334). Not a single counselor was aware of clients' desires when "the client most wanted to discuss child's medical status, financial cost associated with the disorder, or relationship with spouse."

Both professionals and clients were more likely to be aware of the topic each wanted to discuss when the client had a relatively low risk (less than 10 percent) of having a child with a birth defect, when the client had high income and education, and when the counselor had received training in counseling techniques. We believe that the same associations hold true today.

Changes in both the counselor and the client populations during the 1970s and 1980s may have led the counselors to make a more accurate reading of clients' needs and concerns. As we saw in Chapter 3, today greater proportions of counselors are trained in interviewing techniques and the psychological needs of clients. Meanwhile, the growing number of clients whose sole risk factor is maternal age means an increase in the number of patients with low risk and high educational attainment (the ones most likely to have postponed childbearing and to know of, be insured of, and demand prenatal diagnosis). These changed demographics suggest a better "fit" between counselor and client in session topics addressed. Ironically, democratizing access to prenatal diagnosis will heighten the challenge to counselors of accurately identifying clients' concerns.

A final possibility is that the limitations inherent in a forty-five- to sixty-minute session preclude discussing more than a fixed set of topics. It is plausible that logistics, not psychological discomfort, dictate counselors' semiroutine omission of certain topics.[2]

THE CONTENTS OF A "GENERIC" SESSION FOR ADVANCED MATERNAL AGE

Responses analyzed in this chapter came from thirty counselors who both answered the final standardized questionnaire and counseled for advanced maternal age. Of these, twenty-three were in clinics that provided both CVS and amnio (henceforth called "CVS counselors") and seven in clinics that offered only amniocentesis ("amnio counselors"). There were no major differences in their response patterns.

We showed counselors a list of sixteen topics (see Appendix B and Tables 4.1 and 4.2) and asked, "In an ordinary prenatal diagnosis session for maternal age, what points do you think most important to cover? Do you cover the following points usually, sometimes, rarely, or never?" After the counselor had responded to this question, we asked, "Do you discuss the possible effects of a disorder on the child's or the family's life? What about the economic burden of the disorder?"

Table 4.1 summarizes the CVS counselors' responses. Although no small-scale study such as ours can be statistically significant, we believe a large-scale sample would offer similar responses given the lack of variability we encountered among counselors from different regions and backgrounds. All counselors made it clear that they always answered any and all client questions despite a counselor's response of a "less-than-always" inclusion of a specific topic.

Table 4.1

Topics Covered in Prenatal Counseling Sessions at Institutions That Offer Both CVS and Amniocentesis (N=23)

TOPICS	ALWAYS/ USUALLY	SOME- TIMES	RARELY	NEVER/ NO	MISC.	N/A
a. How amnio feels	22	1				
b. How CVS feels	18 3*			1		
c. Need for post-CVS AFP test	21				1	1
d. AFP false-positives	15	2	1	1	2	2
e. CVS false-positives	20	2				
f. CVS/amnio complication rate	23					
g. Describe Down's syndrome	18	3	1		1	
h. Describe other genetic conditions	16	4	3			
i. Describe sex chrom. abnorm.	13	6	3	1		
j. Describe neural tube defects	20	2	1			
k. Age-related Down's risk	16 5**				2	
l. Other risk rates	5**					
m. Take family history	23					
n. Choices if abnor-mality is found	17	3		1	2	
o. How an abortion is done	7	5		11		
p. Describe sonogram	23					

* CVS patients only
** Joint k and l

CVS counselors universally took family histories, described what the relevant procedure (CVS or amnio) felt like (although amnio candidates might not hear about CVS), the complication rate, and the need for CVS clients to have a serum AFP at a later stage of the pregnancy to identify neural tube defects. Only one counselor stressed to CVS clients that the AFP test is optional. All counselors always described the sonogram to the diminishing number of clients who were not familiar with this procedure and had not had a sonogram to verify the date of the pregnancy.

Even completing such a routine task as taking a family history could pose difficulties. At clinics with a primarily poor or recent immigrant caseload, counselors not infrequently found that for "some clinic patients there is not a lot of information about the father, many half-siblings and those of father's are not known, and repeats of family tales are vague."

Regardless of their clients' backgrounds, however, counselors laughed in recognition when we shared the following account by an amniocentesis counselor:

I can't tell you how many referrals for AMA (advanced maternal age) have a polycystic kidney history, or a cousin with—, or at the last moment they say, "Oh, by the way. . . . " It's sort of as if their fear that it might be significant keeps them from saying it earlier in the session, while their honesty makes them say it eventually. Sometimes I have to schedule a second session. . . . One woman said, "I forgot. I had a little brother with physical abnormalities—but my mother said it was oxygen deprivation" [in an aside to interviewer, "as if these abnormalities were caused by oxygen!"]. We proceeded upon the assumption of an unbalanced translocation. Another staid suburban woman sent her husband and children out to the car, then told me that the father of her fetus was most likely someone else!

Essentially all CVS counselors described the possibility of a finding of mosaicism with CVS. Two-thirds of the counselors mentioned the possibility of false positive results with AFP; two other counselors informed clients that maternal blood AFP is less sensitive for neural tube defects than amniotic fluid AFP obtained with amniocentesis. As to specific anomalies tested for, four-fifths (19) mentioned neural tube defects, especially spina bifida, and Down's syndrome. Description of Down's syndrome was tailored to the client's frequently considerable knowledge.

Sixteen counselors added that other chromosomal and genetic defects exist; eight did not elaborate on these, but six counselors specifically mentioned Trisomy 13 and 18 and one mentioned cystic fibrosis and hemophilia. Three counselors answered that whether or not they described other conditions "depended upon the patient's needs"; three more said they rarely described other chromosomal or genetic defects.

Sex chromosomal anomalies were unlikely to be singled out: of thirteen counselors who usually mentioned them, only five "always" and one "mostly" did so specifically. Five lumped them in with a residual category, and two accorded them "brief mention." The ten other counselors infrequently or never mentioned these conditions.

The client's chromosomal risk level was always addressed. Sixteen counselors always provided clients their specific risk for Down's syndrome; five lumped their risk with levels of overall risk of chromosomal abnormalities (approximately twice that for Down's syndrome alone). Two counselors mentioned that all clients received this information before the session via information packets and films. Informing clients of their overall risk levels was neither universal nor client-specific: two counselors each either "sometimes" or "rarely" mentioned this, gave a general population risk for abnormality of 2 to 4 percent, or said vaguely that "many other things may happen" in the course of fetal development.

Table 4.2 indicates that the seven counselors at institutions that offer only amniocentesis described abnormalities in greater detail than CVS counselors. This is probably because they had more time to do so since they spent little time on CVS-related topics. Thus, the amnio counselors were more uniform in their level of description than were the CVS group. All counselors always described Down's syndrome and neural tube defects; six always mentioned other specific genetic defects; five always mentioned six chromosomal abnormalities.

CVS counselors displayed more variability in discussing specific defects other than Down's. Barely more than half mentioned the sex chromosome syndromes. In this respect, they more closely resemble the amnio counselors studied by Rothman (1986) than the amnio counselors in our study. Rothman (pp. 37–38) found that counselors avoided issues of ambiguous results, such as the variable expression of the sex chromosomal anomalies. But the counselors we surveyed had no hesitation dealing with other ambiguous issues, the problems of mosaicisms and of false positive results. We think that time pressures (there is only so much information that can be covered in one session) rather than possible psychological discomfort explain why many counselors lump most possible defects into one residual category.

Two amniocentesis counselors who practiced in settings with large numbers of foreign-born clients faced a more challenging situation:

• When foreign-born, they say "There is no—in my country." So I say, look, there the children are born at home and if they have a heart defect, they may not live to be diagnosed. Here, babies are born in a hospital, and they are treated and survive. With native-born [clients], it depends. Where relevant, I discuss the effect on a family.

• A lot of people don't know what a certain syndrome is. People come with their own definitions [of a disease], personal or cultural. Our specific information challenges this.

Asking all clients at the outset what they want to discuss is not a serviceable option. Many people don't know what questions are important enough to discuss (see Chapter 9). It might be possible to distribute a checklist to clients listing "optional" session topics and asking them to specify any they wish to discuss. Although this procedure runs the risk of suggesting to clients that nonlisted

Table 4.2
Topics Covered in Prenatal Counseling Sessions at Institutions That Offer Only Amniocentesis (N=7)

TOPICS	FREQUENCY TOPICS MENTIONED					
	ALWAYS/ USUALLY	SOME- TIMES	RARELY	NEVER/ NO	MISC.	N/A
a. How amnio feels	7					
b. How CVS feels	1 1[a]	1	1			3
c. Need for post-CVS AFP test	2 1[a]		1			3
d. AFP false-positives	5		1			1
e. CVS false-positives	1 1[a]		1			4
f. CVS/amnio complication rate	7					
g. Down's syndrome	7					
h. Other genetic conditions	6	1				
i. Sex chromosomal abnormalities	5	1		1		
j. Neural tube defects	7					
k. Age-related Down's syndrome risks	6 1[b]					
l. Other risk rates	4 1[b]	1			1	
m. Take family history	7					
n. Choices if abnormality is found	6	1				
o. How an abortion is done	2	2		3		
p. Describe sonogram	7					

[a] When applicable
[b] Joint k and l

topics are not acceptable, it might address critics' concerns that sessions are not sufficiently "client driven."

CHOICES IF AN ABNORMALITY IS FOUND

Rothman (1986) noted the disparate ways in which counselors addressed the emotionally charged subject of what choices a client had should a fetal abnormality be discovered. We, too, found that the topics of clients' choices in the event of fetal abnormality and specific details about abortion procedures elicited the greatest variation in frequency and extent covered. Seventeen counselors discussed choices the client faced if an abnormality was found, with six counselors raising the subject if the client did not. Four infrequently or never mentioned those options unless a client asked; and two informed clients that "there's no cure for an abnormality" or "if one's found, you will receive further counseling."

Neither was it standard practice spontaneously to offer specific descriptions of abortion procedures. Eleven counselors never covered and an additional five only "sometimes" covered this item unless asked. Only three said they "usually" covered this topic, while an additional four always asked if the client wanted this information.

The following selection of responses, all from CVS counselors, illustrates this variability:

- [Re: Fetal abnormality:] What are their choices. . . . I don't raise it in terms of spelling it out: "If there is any problem, we'll invite you back for further counseling; we'll deal with it then."
  [Re: Abortion procedure:] No, they're scared enough.

- [Re: Fetal abnormality and abortion procedure:] I will talk about termination. Some patients say "I don't want to think about it now. If it happens, I'll terminate, but no details now." Others want details.

- [Re: Fetal abnormality:] I do raise it if they don't. I'll ask if they've thought of what they would do "if"—because clinic patients may not know they have choices. I've had patients change pre- and post-procedure when they've had abnormalities—both ways.
  [Re: Abortion procedure:] I'll ask if they want to know. Some do ask.

- [Re: Fetal abnormality:] 100% of the time I raise it, using the word "abortion." I think that's very important. There's a new booklet [for staff] and throughout it uses the word "interruption" [shows booklet to interviewer]. If these resources won't use the words "termination" or "abortion" with us the counselors, they won't use it up front.
  [Re: abortion procedure:] I always bring it up, but sometimes in a superficial way.

- [Re: Fetal abnormality:] Always. I tell them, "[When] the results come, we'll call you. The choice of what to do is entirely yours. We'll arrange for termination if you want it and your OB won't help you." This is very important as some O.B.s welsh out and

won't follow through; they'll arrange for the test but that's it where they're concerned. [We feel] It's your life, it's your choice.
[Re: Abortion procedure:] We don't talk unless they ask. We'll answer any questions.

Only two of the seven amnio counselors always asked clients if they wanted to know how an abortion would be performed. One-quarter of the CVS counselors and one of the seven amnio counselors did not discuss choices if an abnormality were to be found. Only six of the twenty-three CVS counselors deemed it essential that pre-procedural clients confront the fact that abortion was realistically the sole way to avoid the birth of a baby with a major abnormality. Another ten counselors ordinarily mentioned this point. Fully two-thirds of both the CVS and the amnio counselors in our study did not routinely describe abortion procedures.

Something more than time constraints appears to inhibit the discussion of the specifics of abortion procedures or of the options available in case of an identified fetal abnormality. If we can distinguish between counselors' discomfort associated with a given topic and the discomfort caused by the perception (true or not) that discussing that topic occasions distress in a client, we believe that the latter better accords with what we heard. Several counselors stated that their behavior was responsive to clients' requests, as when the client says that she does not want specific information at this point.

These counselors echo several interviewed by Rothman (p. 39) who suggested that many pre-procedure clients do not want to know in advance all the decisions they might be asked to make or all graphic details of a late abortion, a procedure that very few clients will ever experience. The counselor who said she does not spontaneously raise the options to be considered in case of abnormality because her clients "are scared enough" spoke for more than herself. In short, counselors' avoidance of certain topics may be due to the desire to spare clients unnecessary distress. It may also be due to the politically sensitive nature of abortion.

Probably the counselors are accurately perceiving their clients' emotional state. Still, we must question whether at the same time they are being overly cautious about raising an uncomfortable truth. If clients are too scared to consider the implications of their choices, are they capable of making a truly "informed" choice to use or not use prenatal diagnosis? In some states, anti-abortion activists have succeeded in requiring that abortion counselors supply overly detailed descriptions of the procedure; this is regarded as a means of discouraging elective abortions. However, the genetic counseling profession has an obligation to consider what amount and kinds of information a prenatal diagnosis client should reasonably receive. Describing a second-trimester abortion to a woman who must decide between CVS and amniocentesis seems enlightening rather than directive. In our opinion, this information should be as available as the comparative miscarriage rate and the possibility of false positive results (see Chapters 9 and 11).

We asked whether the counselor discusses the possible effects of a disorder on the child's or the family's life or mentions the economic burden. This question also elicited a variety of replies. At the outset of the interview, we emphasized that all questions pertained only to a pre-procedural counseling session for a client of advanced maternal age. Despite this stipulation, only seventeen of the thirty counselors limited their comments to this type of session. Thirteen counselors replied that a disorder's effects "are only rarely or generally discussed pre-procedurally, but in much more detail at sessions after an abnormality has been identified."

Two counselors said they go into more detail when a couple is undecided. "I'll give the scenario of each possible outcome: miscarriage, second-trimester abortion, bearing a child with a problem. We do spend most time on medical aspects, but we discuss others."

Another counselor tied this information to the discussion of risk: "Sometimes when we're talking about numbers, I tell them it's a risk for different things: a miscarriage is a miscarriage, but an abnormality is a lifelong problem. I don't think it's fair to speak about economics."

Note how information may be conveyed: procedural risk is a one-time shot, whereas abnormality is an open-ended process. Counselors who address this issue point out that having an abnormal child involves a long-term commitment and psychological burden, with perhaps lots of additional medical care and extra schooling. They emphasize, however, that neither this consideration nor financial burden is the decisive factor in deciding whether to abort an abnormal fetus.

It is difficult to walk the line between enabling an informed decision and being directive:

I usually try to think of this as balancing the scale. If someone is leaning against amnio, I say that some of these [disorders] can be devastating not just to the baby and yourself but to the family unit. In most cases this has no effect, since most come in decided. *Only those truly undecided can be helped to decide for* (emphasis added). Some will . . . go home and discuss with their partner. That can be significant as they use the partner as the decision maker. The effect is just as likely to be pro as con.

Counselors basically tailor this information to the client's needs and preexisting levels of knowledge. "It varies with patients. Some have a very good idea of what it is like to be around a handicapped child. Those who work with them tend to run for CVS and amnio; they're nervous. To others, we explain that some conditions are more severe, some less."

RELIGIOUS OBJECTIONS TO TESTING AND ABORTION

We asked genetic counselors, "How often do people bring up religious objections to abortion? How do you handle it?" This issue may be encountered either before initial testing or, if an abnormality has been found, while discussing options. Indeed, many of our respondents elaborated more on religious objections to testing than they did on objections to abortion. The thirty-three counselors who answered this question have variable reports on what happens in practice. Even at the same facility, counselors will give different estimates of the frequency with which religious objections are voiced.

It is difficult to distinguish between those clients who object to abortion on religious grounds and those who simply say, "We're not comfortable with abortion." Eighteen or just over half the counselors we interviewed said they rarely encounter this attitude. Five noted that self-selection operates: people do not come in for testing if they have already ruled out abortion. One counselor estimated that maybe one-fourth of the 10 percent who refuse testing do so for religious reasons. Another counselor with ties to a pediatric clinic saw clients who might not have presented themselves except they already had a child with a familial syndrome. In this case the mother was not pregnant, but the parents were considering whether they should attempt another pregnancy, knowing the odds of having an affected child: "We'll discuss prenatal diagnosis and options: donor insemination, adoptions. Several have done that [adoption] rather than have another child."

An additional five counselors replied that in general clients do not use religion in the wording of their objection. Instead, they say they are not comfortable with abortion.

Five counselors described clients who say "it's up to fate" or "we'll accept what God gives us." Three of these counselors commented on the difference between patients funded by governmental programs including Medicaid and those covered by private insurance. Government-funded patients more frequently mentioned religion than did private patients.

At [the university hospital] they were much more apt to bring up [religion] as an issue. They feel it's fate, it's in God's hands if they're meant to have a child with Down's, a birth defect, etc. . . . The patients here [a private suburban hospital] are less likely to leave things to "fate." Here I haven't had a patient yet who's brought up [religious objections]. They'll keep information on their pregnancy from other family members if other family members are opposed to termination and won't support them in this decision.

On the other hand, eight counselors found religious objections "reasonably frequent." Two counselors said "10 percent." Another two answered they rarely encountered such objections. Religion is more often a salient factor in smaller cities than in large metropolitan areas. A counselor at a hospital in a smaller city said she ran into religious objections "25 percent of the time." Another who had moved to a major metropolitan area found that in the big city termination seemed always to be an option, while in the smaller city where she had worked before, religious objections were common. Indeed, in her first city a client who decided on a very late abortion because of a neural tube defect "wanted to have a priest baptize the baby."

A counselor at a New York City hospital where the clientele is approximately 90 percent Catholic (mostly Hispanic) estimated that 20 percent of all potential clients refuse testing. She placed religion first among the reasons for refusal. "They may say, 'I am here because my doctor says I must, but I'm so against abortion I don't even want to be here.' " Reason number two for refusal was "fear of needles, which really indicates a fear of high technology," and reason number three was simply that "they don't feel it necessary for their lives." A counselor whose clientele was largely Italian Catholic offered similar remarks. Eastern European Catholics, however, are as likely to test as other groups, according to our interviews.

If it is not morally opposed to abortion, religion can be a source of support for couples facing an abortion for abnormality: "After we've found an abnormality, religion is always brought up by a couple. In crisis situations they want validation, that what they're doing is not horrible. Certainly they will turn to a rabbi, who will be accepting. Fewer would turn to their priests."

One counselor, however, preferred to see clients follow their own reasoning rather than the dogmas of their church—even if this compromised her own professional nondirectiveness:

In one sense I am totally non-directive. In another sense I direct them to direct themselves. If they're in distress, I try to support them so they can make their own decisions. Usually it's the Catholic women who are the most tortured. . . . They have had such conflicting messages and have been through so much in terms of theology, etc., plus their childhood upbringing. What they really want to do or think vs. what they feel they *should* feel, is a major conflict.

Another counselor noted that where abortion is not an option, she explores with her clients the community resources they can access if needed.

In New York City, several of the counselors we interviewed worked with Hasidic Jews, a sect that opposes both birth control and abortion. On the one hand, Hasidic Jews are helped by a strong community network. On the other, the stigma of a child with an abnormality may make it difficult to arrange marriages for the other children in the family since the family is now viewed as tainted. Such families will try to hide the disabled child and may find themselves very isolated. The repercussions for the family of having an affected child are so high that many Hasidic women will surreptitiously come for prenatal testing. Some even do so with the blessings of their rabbi. These women (and their rabbis) strongly prefer CVS to amniocentesis since CVS gives them the option of an early abortion (see Chapter 8).

Viewing another parent's plight with an affected child may also affect one's own decision. Leslie, a client at a prenatal diagnosis clinic we studied, found out that her fetus had a neural tube defect, but as a Catholic, she decided not to abort. According to the genetic counselor we interviewed, the doctors tried to persuade Leslie to have an abortion, thinking she didn't understand the implications of her decision. But her genetic counselor supported her decision not to abort. Leslie gave birth and took the child home; the baby did not do well. Some time later her neighbor Maria, also a Catholic, came in for prenatal testing at the same clinic. Maria's fetus was diagnosed as having Down's syndrome. Although opposed to abortion, Maria terminated her pregnancy. What she had seen of the suffering of Leslie's child, as well as the family's suffering, made up her own mind.

One thing united all counselors who discussed religion as a possible issue: a "live and let live" attitude. As long as a couple was comfortable with the basis for their decision, the counselor was, too:

As long as I get across to them the various pros and cons and what we're offering, that's fine. We had a very religious couple who have carried [to term a fetus with a] very severe defect—trisomy 13 or 18, I forget which, and also a Jewish couple who had had a child who died of Niemann-Pick disease [a metabolic disorder more common among Jews]. It usually doesn't come down to religion: the couple just feels they can't go through with an abortion.

We don't know, at the social-psychological level, how religion influences people to decide for or against abortion. When a woman who was brought up in a church decides against abortion for reasons that appear personal, we don't know what role religious socialization actually played in her decision. Nor do we know why some people will go against the teachings of their clergy in this matter.

COUPLE DISAGREEMENT

Most genetic counseling research has focused on the reactions and perceptions of the female client. On the one hand, this is understandable: after all, it is her body that is being invaded. She is the more accessible of the two parents and the one always present at counseling sessions. On the other hand, many prenatal genetic counseling sessions and pre-procedural sonogram appointments involve couples. Certainly, when a bad result has to be imparted and discussed, counselors try to involve both parents in deciding how to proceed.

Clearly, in confronting testing and abortion decisions, couples deal with potentially polarizing issues. Yet the question of couple agreement on relevant topics has been studied infrequently. The few researchers who have explored the topic have concurred that couples who disagree are not rare. This is not intuitively obvious; one could argue that in a society where voluntary assortative mating is the rule, people might select as mates only those who agree with them on fundamental reproductive issues. That does not appear to be the case.

Sorenson and Wertz (1986), in a study of nearly seven hundred couples who sought genetic counseling between 1977 and 1979, found that a large minority, if not a majority, of the couples disagreed on major reproductive topics. Fifty-five percent identified different reasons for seeking counseling, while 45 percent identified the same. Forty-four percent "perceived the same level of risk (high, medium, or low) of having an affected child. . . . Agreement on the seriousness of eleven potential problems occasioned by an affected child ranged from 55% to 67%" (p. 549).

Seven to ten days after counseling, the percentage of spouses agreeing about their genetic risk level went up, from 44 to 52 percent. This shift was statistically significant, but clearly it left nearly half the couples in disagreement on risk perception. Rather high levels of postcounseling disagreement remained on the ideal number of children, long-term reproductive plans, and the potential problems in raising an affected child.

The least shift toward agreement and the greatest remaining disagreement occurred in the category of medical and care problems (as distinct from "personal concerns"). After counseling, 37 to 39 percent of the couples still disagreed whether the four listed problems (medical care for child; caring for child at home; educating child; and care for child as an adult) were "serious" or "slight or no problem" (p. 553). Sorenson and Wertz conclude, "There is, in general, as much disagreement on these issues between spouses after as before counseling" (p. 549).

The stress on counselors arising from mediating between husbands and wives has even more rarely been scrutinized. With the transformation of the genetic counseling field, female counselors now conduct the great majority of initial prenatal counseling interviews. Given the male/female communication dynamics in our society, we would expect additional stress to originate when the "expert" is a woman and the (secondary) layperson is a man, especially when a female counselor perceives the husband as bullying the wife. Imparting genetic risk information is impersonal; mediating between a husband and wife and attempting to be even-handed and affirming of each partner rank among the most stressful professional challenges a counselor may confront.

We explored couple disagreements through the counselors' eyes. Bear in mind that counselors do not see a representative universe of pregnant clients. Many potential clients decide on their own accord that they do not want counseling or testing. An indeterminate proportion of those who refuse do so because their partners disagree on its necessity or desirability.

We asked genetic counselors, "Do you sometimes see disagreements between spouses about either the test or the abortion decision?" Of the thirty-one replies we received, the most succinct yet comprehensive was, "Yes—about which tests to do, whether to have an abortion, arguments about perception of risk or impact on their lives of a child with an abnormality!" In other words, about everything.

Counselors' perceptions of how often disagreements were encountered varied widely. Six counselors answered on some variation of "rarely": "5 percent," "every two months" (disagreement about having the procedure), "I don't recall any about termination." Four counselors commented: "Yes! I don't think this is unusual"; "Fairly common, if you mean do any couples disagree: even mild is 40–50%. Diametrically opposed—much rarer"; "More agree than don't, but a substantial proportion disagree." One counselor who reported only rarely seeing spousal disagreement had two colleagues who reported frequent instances. It appears that conflict is in the eye of the beholder. In this case, the proverbial glass is either half empty or half full, depending on the genetic counselor who witnesses these disputes.

Ideally, such disagreements are aired *before* testing, so that some agreement or accommodation can be reached before a diagnosis of defect highlights these differences. To accomplish this agreement, counselors will ask direct questions such as whether the couple has discussed what they would do "if." As befits their training and orientation, counselors encourage partners to speak to each other, trying to affirm that "each person has their ideas for different and good reasons." For the diametrically opposed couple, counselors emphasize that they should come to some sort of resolution before testing.

Where conflict is very intense—"such as conflict about whether to be pregnant" or "if you abort the baby, I'm leaving you!"—counselors try to refer clients to other therapists or to clergy. One counselor reported, "They'll resist referral for therapy, and I think if we weren't called counselors, we'd lose them." Other counselors commented,

- Mostly beforehand, I say "You don't have to make hard and fast decisions before the procedure is done, but you have to explore the depth of the feelings and understanding of each other."

- Frequently, I think, they fight probably in general and when they get in here, why should they change?

- I ask each partner, "How will you feel about your partner if this results?" If people won't consider termination, I say "Sometimes then amnio is not used, although there are other reasons to perform the procedure."

Pressure from the husband about testing may work both ways. Culture plays a part here:

- The wife didn't speak English. An Indian couple, he translated and he'd say, "She understands." When I asked if they wanted amnio, he said "Yes." I said, "Ask her." It was clear the patient wasn't making the decision. It was morally horrible to see a patient subjected to an invasive procedure without her informed consent. Usually I can see an affirmation in their faces, but not in this case. We often deal with cultural beliefs, to have the man speak for the woman.

- Several Hispanic ladies call and say, "My husband won't let me have the test".... Sometimes at the start of an amnio session a husband says, "The ultrasound looks great. Why have amnio?" We counsel and leave them alone to review the risks.

Sometimes it is the counselor who is under pressure. The most extreme instance reported was one in which the wife wanted a child and the husband did not. Over the telephone he tried to bribe the counselor to change a normal to an abnormal finding so that his wife would abort. The counselor got the couple into therapy.

Eight of the thirty-one counselors mentioned encountering some variant on the sentiment "the woman makes the final decision." Most counselors supported this attitude, for generally it is the woman who will raise the child and there is a high rate of disruption in families with a handicapped child. But one or two counselors often perceived this handing over of responsibility as fake. One counselor could not ideologically accept a husband's giving his wife the final decision to terminate:

I don't understand how for a termination someone can just turn the decision over. . . . I think a compromise would be better.

[*Interviewer*:] What kind of compromise would be possible?

I want them to support each other in the decision whatever it is: "our decision together" and not place the blame on the other. I had one couple where the husband said blatantly, "Go ahead with the procedure, but if you miscarry, there'll be hell to pay!"

Counselors feel keenly that the couple should make these decisions jointly. Renouncing responsibility does not strengthen the marital unit.

The husband is not being supportive, and I think it's hard for a joint venture like this to go unsupported. I think women fear they'll lose some part of the relationship if they make the "wrong" decision, that their spouse will think less of them, e.g., "I thought you didn't care!" "Yes—but I never thought you'd do this!"

This is an example of the double bind, a mixed message: "You're free to decide, but it had better be my way!" One counselor replied, "Yes, but what are the consequences of her action? If she has a defective baby, will you take a powder? [i.e., disappear from the scene]. I had a couple where one says [he or she] can handle the situation, the other says not."

A variant on the scenario of a husband's leaving the final decision to his wife was that of detaching himself from the situation as much as possible. This could be viewed as an espousal of the feminist position, "It's your body, it's your decision," but the underlying messages appeared more complex. Arguably, these ranged from anxiety plus denial to a covert struggle for control. Certainly, a husband who brings papers from work and reviews them while the counselor by default talks to the wife (several such men were mentioned by one counselor) would appear to be distancing himself from a stressful topic.

At the other extreme, the same counselor noted, were husbands "who will completely take over. They tell their wives, 'You will do this, you will do that.'

Very paternalistic. It's interesting." For genetic counselors this is a call to moral battle in defense of women's rights.

A final moral dilemma was offered when a nurse who was a hemophilia carrier had a husband who in the words of the counselor "absolutely tuned out: [he said,] I won't be part of this decision." Not until 1985 were the concentrated clotting factors, which were first available in the 1970s (and which transformed the lives of hemophiliacs), freed of the HIV virus. Nearly every hemophiliac born before then had been infected with the virus. At the time this couple was facing the termination question, the counselor described the wife as torn between wanting to please her anti-abortion husband and wishing to avoid having a child with a very real risk of AIDS along with the pain and transfusions ordinarily accompanying the genetic disease.

There is no such thing as a compromise on the decision of whether to abort. Five counselors reported that when a couple with an initial disagreement about a hypothetical situation confronts an actual diagnosed abnormality, the anti-abortion spouse generally changes. Sometimes this occurs without any additional discussion. A younger man from a conservative culture married to an older woman, also an immigrant, had said pre-procedurally that he could not be reconciled to terminating a pregnancy. Yet when the couple was informed that Down's syndrome had been diagnosed, the husband surprised the counselor "and I think the wife, too" by saying, "I guess we should call the O.B. to set up an abortion." The counselor opined that at the first session the husband had to assert his male authority, but that at the second session, as a caring husband, "how could he let his wife's first child at this age be abnormal?"

In another case, both the husband (a lay pastor) and the wife had agreed before the procedure that they wouldn't abort for Down's syndrome. After the bad diagnosis, he acceded to his wife's insistence that they abort. Here the counselor had the sense that the wife had put on her earlier anti-abortion attitude for the husband's benefit, with her true feelings surfacing later.

The decision may go the other way, albeit more seldom. In one case, with a finding of Trisomy 18—a lethal disorder—"the wife who would have had the abortion acquiesced to the husband, a gentle 'couldn't harm a flower' person. There was no adversarial fight or religious issue."

Religious differences may have contributed to two reported instances of intense disagreement persisting after the finding of an abnormality. In both cases, the Catholic spouse was against termination and the non-Catholic in favor: in the one case, a wife was already caring for two children with cystic fibrosis, and in the other the husband said they couldn't afford a second child with *cri du chat* (a rare congenital disorder often accompanied by heart defects and mental and physical retardation); their first such child had died. Additional counseling had been set up with a priest in one case and with a psychiatrist in the other.

Ethnicity and marital status also play a role. While one counselor reported that her unwed Hispanic clients would not terminate a pregnancy because they feared losing their boyfriends, another counselor described how one Hispanic woman had prenatal testing at her private doctor's office without letting her husband know. When Down's syndrome was confirmed, she had an abortion while he was at work and told him she had had a miscarriage.

Inevitably, there are stories about couples in which the wife refuses testing, despite the husband's pleading, and subsequently gives birth to a child with a diagnosable defect. The two counselors who mentioned such cases did not mention any long-term followup on the state of these marriages, although in one the wife said she had worked through her denial of the child's condition (while the husband presumably was still working through his). In another case, the couple divorced after a strong disagreement on aborting an affected fetus.

Despite a decade's additional discussion in the popular as well as the academic press, the issues Sorenson and Wertz identified in the late 1970s as evoking prolonged and resistant disagreement among spouses have remained divisive: the perception of risk and the assessment of the impact of a defective child on the family's life. Couples appear similarly far from achieving consensus on the issues raised by prenatal testing: the need to test and the will to abort an affected fetus.

More research is called for. Long-term followups on satisfaction with the final decision, with the quality of the available counseling, and with the marriage itself might suggest ways to minimize the psychological costs to the couple of this conflict. Did satisfaction with the marriage two or more years after the signal pregnancy correlate at all with the amount of counseling received, with the varieties of counselors seen, with the sameness of the spouses' religious beliefs or affiliations, and, of course, with the outcome of the pregnancy?

Additional questions for future research include the influence of the counselor's sex on the counseling process. Do counselors exhibit a bias in favor of the spouse of the same sex? Do male and female counselors differ in how they mediate disagreements?

Answers to both sets of questions could enable counselors to achieve two goals simultaneously: expediting agreement between partners at the lowest psychological cost possible, and minimizing the stress on the counselor as he or she acts as mediator.

HOW COUNSELORS EVALUATE THE COUNSELING SESSION

Question: What makes for a good counseling session? A bad session? What do you look for in a client?

Given the goals of genetic counselors—imparting as full information as possible, understanding and meeting client needs, and assisting clients in reaching the "right" decision for them—it is to be expected that the most popular set of responses to what defines a good session would involve communicating information. Thirteen of the twenty-eight counselors who provided responses to this question replied with some variation on "I've brought up all the important points" or "The client seemed to end up with a good understanding of her particular situation." Three excerpts will give the flavor of these responses:

- A sense of people having learned something, having acquired useful tools to make decisions, an understanding and reasoning.
- I had a real good one this week. When all issues have been adequately covered—or uncovered; when I feel they've learned or got something to take home to think about, without devastating them: something to give them hope. I'm thinking of a case with irradiation exposure in early pregnancy where the risk was much lower than they thought.
- One patient said, "I don't want to have amnio, and I feel so bad since you worked so hard at explaining." I said the point was for her to understand the choices.

Counselors also hope to establish a rapport with their clients, both to assure themselves that they have identified their clients' concerns and perhaps to exercise the expressive openness that is their stock in trade. Seven counselors (one-quarter of the respondents) described their sense of having achieved easy communication with their clients in a good session:

- For me the easiest sessions are when people are open and up-front on what they're going through. If a patient is quiet and sullen, I know it's like pulling teeth to guess what they need. I also want to feel I have made a difference to them, like the couple who disagreed on amnio: I think I made it safe for him to disagree with her. It later came out that the wife was Catholic and would have had difficulty in termination.
- If I felt that people first have a good or better understanding of the material for the decision. Another sign is if the couple showed relief after discussing their fears and anxiety, that they feared something they had done might have harmed the fetus, and I told them this was not so. I want to just facilitate looking for understanding.
- A good session is where the couple is very expressive about their feelings about the procedure, they're open, they understand everything, even firing a slew of questions. When the rapport is easily established, and you've helped a couple come to an understanding.

Similarly unsurprising were the seven replies that identified a good session with a client's or a couple's reaching a decision with which she/they were comfortable. "Getting across the information to patients, and they understand it. They make the decision best for themselves. I know these are the canned phrases from graduate school!"

Counselors appreciate clients who are interested in what is being discussed. "I like a client who's interested in getting the information or support or something we have to offer rather than showing up because the doctor told her to."

Indeed, one counselor explicitly mentioned preferring "patients who are somewhat informed before coming in and show an interest in learning."

Although the descriptions of what makes for a bad session are somewhat more variegated, they essentially come down to the opposite of what makes for a good one. Frustration is contained in the half-dozen responses that bemoan a client who resists information, whether from disbelief in the reality of genetic defects, a desire just to sign the consent form and walk out without a lecture, or psychological denial.

- A bad session is the reverse [of good understanding and rapport], or when the client says "I know everything" and doesn't listen—and then, when you call to give results, she asks, "What did you test for?" Sometimes a patient will call back and say, "I'm upset we discussed this."
- A bad session is when I know people are keeping things back, one spouse is hostile, or people say they know everything and just want to sign the consent form—and I know this isn't true.
- Sometimes I have patients with negative attitudes: what I say, they'll reject. They don't believe in the reality of risk: "My mother is fine," or "God won't punish me," or "All my 10 kids are fine, why should this one be different?"

In other cases, the counselor feels she has succeeded only partially in communicating what she hoped to owing to factors outside of her control:

- I tend to blame myself if I present the information in a way they can't comprehend to make the decision, especially since my mother tongue is not Spanish. . . . The one thing that makes me frustrated: you can't get any feedback. You don't know what they're thinking: are they frightened of the test? I will describe a few categories of women who refuse testing, and I will ask if any fit them.
- Bad: I've had clients who speak another language or are mentally retarded, and they have to sign an informed consent form, and they're basing their decision just on what the doctor says to do. With the retarded, it's very difficult to get across the concept of risk. They have no biology understanding. I have had one retarded woman who told me, "I don't want a child like myself." So I knew she had some understanding.

Client hostility understandably makes for a bad session. This may occur "when the patient is angry because she came against her wishes" or "anytime there's a confrontation." Sometimes it is difficult to judge whether hostility or differences in communication style or culture is responsible for a client's non-communicativeness. "No matter what I do, I cannot draw anything out of them, cannot engage them in a communicative discussion. I can't tell how they're reacting."

Counselors are sensitive to their own inadequacies:

- Bad is where I feel pressed for time, or I feel tired, need to get a patient out quickly, doing only what is required rather than that little extra or emotional support.

- Bad is when their questions are not answerable by a test. "I had a child with X disease"—and we say, "That's not yet testable for." "I understand, I just want the test." Leaves you feeling they haven't taken in that we can't answer their first question.

- The worst is when there are hidden issues which never come to light; we don't hit on the true reasons for their anxiety. There are all kinds of bad counseling sessions. For the counselor, it's hard when you empathize with the wife of an unfeeling husband and you're trying to be objective—which you can do, but it leaves a bad taste in your mouth. There are a lot of nasty people around.

- People come in with different agendas from mine. Some are nitpickers, some monopolize everything or get hung up on some statistic—hound you on statistics or data. If it interferes with the session, I suggest we go on and return to it later. . . . What I hate is someone who comes in without her husband and then says, "I want to go home and ask my husband what he thinks." I think, but he hasn't been to the session! I'll try to use the phone, if indicated.

Paradoxically, one kind of bad session can result in a counselor feeling useful: where the client is being coerced and is unable (without support) to assert herself: "One woman was clearly unhappy with CVS, which her husband wanted. On the phone she kept expressing misgivings, so I finally said, 'I hear you don't want CVS and are more comfortable with amnio.' She was so grateful."

In summary, it is clear that counselors want clients who come in with some (accurate) understanding of why they are there, a desire to learn more about their particular situation, the ability to articulate their needs, and the ability to make a decision on grounds that seem rational to the counselor. A session may be termed "bad" "when the client makes a decision based on what I consider a trivial reason, for example 'the needle will hurt' or 'my doctor said I had to have this test.' " Actually, fear of the needle is quite common among patients.

HAS SESSION CONTENT CHANGED OVER TIME?

Judging from our respondents' answers to a questionnaire adapted from Rothman's, we found that the introduction of CVS had occasioned little change since the early 1980s in the content of a pretest session for clients of advanced maternal age. Both CVS and amnio counselors still spend most of the session taking family histories, explaining risk levels for birth defects (generally singling out that for Down's syndrome), and describing how the procedures feel and their associated complication rates. The extensive coverage of prenatal screening in the popular press and in women's service magazines such as *McCall's*, *Redbook*, and *Good Housekeeping* has increased clients' sophistication. With rare exceptions, however, the added knowledge does not appear to modify the session content appreciably.

One exception is the clients' greater familiarity with Down's syndrome, a result both of the open discussion of the syndrome by several prominent families about affected family members and of the television series "Life Goes On."

This show starred a very likable, high-functioning teenager with Down's syndrome. The show's producers have publicly admitted to exaggerating the capabilities of its star. Yet, this show had led some families to decide against testing for Down's syndrome or against aborting a fetus with this condition, forgetting that there is a very high degree of variability in the severity of this disorder (Burke, 1989; Horowitz, 1989).

In addition, counselors are less frequently called on to describe the sonogram procedure. It is increasingly rare to encounter a client who has never had a sonogram before or heard one described by a friend.

As we have suggested, in our view the contents of the standard genetic counseling session should be expanded to include more explicit information on certain topics, including the different abortion procedures in the second and first trimesters. In Chapters 8 and 9 we discuss abortion views and experiences. In the next chapter and those that follow, we shift our focus from professionals who provide counseling for prenatal testing to the women who undergo these procedures—the clients.

NOTES

1. Because these sessions were not for prenatal diagnosis, the specific topics and specific findings may not be applicable to the client who comes for reasons of advanced maternal age alone. Hence, we examine only Wertz and her colleagues' analysis of agreement rather than their findings about the "popularity" of specific topics.

2. Of course, psychological discomfort may still be a problem. This is particularly true for genetic counselors fresh out of school. Such counselors, largely women in their mid-20s, may find themselves inhibited in discussing potentially explosive reproductive issues with clients who are fifteen years their seniors (Seymour Kessler, personal communication, August 1993).

5

Reactions to Amniocentesis:
The Early Years

In 1982, when we started our study, amniocentesis was a relatively new technique; only 2 percent of all pregnant women aged 35 and over were using it. There were few studies of its social, psychological, or ethical implications. Historian Jean Ashton (1976), recalling her own experience with amniocentesis, called attention to "the gap between the achievements of science and the emotional equipment we have to absorb them" (p. 6). Rothman (1983), pointing out the lack of cultural guidelines for dealing with the new technology, spoke of "amnio and anomie." Rapp (1988b) referred to early users of amniocentesis as "moral pioneers." She voiced the dilemmas raised by the new technology:

Does amniocentesis offer women a "window of control," or an anxiety-provoking responsibility, or both? Is there a transition for those who use prenatal diagnosis between an image of mothers as all-nurturant, self-sacrificing madonnas, and mothers as agents of quality control on the reproductive production line? . . . It is perhaps part of the larger meaning of motherhood in an age of high female labor-force participation rates; later marriages; high divorce rates; smaller families and later childbearing (at least for some Americans); and an increased use of legal abortion. In this context, a decision to bear or not to bear a child with serious health problems in a society which provides meager services for disabled children and their families takes on new meaning. (pp. 109–110)

To find out how those at the front line of the new technology viewed these issues, we interviewed twenty-four women who had had amniocentesis. We used a snowball sample. Twenty-one of our twenty-four respondents were aged 35 or over at the start of the studied pregnancies. All but one had at least a bachelor's degree and eight had a Ph.D. Two of our respondents chose to become single parents, one following an unplanned pregnancy, and the other becoming pregnant through artificial insemination in a physician's office. Four respondents had used amniocentesis in two pregnancies each. Of the total twenty-eight pregnancies for which amniocentesis was used, twenty-four were planned. Seven pregnancies, including three of the unplanned ones, were first pregnancies. All the diagnoses were negative (that is, no abnormality was detected), and all the babies were born healthy. Four were born after completion of the study.

THE DECISION-MAKING PROCESS

In our sample, by the early 1980s knowledge of amniocentesis was so widespread that many respondents took it for granted. Fourteen of the twenty-four women first raised the question of amniocentesis with their physicians. In another four cases, the respondent and her husband raised the possibility jointly. In three cases the respondent or the couple initiated consideration jointly with the doctor. In only two cases did the doctor initiate consideration. Some respondents had trouble remembering who suggested it first: "I don't know who first raised the possibility. I think everyone assumed it would be done."

Why did they seek the test? In six cases, the decision was partially motivated by a specific concern, such as a history of birth defects in the family. The large majority, however (eighteen women), chose to have amniocentesis merely because they knew it was available and because they believed that at their age the statistical odds of birth defects were sufficiently great to warrant it. If age were not positively associated with increased risk, few of our respondents would have opted for amniocentesis. The three women who had amniocentesis before age 34 were among the most emphatic in their desire to avoid having an affected child.

None of the women in our sample had chosen amniocentesis because she or her husband was a known carrier of a genetic defect. One couple, Bobbie and Greg, had had a child with a neural tube defect in which the exact contributions of heredity and environment were unclear. Harriet's husband, Carl, had had a child in a previous marriage who was reported as not developing normally but who had not been diagnosed as having a recognizable syndrome. Another woman, Maureen, had been RH-sensitized as a result of medical error in her first pregnancy. In each subsequent pregnancy, there was a possibility that her antibodies might destroy the fetus's red blood cells. Maureen had to have amniocentesis repeatedly throughout her second and third pregnancies, seventeen times in all.

Although no one reported actual disagreement with her husband on the initial decision to have amniocentesis in only sixteen of twenty-two married couples were both spouses equally favorable or enthusiastic. In three cases the wife was more favorable than the husband; in three cases the reverse was true. In two of the former cases the husband believed that the likelihood of a defective fetus given the family history was too small to worry about, but if his wife wanted reassurance, that was acceptable. One husband, though not opposed to abortion, felt he could accept a disabled child. The wife knew she couldn't face that possibility, and she felt that her husband erred in assessing that he could. Where the husband was more favorable toward amniocentesis, the couple had different views on the acceptability of abortion.

The reasons respondents gave for having amniocentesis reflect their concern about birth defects:

- Having waited so long to have a family, I wanted to make sure that the baby would be without major birth defects.
- I was aware of the increased risk of Down's syndrome at my age, and I was certain I didn't want to rear a child with that condition.
- I decided to have amniocentesis because of my age, and because of a strong desire to have a healthy child.

For the two unmarried women in our sample, having to raise the child as a single parent also weighed in. They felt that the burden of coping with a disabled child would be unmanageable in this situation.

Some people viewed amniocentesis as a kind of insurance against birth defects. Two women, both of whom had previously had healthy children, mentioned that they would not have become pregnant if this option had not been available. One indicated that she and her husband wanted this baby only if it was healthy since, as she put it, this was an "elective" baby, not a "necessary" one.

Studies suggest that prenatal genetic counseling does not contribute significantly to decision making about amniocentesis. Dutch geneticist Marianne Verjaal and her colleagues (1982) found that, although counseling improved the clients' knowledge, it did not affect the decision-making process. Wertz and her colleagues (1986) found that in approximately three-quarters of all cases, either the counselor or the client, or both, was not even aware of what topic the other wished to discuss (see Chapter 4).

For most couples in our study, prenatal genetic counseling was not necessary in order to arrive at a decision to have amniocentesis. Ten of these felt that counseling served some use in reinforcing a decision already made. However, two couples felt it was a waste of time, and three more persevered in their decision to employ amniocentesis despite efforts by doctors to dissuade them. One woman, a demographer, had researched the literature so thoroughly that she was able to demonstrate to the head of the genetics unit of a large medical center that his calculation of the procedure's risk was misleading. He had been using figures that lumped together both trivial side effects and such a major one as a miscarriage. By limiting consideration to only the major effects, they could see that the risk of an abnormal fetus outweighed the procedural risk. Another demographer, who also used a large medical center, thought "the medical personnel involved were chillingly confused about the various risk factors." Five couples found counseling useful in arriving at a decision. One couple apparently found that it was just one more factor along with their own reading, the accounts of friends, and their own "gut" feelings.

Although amniocentesis is used to diagnose hundreds of genetic and chromosomal defects, including anencephaly and spina bifida, the overriding concern among the women in our sample was Down's syndrome. No other defect besides Down's syndrome was mentioned by those respondents who had no history of birth defects. One woman, a nurse, didn't even know that other disorders could be diagnosed with amniocentesis. Because the incidence of Down's syndrome is known to increase with age, in some views it has become the ultimate nightmare for childbearing women in the middle 30s and beyond.

Some users believed erroneously that amniocentesis would screen for all major birth defects, guaranteeing a healthy child. In fact, after the results of the amniocentesis were in, anxiety about other birth defects and complications persisted. Both perceptions—that Down's syndrome was the major risk to the baby and that amniocentesis would assure peace of mind about the baby's health—reflect a construction of reality that is largely an artifact of the procedure itself. Amniocentesis is used primarily to screen for Down's syndrome, with the result that other disorders are downplayed. However, when the results are announced the couple is often told not, "No Down's syndrome or other detectable abnormalities were found," but "Congratulations—you have a healthy baby." Hence, we found a widespread belief that from that point on the pregnancy (which may have been in the fifth or sixth month) was "in the clear."

AMNIOCENTESIS AND ABORTION: SINGLE PACKAGE OR SEPARATE DECISIONS?

Did the decision to have amniocentesis imply a commitment to abort an affected fetus? Not necessarily. To be sure, most couples, when deciding to have amniocentesis, were firmly committed to aborting in case an abnormality were detected. At the time they opted for amniocentesis, eighteen of our twenty-four respondents were prepared to have an abortion without further ado. One respondent said: "I do not understand those who would want amniocentesis if they are not willing to abort." This did not mean it would be an emotionally easy decision, but merely that the respondent had come to closure in her mind. As we will see below, however, even a firm commitment to abortion may change as the pregnancy progresses.

For others the decision on amniocentesis was perceived as separate from the decision on abortion, and the decision to abort was by no means automatic. At one end of the spectrum we found women who were firmly opposed to abortion in their own case, though usually not in principle. Three of our respondents maintained that they would not consider abortion; these women planned to keep the baby no matter what. One said, "I was raised Catholic, but have not practiced in fifteen years. I did not feel I could have an abortion, although I strongly believe in a woman's right to choose an abortion." Two others were prepared to keep a Down's syndrome baby but would abort one with a more serious defect such as Trisomy 18.

Women who opposed abortion viewed amniocentesis not as a precaution against birth defects but as an early warning system. The function of amniocentesis in this case was to give the parents a chance to adjust emotionally and pragmatically to raising a handicapped child. One respondent said,

We wouldn't have aborted a baby with Down's syndrome. We would raise it. But knowing ahead of time would make it much easier: we could read about it and prepare for it. In a way, it's like a death in the family: A sudden death is much harder to cope with than a death for which you have been prepared by a long illness. Knowing ahead of time makes it less devastating. I am a very organized and meticulous person. That's why I wanted to know ahead of time.

Given the undercurrents of disagreement between spouses with respect even to testing (see Chapter 4), it is not surprising to find that only two-thirds of our respondents reported total agreement with their spouses with respect to abortion. In one case, the wife reported she was favorable, but her husband admitted to feeling ambivalent. In four cases, the husband was more favorable than the wife. Two respondents reported they didn't know if their spouses agreed with them: one said merely she didn't know, and the other that it was never discussed. How, we may ask, is it possible for a husband and wife to seek amniocentesis and yet not discuss the possibility of abortion? Perhaps the spouses suspect that they in fact disagree and choose to avoid a bitter confrontation over a contingency that is a remote possibility. (Only 2 percent of amniocenteses reveal a defective fetus.) Inasmuch as there can be no compromise on the issue, this behavior will probably avoid outright strife.

Occasionally, when husband and wife disagreed about aborting a defective fetus, the amniocentesis decision became a major issue affecting the foundations of the relationship. Bobbie is Catholic by background, although she no longer practices. Bobbie and Greg's first baby was born with a birth defect (omphalocele, a protrusion of the organs in the abdominal cavity through the abdominal wall) that was later corrected surgically. Bobbie told us that in her second pregnancy she was ready to accept a defective child, but Greg was adamant about having an abortion. Bobbie was prepared to go along with the abortion for his sake. As she put it, "It is very important to me to have an intact family . . . as opposed to the marriage splitting up or as opposed to having the father so alienated that he can't relate to the child in any significant way." Bobbie was prepared to forego the pregnancy in order to keep her marriage. They had a healthy child, but were later divorced anyway.

By the time the results of amniocentesis are available, the woman may be past the midpoint of the pregnancy. The deadline for legal abortion (twenty-four weeks in most states) is rapidly approaching. Moreover, in the interval between the amniocentesis and the announcement of the results, quickening (fetal movement) begins and with it the mother's physical awareness of fetal life. At this point maternal bonding may overwhelm previous considerations. As the waiting period progresses, anxiety may increase together with ambivalence about abortion—even among those women who initially felt firmly committed to it. As Ashton (1976, p. 5) notes, "It is one thing to contemplate the abortion of a defective or unwanted fetus when the only signs of pregnancy are frequent urination and sleepiness, symptoms that seem to belong only to your own body and can be classed with runny noses and stomach aches. Once the fetus has quickened, however, the situation seems radically different." Physicians Bernard Adler and Theodore Kushnick (1982, p. 97) have found that "the decision to terminate a pregnancy because of a chromosomal abnormality is one of the most shocking and traumatic experiences that couples endure in their marriage." Women awaiting the results of amniocentesis while feeling the fetal movements grow stronger each day appreciate and dread this eventuality, even if at the beginning of the pregnancy it seemed remote.

In our sample, several women found their resolve to have an abortion weakening. Maureen, who had to have amniocentesis repeatedly throughout two pregnancies, said that both she and her husband were committed to abortion in theory. She noted, however, that "it is easy to be positive in theory . . . I think my husband was terribly afraid that I would not go along with the abortion if the child was very badly damaged." Joan expressed the change in her feelings more dramatically:

[Initially I thought that] if I were carrying a retarded child I would admit myself to a hospital immediately [to have an abortion]. However, by the time the results came in (the 24th week) the baby had been leaping in my womb for a month. Pride of authorship and female hormones took over. During one of the sleepless nights before the results were in I decided I would raise the child if it looked like E.T.

During the waiting period, more than ever before, Joan had come to grips with the meaning motherhood held for her. She realized that she could love—would have no choice but to love—a less than perfect child. On the verge of the last trimester of her first pregnancy, motherhood had finally become unconditional.

In our sample, all the fetuses turned out normal, and no one had to confront the dreaded decision on abortion. The relief felt after receiving normal results was powerful. One woman reported that she cried when she heard the results on the telephone.

ANXIETY AS A DIMENSION OF SUBJECTIVE REALITY

The likelihood of detecting major birth defects, especially in pregnancies where the only known risk factor is the mother's age, is small. It is not surprising

that the common justification for undertaking this potentially hazardous, unpleasant, and costly procedure is to set the mother's mind at ease. Some early
studies reported that amniocentesis made a significant contribution to the psychological well-being of those pregnant women who were at greater risk of
having an abnormal baby.

Other research, however, shows that amniocentesis does not decrease maternal
anxiety. Genetic counselor Alma Chervin and her colleagues (1977) found that
before having amniocentesis women expressed only a moderate degree of anxiety about the possibility of abnormality, but the anxiety increased considerably
after the procedure was done and before the results were received. Physician
Giovanni Fava and his colleagues (1982) report that, while women who had
amniocentesis found that their apprehension decreased significantly after the
results were known, it also decreased to the same extent in a matched control
group of pregnant women who did not have amniocentesis. They conclude,
"Contrary to expectations, changes in anxiety and depression (and the corre-
sponding well-being scales) which occurred after amniocentesis did not differ
significantly from changes in the control group from the first to the second
trimester of pregnancy" (p. 511).

Our research suggests that over the entire pregnancy, amniocentesis may
heighten rather than reduce anxiety. We found that, while the good news "You
have a healthy baby" was invariably greeted with relief, the fact of having
amniocentesis, coupled with the seemingly interminable waiting period, increased anxiety up to that point. Apprehension centered on two main concerns:
the possible risks of the procedure itself and the diagnosis of abnormalities.

Women who undergo prenatal diagnosis subjectively estimate the chances of
major complications arising from the procedure. To some, the risks seem neg-
ligible; to others, they are overwhelming (see Chapter 7). The doctor's reputation
(and therefore his or her power as an authority figure), the figures on risks
supplied by the genetics unit, and the experiences and opinions of others in their
informal network who have had amniocentesis buttress the client's construction
of reality.

Among our respondents, the perception of risk as well as the anticipation of
pain varied widely. At one extreme we found four women who were confident
on both counts, the baby's and their own: "I wasn't scared at all. I didn't worry
about possible miscarriage because I knew the possibility was very small. I did
see the big needle being stuck in my body—I insist on seeing everything that
goes into my body—but it was over in a couple of seconds. . . . It was not very
painful at all. . . . It was really pleasant." Another woman said, "Everything
about the amniocentesis was positive. It was not painful at all. I wasn't nervous
beforehand or at the time. I didn't worry about damaging the fetus because the
doctor came so highly recommended and because of the sonogram. . . . I was
very impressed with the unit and with the doctor. . . . So I wasn't frightened at
all."

On the other hand, most of our respondents (nineteen) reported some apprehension, while several reported overwhelming fear. This centered primarily on the baby but also on themselves. One woman said: "I was very scared; I was white as a ghost. I wasn't very thrilled about it. I worried about the pain. . . . Also, I was very scared about the possibility of miscarriage. Everybody I know who had amniocentesis was scared about that . . . I had heard of miscarriages because of amniocentesis."

Maureen, who had seventeen amniocenteses through two pregnancies, never got over the fear as well as the pain:

It never got any easier. The worst part was fear for the baby. It was painful but pain is transient. And in fact the pain was overwhelmed by the tensions. . . . I was always very tense, which meant it would hurt more because of my tense muscles. But the worst part was the idea that the baby could be stuck by that needle. I felt guilty, too: I had chosen to do this to my babies. . . . You don't get over that fear. I don't think it was any easier for me the ninth time than the first. You never get used to it. . . . Toward the end, when the baby was bigger, the doctor would say, "The worst they'll get is a hand or a foot." True, that is better than pricking the baby's heart, but it was no consolation to me. . . . I had very active babies; they kept moving around. . . . I look at Kelly now and I think about how she scooted around and missed that needle nine times.

In contrast to the perception of procedural risk, which varied widely, we found almost universal anxiety about the possible diagnosis of abnormality and about having a late abortion. During most pregnancies, women do not think much about birth defects because there is nothing they can do about them. One woman noted, "In my first pregnancy I didn't worry about a defective child for some reason, although I was only three years younger." Once a woman has had amniocentesis, however, and is hanging by the phone—in the early years of amniocentesis for a period of up to six weeks—waiting for the results, she cannot evade those fears. The experience of amniocentesis has the unintended consequence of dramatizing what would otherwise be diffuse, low-level anxieties. Some women reported that they ate often or prayed a lot during this period. One woman told us,

Waiting for the results was difficult. After three weeks I was a little nervous and tense, resulting in a couple of sleepless nights. I was constantly thinking about how I wanted things to go well and about the possibility of aborting the fetus if results were poor. I had to fight off phoning my doctor's nurse to see if we heard anything.

The experience was summarized by another respondent as follows:

I still have mixed feelings about amniocentesis. . . . Amniocentesis makes you confront all the things that could go wrong. Normally during a pregnancy you don't think about what could go wrong. You sort of take it for granted that everything would be O.K. But with amniocentesis you can't take it for granted. You are doubly grateful for having a healthy baby.

At least for some women, then, amniocentesis unleashed terrors that previously had been absent or suppressed.

While the relief that follows notification of "good news" was palpable, the rest of the pregnancy as well as the labor and delivery were not completely worry-free. Most women were aware that amniocentesis did not screen for all congenital abnormalities and that birth-related complications were still possible. Anxiety was therefore not totally eliminated; it was reduced only by those factors that the procedure itself had underscored. Thus, in our sample amniocentesis could not be said to reduce anxiety and to contribute significantly to a woman's peace of mind during pregnancy.

BONDING

We thought that initially amniocentesis would decrease the woman's identification with the pregnancy since she might have to terminate it. We assumed that the "good news" results would allow positive feelings about the pregnancy to find natural expression and would facilitate maternal bonding. However, only two women in our sample reported that they "avoided acknowledging the pregnancy" to themselves or to others until "it was clear that the pregnancy would proceed." Overall, we found that bonding tended to proceed at its own pace independently of the amniocentesis.

Before the amniocentesis, an ultrasound is performed to determine the exact location of the fetus and the fetal age. In the early 1980s ultrasound was not done routinely. Most women had no way of anticipating its emotional impact. Yet we found that the ultrasound, a mere appendage to the drama of amniocentesis, had a greater emotional effect than the more complicated and glamorous procedure. Through the ultrasound, the mother was able to see her baby for the first time, usually before quickening had started. As one woman reported, "It was reassuring to see the baby was 'normal,' at least in relation to size, body parts, etc."

Sixteen of our twenty-four respondents reacted to the sonogram with increased identification with or appreciation of the fetus. Seven of them reported themselves "thrilled," "amazed," or "excited" to see the fetal movements in utero, and four found that the procedure made the fetus seem more real, a person who had to be taken into account. For three women the confirmation of the pregnancy led to increased bonding. Typical comments included, "It was really exciting. . . . He actually waved his little hands at us," and "I felt having the sonogram to be a high—a realization of the real viability of my child. I believe it facilitated some bonding." One woman perhaps spoke for many when she stated, "It made abortion—the thought of it—almost impossible" (see Chapter 9).

Ultrasound has its dark side. Should an abortion be necessary or should a miscarriage occur, the subjective reality of the fetus makes the loss more painful. Instinctively aware of this effect, three women in our sample said that they had intentionally avoided looking at the picture or thinking about it for fear of worsening the pain of a possible loss. Maureen, who experienced multiple sonograms and taps, each time with renewed apprehension about the fetus, stated,

I didn't want to see the baby on the screen. I wouldn't let the doctor give me the picture. I thought, "What if it is really a person? How could I ever abort a person?". . . . But the doctor handed me the picture and said, "You are carrying this baby. It is inside you. Take this picture and go home with it." He made me face it. . . . And actually he was right. Seeing it did not make it any easier for me to make a decision about abortion, but it did make me more determined to go through with the abortion. . . . I thought, "It's a person! It is not a blob, it's a person who would have to survive [with a deformity]."

For those with less reason to be concerned about the fetus's health, the ultrasound may provide a thrilling emotional experience that facilitates bonding, but only with the doctor's cooperation. The sonogram is not meaningful by itself. The picture is too blurred and the fetus too small (perhaps only a few inches) to be identified by an untrained viewer. Some sonographers do not interpret the image for the client because they believe it would make a possible loss more painful. Two women in our sample, whose doctors did not explain the picture, were disappointed at the sonogram. In one of these cases the woman's anxiety actually increased: she feared she had a tumor, not a baby.

The amniocentesis itself had considerably less impact. Our respondents denied that it made an appreciable difference in their feelings of intimacy toward the baby. They did, however, acknowledge that the results had a positive effect on their emotional well-being in the latter half of the pregnancy. They used similar comments to describe their feelings at this point:

• It greatly increased my happiness during the second half of the pregnancy.

• Joy and relief that the baby would be normal. Freedom from anxiety to enjoy the pregnancy.

• Now that we could put the worries behind us, we were free to enjoy the pregnancy.

Two women said that knowing they had a healthy baby made them more determined than ever to keep it that way. One of these women said that she refused painkillers during labor for this reason. The other, who went into premature labor at six months, said that "knowing the fetus was normal, I felt it was worth taking precautions (bed rest, anti-contraction medication) to save the pregnancy. I might not have worked so hard if there had been a suspicion the fetus was abnormal."

For another woman getting the results of amniocentesis meant that now that she knew she was going to keep the pregnancy, she was able to plan for the baby. She reported, "The amniocentesis was a watershed; it helped me to get through the normalcy of the rest of the pregnancy. It meant that I could plan.

There had been a lot of uncertainty surrounding this unborn child, whom we had been trying to conceive for four years. Now I could finally plan for him."

How did women account for the apparent inconsistency between the medical reassurance that everything was fine and the lingering concerns about possible birth defects and complications? Of course they knew that other things could still go wrong with the pregnancy and the birth. Yet, several women reported that they were greatly pleased with themselves because they had acted "rationally" and "responsibly"; the rest was beyond their control. As one woman said, "It was great to find out everything was fine. From then on I didn't worry about losing the pregnancy. I had confidence in the doctor and confidence in myself. I was doing everything right." Another said,

It's a feeling that I have a responsibility and I have fulfilled it. I have done all I can do that is medically feasible and advisable, at my age, to ensure that any baby that I have will be fine. There still may be defects beyond the amniocentesis—indeterminable ones. But as I say, I have done what I can. . . . And I can't blame myself for what I couldn't have done.

The feeling of well-being in the second half of the pregnancy was partly a natural occurrence and partly a product of the amniocentesis. While the results reassured the couple that they could continue the pregnancy, complete reassurance is impossible. The period following the announcement of the results was subjectively contrasted with the period immediately preceding it, which had been one of heightened apprehension. The contrast served to increase the women's happiness about the pregnancy. The procedure itself both generated intense anxieties and then acted to relieve those anxieties. It is also well to remember that happiness tends to increase for most pregnant women in the second half of the pregnancy (Fava et al., 1982).

The meaning of amniocentesis, like that of pregnancy itself, is subjectively constructed by prospective parents, medical practitioners, and researchers. Each brings her own predisposition and values. While the medical literature has viewed amniocentesis as a major advance in prenatal care (Golbus et al., 1979), the sociological literature has raised questions about its physical and psychological risks in the context of the overmedicalization of pregnancy. Our early study showed that, whatever the numerical risks, women who underwent the procedure assessed and internalized them in their own way. Often spouses interpreted the risks differently, as did women and their physicians or genetic counselors. We also found that the link between amniocentesis and abortion was problematic and was likely to change as the pregnancy progresses. Finally, while couples sought amniocentesis in order to reassure themselves that the fetus was normal, the procedure had the unintended effect of heightening concern about the baby's health.

Our interviews revealed that amniocentesis was welcomed by many women, and yet caused unforeseen tensions and fears. By focusing on problems about which pregnant women could "do something," the test provided an illusion of control over the pregnancy. Yet when the import of motherhood became clear to these expectant mothers, as it inevitably did, the awfulness of the "solution" also sank in. Amniocentesis did not usher in an age of motherhood-as-quality-control. Rather, it shifted some of the responsibility for the life, death, and health of the fetus to the parents.

From the clients' viewpoint, the major issue that emerged from our early interviews was widespread dissatisfaction with the lateness of the procedure and the length of the waiting period. These concerns, at first not given voice in the medical literature on amniocentesis, eventually motivated the search for an earlier procedure.

We also found a need to improve access to the technology and to support decisions made as a result of its use. Access not only refers to facilities and medical insurance, but also includes complete and accurate information on the risks and implications of the procedure. The issue of access is discussed in Chapter 6.

6

Who Uses Prenatal Diagnosis: Innovation

Kate's Story: "I Told the Clinic I Wouldn't Settle for an Amnio"

Kate, a busy, successful entrepreneur, describes herself as "not a mother type": she didn't care whether or not she had children. Her husband, who had older children from his first marriage, "pushed" her to become pregnant at age 37. When Kate found out how late in the pregnancy amniocentesis is done, she refused to have it. "I wouldn't have a fifth-month abortion. I asked what do you have that's earlier? I told the clinic I wouldn't settle for an amnio." The clinic's staff told her about CVS but cautioned that it was still an experimental procedure with potentially high risk. She insisted on CVS.

Vickie's Story: "Chromosomes Are the Least of Your Problems"

Vickie, a nursing professor, felt her biological clock was running out. "I had a feeling of safety at 35; 36 was too late in my mind." She had to persuade her reluctant husband, an engineer, to have a family. When she got pregnant, they decided she would have amniocentesis and abort if an abnormality were found. "Since he wasn't thrilled about having a family," Vickie says, "that additional burden [a disabled child]—I didn't know how he would take it." She found it stressful to conceal her pregnancy for sixteen weeks until she was sure she would keep it.

Vickie found out too late about a new CVS clinic. She regrets missing the chance to have that procedure. "The idea of a 16th-week pregnancy [with amnio] before you even get a confirmation of O.K. child or not O.K. child! You are feeling life! . . . Obviously CVS would be far superior."

Vickie felt that her obstetrician "was cautious not to give me anything that would cause me to say he made me decide or he told me to do something like that. It was really uncomfortable. . . . Obstetricians are so lawsuit-conscious that they can't even tell you what they think. . . . He didn't even make eye contact. He gave me research reports to read and he said, 'You decide.' Chorionic villus biopsy was brand new. . . . There was no track record." She feels that his impersonal and unsupportive attitude, motivated by fear of malpractice suits, drove her away.

In the end Vickie decided not to have either test. While she was evaluating the risk information, Vickie says, "It occurred to me that I might be ruling out a chromosome or another specific problem and that was it. And to feel *that* would make it 'safe' in relation to the risk [of the procedure]— I didn't think the benefit outweighed the risk. So I decided not to do it." As a pediatric nurse, Vickie knew that many health problems in children can't be ruled out by prenatal diagnosis. She points out, "One thing that has to be put into balance is that [if you are concerned about having a healthy child] chromosomes are the least of your problems. They are not of course something to belittle, but there are so many other possible outcomes."

Vickie also felt that the pre-procedure sonogram "assembly-lined" and "processed" her—"counterbalanced" her, in her words. She walked out of the clinic without having the amniocentesis. She had a healthy baby girl.

By 1986 CVS was available in some cities on an experimental basis. Many physicians regarded it as the answer to women's prayers and expected that it would supplant amniocentesis (see Chapter 2). We set out on the second phase of our study to discover how women in fact decide which test to have—or whether to have any invasive test. Only individual variation fully explains why some women, such as Kate, overcome providers' misgivings to gain access to an experimental procedure, while others, like Vickie, refuse any testing. Yet, the patterns of use emerge clearly.

The phrasing of these questions indicates our expectation that pregnant women over a certain age "should" have the test. Studies have inquired, not why some women opt for this procedure, but why many don't. Refusal requires scientific as well as personal explanation because it violates the norm. Vickie, who is knowledgeable and ultimately secure enough to breach the norm for good reasons, still does not question it. She says that if she gets pregnant again, she *may* have amniocentesis or CVS, but she is not sure.

ADOPTION OF INNOVATIONS: THEORETICAL CONSIDERATIONS

Social scientists have long been interested in the patterns of diffusion of technical innovations, from new breeds of corn to educational computer software. Sociologists Everett Rogers and Floyd Shoemaker (1971) suggest a model of innovation diffusion that follows a bell-shaped curve. As knowledge about the innovation accumulates and access to it becomes easier, more individuals adopt the innovation in any given time period. The rates of adoption first accelerate, then decline as the potential market for the innovation becomes saturated.

Rogers and Shoemaker classify potential adopters into five categories: innovators (those who are always eager to try out new ideas), early adopters, early majority, late majority, and laggards or the last holdouts. Studies consistently show that early adopters rank higher on the socioeconomic scale than late adopters and holdouts. Not only do the affluent have greater resources that allow them to purchase the new product or service, but also the more highly educated are more attuned to the mass communication media. They are better informed about new developments, understand the complexities of using them, and are more likely to take the risks associated with innovation.

The underlying assumption here is that innovation is a good thing: people *ought* to try new things. Progress depends on it. Better educated and wealthier people presumably are ''smart enough'' to know what is good for them. Indeed, much of the older literature is based on studies of agricultural innovations, such as high-yield hybrid corn. These innovations *were* fairly safe and, on the whole, beneficial. No one questioned that adoption was rational behavior and resistance, irrational.

The case for medical technologies, particularly those with high stakes such as prenatal screening, is less clear-cut. Not only do they carry physical risks, but also they entail psychological costs and raise troubling ethical dilemmas. Furthermore, there is little evidence that they improve the overall outcomes. To many, these are unwarranted and potentially dangerous technological interventions—another step in the medicalization of pregnancy and childbirth (Hubbard, 1984; Rothman, 1986). Yet the patterns of use and nonuse fall along class lines, as the early innovation studies predicted.

CLIENTS' SOCIOECONOMIC CHARACTERISTICS

Who uses prenatal diagnosis? Or, as the question is most often phrased, who does not use it? Medical sociologist William Metheny and his colleagues (1988) surveyed all women aged 40 or older who gave birth to a liveborn child in the state of Michigan in 1981. They found that, by comparison with women who had undergone amniocentesis, those who declined to have it were less educated, more likely to be members of minority groups, and less likely to have medical insurance. They were also more likely to be ignorant of the relationship between maternal age and chromosomal abnormalities, more concerned about the risks of the procedure itself to the fetus, and more averse to abortion for any reason.

Sociologist Troy Duster (1990) has studied clients of genetic service centers in California. The centers, whose programs include public education as well as prenatal testing, are subsidized by the state. Yet Duster found that women who received amniocentesis in the 1970s were twice as likely as other California women to have high-level jobs and high incomes. He concludes, "In short, class position and age in combination explain most of what is happening here. No matter how much information is provided to working class women . . . they are far less likely than middle-class women to have amniocentesis" (pp. 64–65). Physician Mitchell Golbus and his colleagues (1979), analyzing three thousand women who had amniocentesis in San Francisco, similarly found that "the lower socio-economic groups have yet to use prenatal diagnosis facilities as fully as those in the higher socio-economic groups" (p. 158).

Rapp (1988b) has studied genetic counseling in New York City clinics that serve minority group members, the working class, and the poor. Many of the clients in these clinics are covered by Medicaid. Rapp reports that about 50 percent of public clinic patients and about 10 percent of private patients break their appointments for genetic counseling. Of those who come for counseling, about one-quarter do not go on to have prenatal testing.

Rapp suggests the motives of those who refuse testing. She points out that these people have seen first-hand the consequences of the *social* handicaps that hamper minority group children. Compared to the effects of prejudice and poverty, "chromosome defects seem a weak explanation for the problems that children may suffer" (p. 113).

Women who do not even telephone or walk in to inquire about prenatal diagnosis are presumably a diverse group. Some pregnant women are ignorant of the tests, unable to afford care, or too troubled to admit they are pregnant. Other women who reject testing are those who for religious or moral reasons will not countenance abortion. Since consideration of abortion is built into prenatal diagnosis, women for whom termination is not an option are likely to stay away (Ekwo et al., 1985).[1]

In our survey we were interested not just in the characteristics of prenatal diagnosis users but, in particular, in the differences between women who have CVS, the newer method, and those who have amniocentesis, the more established one. The relationship between socioeconomic status (SES) and innovation, or utilization of the newer method, confirmed the prediction we made on the basis of the literature: the higher the socioeconomic status, the more likely is the woman to have CVS. (See Appendix D for a discussion of our measures of SES.)

In our study only ten women, 8.5 percent of the sample, had the test for reasons other than maternal age, such as a previous history of genetic defects or an abnormally high or low score on a routine alphafetoprotein (AFP) test. This group had a more varied socioeconomic background than those who came for maternal age alone. Because of its small size, this subgroup did not change the overall pattern. Nevertheless, for reasons of clarity we analyzed only the larger group, those who were 34 and older at the time of the test and who had no other reason for it. There were 110 respondents in this category.

As Table 6.1 shows, women aged 34 and above who used CVS had a higher

Table 6.1
Comparison of Socioeconomic Characteristics of Amniocentesis and CVS Users

	AMNIOCENTESIS (N=64)	CVS (N=46)	U.S. POPULATION AGED 35-44 IN 1987
% completed college	57.2	89.1	22.0 (women)
% with some graduate education	41.3	67.4	9.9 (women)
% husbands who completed college	61.0	87.0	31.0 (men)
% husbands with some graduate education	48.5	63.1	15.4 (men)
Mean household income/year	$46,000	$56,000	$39,529
% employed full-time	52.4	54.3	56.8 (women)
Mean # hours/week of employed	24.5	34.5	37.0 (women)

Note: Only women in our sample who were aged 34 and above at the time of the test are included in this table. The U.S. population figures are based on the Statistical Abstracts of the United States, 1988, Table 88 p. 68 and Table 203 page 126. Educational statistics are tabulated separately for ages 35-39 and 40-44. The differences are very slight. The number given here is the average for the two age groups.

socioeconomic status than those who used amniocentesis. Both groups, moreover, were more affluent and better educated than the average American woman. They were disproportionately well educated and well-to-do even by comparison with their own cohort, women aged 35–44. The percentage of our respondents who completed four years of college was two and a half to four times that of other women their age. This difference was even greater for graduate education. Their husbands were similarly well educated.

The mean household income for respondents was approximately $46,000 for amniocentesis users and $56,000 for CVS users. By comparison, the mean income for all households in the United States in 1987 was $32,000, and for householders aged 35–44 the mean was close to $40,000.

Were the women in our sample more career-oriented than the average American woman, as suggested by the "advanced" age at which they were having babies? It's hard to say. The percentage of women employed full time in our sample was similar to that of the general population of women aged 35–44: slightly over half. There were no clear differences in labor force participation either between the amniocentesis and CVS users or between these groups and women in the general population. However, the mothers in our sample had younger children that did other women their age.

How does our sample compare, not with all American women of the same age, but with those who have prenatal diagnosis? Studies show that women from minority groups, rural and inner-city areas, and low socioeconomic strata are underrepresented among users of prenatal services. Although prenatal screening and treatment are funded by Medicaid in most states, many obstetricians and laboratories do not accept Medicaid patients because this program reimburses only a fraction of the full cost of the procedures and the counseling. Medicaid regulations restrict eligibility and access in various ways. In addition, federal programs, including the Indian Health Services, do not cover abortion for abnormality. Hence, poor women face many barriers to access to prenatal screening (Coffman et al., 1993; Nsiah-Jefferson, 1993). This is similar to the inequality of access to other forms of health care in the United States.

Our survey respondents reflect the national pattern of unequal access to prenatal services. Relatively well-to-do, highly educated holders of prestigious jobs, and residents of metropolitan areas, they are in fact quite typical of American women who use prenatal diagnosis.

THE ROLE OF INFORMATION

Access to prenatal diagnosis is only partly a function of cost and proximity. It also entails knowledge about the procedures, awareness of their risks and benefits, and the ability and determination to take control of one's reproductive life. The pivotal role of information emerges when CVS and amniocentesis users in our sample are compared, since the cost of the two procedures at each clinic we studied was equal.

Women who had the different procedures had utilized different sources of information. Nearly half the amniocentesis clients in our survey sample said that they had "always" known about this test, probably by word of mouth. Knowledge of CVS, by contrast, was more likely to have come from the mass media (31 percent) or from the primary-care physician (40 percent). This is consistent with studies suggesting that early adopters often obtain information from the mass communications media, while late adopters "wait" for the news to filter through informal social networks. Many of the amniocentesis clients in our study in fact indicated that they would have opted for CVS had they known about it in time for the earlier procedure.

In Holland, where prenatal services are covered by national health care, physician Helen Brandenburg and her colleagues (1991) studied the role of information in the decision to use CVS or amniocentesis. They found out that women who had CVS had come for prenatal care earlier in the pregnancy and were more likely to be told about CVS by their obstetrician or midwife. Only 29 percent of the women who had amniocentesis had actually chosen this procedure; 71 percent were too far along in their pregnancies and so had no choice but to have amniocentesis. The researchers concluded that women who had amniocentesis did so not out of choice but because of lack of information.

Clearly, obstetricians play a key gatekeeping role in referring patients for prenatal testing (Bernhardt and Bannerman, 1984). Yet pregnant women often rely on their own initiative and determination to secure this care. This is especially crucial when the procedure in question is new, providers and facilities are in short supply, and questions about safety have not been resolved.

Some women may be unusually alert for new information. Carol had amniocentesis in her first pregnancy and found out that her fetus was affected with Tay-Sachs disease. She terminated that pregnancy at five and a half months, an experience that left a lasting emotional wound. The day after she received the Tay-Sachs diagnosis, before the abortion could take place, she watched the ''Today Show.'' ''That's how I found out about the CVS. I called the station for more details. I decided then and there that in my next pregnancy I would have a CVS.'' When she got pregnant again she flew from Phoenix, her hometown, to Philadelphia, one of a handful of cities where CVS was available at the time, to have that procedure. This time the fetus was normal.

CLIENTS' REPRODUCTIVE PATTERNS

Our respondents, like most women who have prenatal diagnosis, are disproportionately well-to-do, highly educated, and well informed. But how do they compare with other American women in terms of their childbearing history? How do amniocentesis and CVS users compare with each other? Understanding these differences will help us to place in perspective their attitudes about pregnancy, disability, and motherhood.

Again, we excluded from the analysis the ten younger women who had come for reasons not related to age. This group included two women who had previously terminated an affected pregnancy, one for anencephaly and one for Down's syndrome; three women who were referred because of a low reading on a routine AFP test; and five women with a family history of abnormalities including Down's syndrome, muscular dystrophy, and Trisomy 18. (This condition, also called Edward's syndrome, is caused by the presence of an extra chromosome 18. It is characterized by severe mental retardation and multiple deformities. Survival for more than a few months is rare.)

Table 6.2 shows the reproductive histories of amniocentesis and CVS users aged 34 and above. Each group had an average of two previous pregnancies, with one living child and one unsuccessful pregnancy. In both groups more than half the present pregnancies were planned. The two groups differed in their experience with abortion. The percentage of CVS users who reported previous abortions for any reason, including fetal abnormality, was 44, compared to 31

Table 6.2

Comparison of Reproductive Histories of Amniocentesis and CVS Users Aged 34 and Above

	AMNIO-CENTESIS (N=64)	CVS (N=46)
% Pregnancies planned	56.3	67.4
If pregnancy planned, how long it took to conceive (months)	6.6	4.6
Mean # of previous pregnancies	2.0	2.3
Mean # of living children	1.4	1.2
Mean # of unsuccessful pregnancies	.8	.9
% who had previous elective abortion	22.4	39.5
% who had previous abortion for any reason (including abnormality)	30.8	44.3

for amniocentesis users. The disparity is even greater when we compare the percentage who had had elective abortions (as opposed to terminations for abnormality): about 40 percent of CVS users, 22 percent of amniocentesis users.

How typical are these women of all American females of childbearing age? Comparisons of reproductive histories with the general population are difficult because the census data on fertility are calculated differently. Nevertheless, overall patterns are similar. However atypical these "moral pioneers" are in social status and access to information, they are quite similar to other women in fertility patterns. Although older than other expectant or new mothers, they have had roughly the same number of children, pregnancies, and abortions as the rest of the population.

At the time of our study, the average woman in our sample was expecting, or had recently given birth to, her second child. The average married American woman similarly anticipates having two children (nationwide there are approximately 2,300 children per 1,000 wives). In fact, women at the end of their reproductive years have had an average of 2.4 children, with higher means for blacks and Hispanics: 2.7 and 2.8, respectively (*Statistical Abstracts of the United States*, 1988, Tables 95, 98, pp. 66–67).

The proportion of planned pregnancies in our sample also reflects that in the general population. Although about half of all pregnancies nationwide are unplanned, many of these pregnancies end in miscarriage or abortion. Among all women aged 35 to 44, about 62 percent of children were wanted at conception and timed "right"—that is, the pregnancy was planned (*Statistical Abstracts of the United States*, 1988, Table 101, p. 68). This is comparable to the rate in our sample.

The rate of abortions in our sample is about the same as that of the rest of the population. All available data indicate that abortions are common in our society. In 1985 there were 1,590,000 legal abortions in the United States. This translates into 28 abortions (compared to 70 live births) for each 1,000 women aged 15 to 44, or 425 abortions for every 1,000 live births. The rate of abortions among minority women is double that for white women (*Statistical Abstracts of the United States*, 1988, Tables 103–105, pp. 68–70).

Our study shows that, despite individual variations, the diffusion of CVS has followed the classic model for the spread of innovation. Initial users are disproportionately drawn from higher socioeconomic strata. These women possess not only money (or insurance coverage) and geographic proximity, but also better information and a determination to seek out and use any new technology that will help them to control their reproductive lives. As the pioneers accrue positive experience with the new technique, CVS, like amniocentesis, seems more "natural" to less well-situated or more cautious women. Use of the technique then spreads to broader segments of the population.

NOTE

1. Many women do not realize that they in fact are undergoing prenatal diagnostic testing or that they theoretically have the option to reject it. Many women who seek prenatal care by week 16 of the pregnancy are offered an AFP test, and nearly all have one or more ultrasound examinations (see Chapter 2). Accepting noninvasive testing may subject women to the very knowledge and decision making that they had sought to avoid by rejecting invasive testing. One of our counselors reported that she had seen only one patient who had decided to continue a pregnancy with Down's syndrome. This patient had not initially elected amniocentesis; she was referred for it after a finding of low AFP.

7

Assessing the Risks

Brenda and Harvey's Story: "The Risk Grows Exponentially"

Brenda and Harvey are a married couple expecting their first child at age 40. They operate their own business. Since they were both home when we called, we interviewed both of them. Both have a professional background in the health fields. They pride themselves on being medically sophisticated. Before deciding to have CVS, they did a computer search on the procedure. Yet, the interview revealed persistent misinformation.

Interviewer: As far as you know what were the odds of your having a child with an abnormality?

Harvey: I don't know. I remember reading the statistics.

Brenda: I know we read it but I don't remember.

Harvey: I think it's 1 in 10.

Brenda: No. I don't think it's that high.

Harvey: It grows exponentially with each year of maternal age.

Interviewer: What were the odds of procedurally caused miscarriage? You researched that.

Harvey: Basically they said it was greater with CVS [than with amniocentesis]. It was like point oh-oh-one.

Brenda: It was like 1 to 2 percent higher with CVS than with amnio. That's what I recall. . . .

Interviewer [to (*Harvey*)]: Did you say point-zero-zero one? That's 1 in 1,000.

Harvey: I don't recall. I did this in June and had some notes, but I don't have them any more. It sounded like there was a greater possibility of miscarriage with CVS, but what it came down to was—it was hard to interpret the statistics because it looked like you have a greater risk of miscarrying if you didn't perform the procedure. [?]

Interviewer. What are the odds of miscarriage with amnio?

Harvey: It's something like ten times greater with the CVS.

Interviewer. Ten times?

Brenda: No, it was 1 to 2 percent greater.

Harvey: No, it was ten times greater.

Brenda: Well, you [have two different impressions].

Brenda and Harvey, an articulate, well-educated couple, provide an extreme example of erroneous interpretation; most prenatal diagnosis users do better than that. Yet, numbers are an abstraction to most people, whether the unanticipated outcome is desired or dreaded. Couples who undergo in vitro fertilization are typically told that the odds of having a baby are quite low—from 10 to 20 percent, depending on the clinic. Yet most couples are optimistically convinced that they will be the lucky ones (Modell, 1989).

Prenatal genetic counseling is designed to supply information to enable couples to make the choice about whether to seek testing and if so, which test to employ. In principle, the decision is made on the basis of a careful weighing of the risks and benefits of each option. The presumed rationality of this decision, and the couple's "right" to make it on the basis of complete information, are cardinal principles of genetic counseling. However, these choices, like all reproductive behavior, are socially constructed. Decisions reflect the clients' backgrounds, the dynamics of the counseling session, and subjective perceptions of the different outcomes.

THE SOCIAL CONSTRUCTION OF RISK: THEORETICAL CONSIDERATIONS

Analysts of risk behavior distinguish between the objective probability of an event's occurrence (for example, the incidence of lung cancer among smokers, the odds of serious injury or death in an automobile accident, or the probability of a child's abduction by a stranger) and the subjective perception of such risks. Studies suggest that the *perception* of risk often diverges from the real odds. The subjective assessment of the odds as high, moderate, or low, and hence their implications for behavior, are influenced by individual biasing factors. These biasing factors include the salience of the risked event in the person's mind, its "anchoring" or the baseline risk with which it is compared, its potential severity, and the degree to which the behavior that causes it is voluntary (Kahneman and Tversky, 1972, 1979; Slovic, 1987; Vlek, 1987).

Salience or *availability* refers to the ease with which instances of the event in question may be brought to mind. The more personal the experience that a person has with an event, the stronger is her tendency to believe that her own chances are greater than average. In making a decision on prenatal diagnosis, a would-be parent who already has a child with a particular birth defect, or who knows such children professionally or socially, tends to rate as higher the numeric risk of having such a child. This person may be more willing to undertake an additional procedural risk in order to avoid such an outcome (Fischhoff et al., 1981; Kahneman and Tversky, 1982; Lippman-Hand and Fraser, 1979; Wertz, Sorenson, and Heeren, 1986).

Anchoring refers to the background risk, the starting point for comparing the odds of the event in question. In prenatal diagnosis, the starting point is the risk of defect in an average pregnancy. The operative rule is that a woman should be offered prenatal testing "when the risk of defect equals or exceeds the risk to the pregnancy of the procedure itself" (President's Commission, 1983). As estimated procedural risk declines, the maternal age at which the procedures are offered has also fallen.

The *severity* of the undesirable outcome is its catastrophic or disruptive potential. An unplanned pregnancy means one thing for an unmarried woman still in school who is facing the decision of whether or not to become a mother now and with this man. It has a different meaning for a married woman with several children who is secure in her identity and her role relationships. Therefore, women at different points in their life cycles behave differently with respect to contraception and abortion (Badagliacco, 1989; Luker, 1976; Rothman, 1989; Zimmerman, 1977). In making decisions on prenatal screening, women consider the severity of the disorder and its implications for the child and the family. In general, people are more willing to risk having children with disorders that cause physical handicaps, such as cystic fibrosis, than those entailing death or mental retardation (Wertz and Fletcher, 1989b). Not only the future demands that may be placed on the family by a given disability, but also the family's perceived ability to cope with the demands, enter into the social construction of the situation.

Finally, people's tolerance for a given risk is affected by their *control* over it, that is, whether the adverse outcome is viewed as an act of God or nature or as caused by voluntary behavior. Engineering educator Chauncey Starr (1969) concludes that people will accept risks from voluntary activities, such as skiing or riding a car without a seat belt, that are roughly 1,000 times as great as they would tolerate from hazards over which they have no control, such as harmful food preservatives and nuclear radiation. Paradoxically, in prenatal screening, this means that some people are more likely to accept the naturally occurring risks of genetic disorders than to tolerate those caused by medical procedures over which they have a choice. Others view as "preventable" the occurrence of those defects that can be diagnosed in utero and hence feel compelled to undergo screening. At the same time, they may be less concerned about illnesses or injuries they do not control, those related to the birth process (Vlek, 1987).

The content of the genetic counseling itself affects clients' interpretation of the risks. Clients often find it difficult to grasp the meaning of probability figures supplied by the genetic counselor, to apply the information to their own decision, and even to accurately recall the numbers shortly afterward. Several studies (d'Ydewalle and Evers-Kiebooms, 1987; Pitz, 1987; Wertz, Sorenson and Heeren, 1986) conclude that discussing in the counseling session whether the couple should have a child, as well as explaining the ramifications of a genetic abnormality for the family's life, influence clients' interpretation of risks. As we will see below, the omission from the counseling session of details about the abortion procedure, should one be necessary, also colors the clients' choice.

CLIENTS' PERCEPTION OF RISK

Socioeconomic Status and Risk Assessment

We asked our survey respondents about their perceptions of the probability of three undesirable outcomes: having a child with a genetic or chromosomal abnormality, miscarriage or damage to the fetus as a result of the screening procedure, and serious complications to themselves as a result of the procedure. For each outcome we asked about their assessment of the numerical odds, on a scale from "1 in 1,000 or less" to "1 in 2." We also inquired whether they viewed this chance as "very low," "moderately low," "moderately high," "very high," or "don't know." The last option was included because at the time of our survey the risks of CVS had not been fully established, and this fact was emphasized to clients who inquired about it (see Appendix A for the survey questions).

While we found only small relationships between income and risk perception, education had a considerable impact. To be sure, clients with different levels of education did not differ in their awareness of the numerical risks, either of genetic defects or of procedural damage. (Recall that, before the procedure, all women had been given written handouts citing the various risks.) Educational level was associated, however, with the evaluation of those risks as high, moderate, or low (Table 7.1). Women whose education included some graduate or professional school were more than twice as likely as those with only a high school education to regard as "low" their risk of having a baby with a genetic defect. They were one and a half times as likely to assess as "low" the potential risk to the fetus and twice as likely to say the risk to themselves was low. Conversely, less educated women were more likely to view the same risks as "high."

Why the differences? Clients find it difficult to apply abstract odds to the immediate situation, a difficulty compounded by the high stakes involved. Fears of having a baby with a chromosomal abnormality or of losing the pregnancy typically exist in the background as low-level anxieties, overshadowed by anticipation and preparations for the baby. The emphasis placed by genetic counseling and invasive procedures on the possibility of loss may transform these fears into dreaded eventualities (see Chapter 5).

Women do not share these fears equally. As one genetic counselor told us, "All pregnancies are precious, but some are more precious than others." Many health care givers believe that late-life pregnancies are somehow more "precious" and would be mourned more keenly because of the dwindling likelihood of having more children. In addition, women presumably are more concerned

Table 7.1
Percent of Survey Respondents Who Perceived Risks as "Low," by Education

PERCEIVED RISK OF:	H.S. OR LESS (n=10)	COLLEGE (1-4 YEARS) (n=50)	GRADUATE SCHOOL (n=59)
Genetic defect (n=117, p <.05)	30	39.6	62.7
Procedure's damage to fetus (n=119, p <.05)	40	30.0	62.7
Procedure's harm to self (n=118, p <.01)	30	24.5	62.8

Note: Each row combines those who answered "very low" and "moderately low." The original question also included the following possible answers: "moderately high," "very high," and "don't know."

about the health of their babies if the child's health would have a greater impact on their life-style.

Critics have charged that, in practice, this translates into a belief that women of a higher socioeconomic background are more concerned about their pregnancies and the health of their children than are poor or working-class women (Simonds and Rothman, 1992). Our data suggest, however, that it is *less* educated women, those of a lower SES, who are most terrified by the prospects of loss or abnormality. There is no reason to believe that better educated women are any less concerned, but perhaps they are better able to place the odds in the perspective of probabilities.

Procedure and Risk Assessment

At the outset of our research, CVS was considered an experimental procedure whose risks were undetermined. In time, as data on the relative safety of CVS became available, this information was disseminated to clients. A typical hand-out to clients in 1987 estimated a loss rate of 1 in 50 to 1 in 100 (1 to 2 percent) with CVS, compared with 1 in 200 (one-half of 1 percent) with amniocentesis. The handout stated, "CVS offers the promise of being as accurate and safe as amniocentesis while permitting much earlier diagnosis." Presumably women weigh the genetic against the procedural risk in making their decision. According to one counselor, "The tradeoff [between CVS and amnio] is the benefit of the timing versus the risk of the procedure. Many women who are seeking CVS are at slightly higher risk—say, somebody who is 40 vs. 33." This counselor, 35 years old at the time, would follow the same guidelines for herself: "Right now, if I were pregnant I would probably have an amnio. Four years from now I would have a CVS."

We expected that women with higher perceived susceptibility to genetic abnormality would opt for the newer procedure which they knew was riskier, while younger women and those with a lower perceived vulnerability would choose amniocentesis. This is not what we found, however. There was no objective difference in susceptibility; that is, the CVS and amniocentesis groups had the same age distribution and history of abnormalities. The numeric odds assigned to the probability of genetic abnormality by both groups accurately reflected the absence of objective difference. *Interpretations* of genetic susceptibility, how-ever, differed considerably—but in the opposite direction from that expected (Table 7.2). CVS users were nearly twice as likely as amniocentesis users to

Table 7.2
Percent of Survey Respondents Who Perceived Risks as "Low," by Procedure

PERCEIVED RISK OF:	AMNIO (N=72)	CVS (N=48)
Genetic defect (n=118, p <.0001)	33.8	74.4
Procedure's damage to fetus (n=120, p <.001)	33.4	67.7
Procedure's harm to self (n=119, p <.001)	33.8	58.4

Note: Each row combines those who answered "very low" and "moderately low". The original question included also the following possible answers: "moderately high", "very high" and "don't know".

rate their genetic risk as "low." The difference in the proportion who rated the risk as "very low" (not shown in the table) was *five times*.

Clients' assessments of the potential dangers of the procedure were also the reverse of what we expected. Again, the numeric odds were assessed accurately; yet, CVS users were nearly twice as likely to interpret those odds as "low."

As a group, CVS users are better educated than amnio users. Could the gap in perceptions between amnio and CVS users be a spurious one, owing to the educational difference rather than to the choice of procedure? To find out, we separated the effects of the procedure from those of education. In each screening group, we found that educational attainment is correlated with a "low" perception of both genetic and procedural risks. This is more pronounced among CVS users than among those who had amniocentesis.

Statistically significant relationships between educational attainment and risk perception emerged only for CVS users, and only with respect to the procedural risk to the fetus (Table 7.3). In this group the most highly educated women, those with some graduate or professional school, were more likely than those with "only" a college education to view the risk of miscarriage or damage to the fetus as "very low" or "moderately low" (74 percent compared to 60 percent) and less likely to view it as "moderately high" or "very high" (23 percent compared to 40 percent). It appears that both education and choice of procedure are associated with the perception of risks.

Table 7.3
CVS Users' Perception of Procedure's Risk to Fetus, by Education (N=48)

	LEVEL OF EDUCATION			
PERCEPTION OF RISK TO FETUS	H.S. OR LESS (N=2)	COLLEGE (1-4 YRS) (N=15)	GRAD. SCHOOL (N=31)	ROW TOTAL
Very low chance	-	13.3	32.3	25.0
Moderately low chance	-	46.7	41.9	41.7
Moderately high chance	-	33.3	22.6	25.0
Very high chance	50.0	6.7	-	4.2
Don't know	50.0	-	3.2	4.2
COLUMN TOTAL	100.00	100.00	100.00	100.00

p= < .001

These findings defy the accepted wisdom about the decision-making process in prenatal diagnosis. Clearly, women do not choose CVS after concluding that it is "worth" taking a higher risk because of their own greater susceptibility to abnormality. Rather, they construe the risk level of the new procedure as acceptably low. Those who, for whatever reasons, have decided to undergo CVS attempt to achieve cognitive consistency and peace of mind by persuading themselves that it is in fact safe.

Outcome Characteristics and Risk Assessment

One factor that influences the perception of risks and the subsequent behavior is the *severity* or impact of the outcome—the "dread factor." In prenatal testing, which is done to avert the birth of a child with a chromosomal abnormality, there are two other potential tragedies: losing the pregnancy through a miscarriage caused by the procedure and having an abortion following a diagnosis of abnormality. For parents who have decided to have testing in order to avoid giving birth to an affected child, the question is which danger is more dreadful— Scylla or Charybdis—miscarriage (with CVS) or induced late abortion (with amniocentesis).

Our interviews reveal that the two outcomes are not feared equally. In fact, since abortion is rarely discussed in the genetic counseling session, many clients have only a vague notion of the trauma it involves (see Chapter 9). But the fear of miscarriage, although it occurs infrequently, drives many away from CVS, if not from prenatal diagnosis altogether. With a very high emotional investment in the pregnancy, these women cannot accept even a slight elevation of risk to the fetus.

Barbara, a 37-year-old professor pregnant with her first child, made an appointment for CVS. She recalls running out of the clinic in tears when she found out during the counseling session that the risks of CVS exceeded those of amniocentesis by about one percentage point: "I know I just said that we didn't want to take any risk at all. But it just seemed that it was marginally less of a risk to do amnio than to do CVS. That's why I eventually had the amnio."

Barbara's decision was "rational" in that, given her low genetic risk, she opted for the procedure that offered the lesser risk to the fetus. She did not take into account the more traumatic nature of abortion following amniocentesis; no counselor had discussed this with her.

Other responses illustrate the role of the psychological *availability* of the event to the interpretation of the odds of its occurrence. Vickie, the nursing professor mentioned in Chapter 6, had cared for many severely handicapped children. During her pregnancy she found herself obsessed by the possibility of a fetal abnormality. By her own admission, she greatly overestimated the odds of this occurrence:

I had lots of exposure to handicapped kids. . . . And knowing that [an abnormality] was possible, I was trying to prepare my husband for it. I think he had the feeling, with all of the focus that I gave it, that I was "planning" on it, that a handicapped kid was a likely outcome. It was really very strange. But if that's where your exposure is and that's where your mindset is—it's like when you are going through medical school or nursing school, you are sure you have every disease you are studying. So being pregnant, I had a lot of concerns that we wouldn't have a healthy baby.

Despite her "obsession," she eventually declined prenatal diagnosis because her professional experience convinced her that no screening could rule out more than a small proportion of disabilities.

While statistics indicate that one out of, say, a hundred women of a given age will get a bad outcome on a prenatal test, for an individual woman the risk may *feel* like 50 percent. A bad outcome is experienced like an on/off switch; either it will happen or it won't: "My feeling is, either the fetus has [an abnormality] or it doesn't. I don't care if it's one in a billion or one in two. If it is a risk that can be avoided, do so." [Christine, age 37, mother of three; had CVS with a normal outcome in her third pregnancy.]

The "pessimistic" perception of risk is especially true for women who have had an abnormal pregnancy, borne a defective child, or may be carriers (Green, 1992). Betsy, a biologist and a mother of two healthy children, terminated her third pregnancy when amniocentesis revealed Down's syndrome. With her scientific background, she was aware of the discrepancy between her emotional perception of risk in any future pregnancy and the actual odds: "My perception of risk has changed. Now when I hear that the danger of something is 'only 1 or 2%' I feel emotionally that that danger is very high. I really do feel as if my risk of having this happen again is 50%, or at least 25% (though I don't believe it intellectually, of course)." This perception gradually declined along with the trauma of the diagnosis and the termination. A year later Betsy conceived again and gave birth to a healthy baby.

Decisions are complicated not only by the difficulty of grasping numerical probabilities but also by the absence, in most cases, of information about the implications of each outcome. Just as few women know what a second-trimester abortion entails, few people understand what it is really like to live with a Down's syndrome child or to watch an adolescent die an agonizing death from cystic fibrosis. Genetic counseling rarely supplies this information (see Chapter 4).

Unlike the rational decision-making model, our data suggest that in real life reproductive decisions are neither "rational" nor simple. The social construction of the risks is affected by gaps in knowledge and by the content and tone of the counseling session. It is also affected by the client's education and her selective exposure to the potential outcomes; by the desire to "do something" about outcomes believed to be under human control; and by the couple's emotional investment in the pregnancy.

COUNSELORS' PERCEPTION OF RISK

The first survey of genetic counselors in the prenatal diagnosis era was conducted by Sorenson (1973). Sorenson, it will be remembered from Chapter 3, received mailed responses from nearly five hundred U.S. counselors, of whom 80 percent were M.D.s and 74 percent were male. They were asked the following question: "If you were considering only the mathematical probability of recurrence of a genetic or chromosomal condition, how would you describe the following recurrence estimate in your own mind?" The results are shown in Table 7.4.

In the early 1970s nearly three-quarters of all genetic counselors regarded a genetic risk of 1 in 100 or less as "low" or "very low." Not until the risk reached 1 in 10 did the majority regard it as "high" or "very high." There was near-unanimity that a risk of 1 in 4 or greater (the actual odds of inheriting a recessive genetic disorder if both parents are carriers) is "high" or "very high."

About five years later Sorenson, together with Wertz and biostatistician Timothy Heeren, surveyed 205 genetic counselors and clients in 544 genetic coun-

Table 7.4
Risk Assessment, "Recurrence of Genetic or Chromosomal Condition,"
Counselors Surveyed by Sorenson, 1973 (N=496)

NUMERIC RISK	RISK INTERPRETATION (%)				
RATIO & %	VERY LOW	LOW	MODER.	HIGH	VERY HIGH
1/200 (0.5%)	50	33	11	5	1
1/100 (1%)	30	43	18	7	2
1/50 (2%)	7	38	35	16	4
1/30 (3.3%)	2	25	41	25	7
1/20 (5%)	1	14	38	37	11
1/10 (10%)	0	2	21	50	27
1/4 (25%)	0	0	2	26	72
1/2 (50%)	0	0	0	3	97

Source: Adapted from James Sorenson, "Counselors: A Self-Portrait." Genetic Counseling, 1973, vol. 1, p. 31.

seling sessions in twenty-five states and the District of Columbia (Wertz, Sorenson, and Heeren, 1986). Following each counseling session, counselors were asked, "Did you give this patient a numerical risk?" (About half did.) "If so, what was it? Do you consider this risk very low, low, moderate, high or very high?" The most common response to risks below 7 percent was "low"; to risks of 7–19 percent "moderate"; and to risks above 20 percent "high." These counselors were comfortable with higher risk levels than were those surveyed earlier.

Rothman (1986) interviewed twenty-five genetic counselors in the early to mid-1980s, in addition to spending a month observing three different counselors at work. She posed Sorenson's original question to her counselors in its exact wording. Whereas in the late 1960s access to amniocentesis was restricted to women with a known familial risk or those who were age 40 and above, by the 1980s amniocentesis was routinely available to women 35 years of age and even younger.

Rothman pointed out that her counselors were far likelier than Sorenson's physician–counselors of 1973 to give "high" risk ratings to risks of 10 percent or less. A 2 percent risk was called "high" or "very high" by almost half her respondents compared to 20 percent of Sorenson's. Conversely, fewer than half of Rothman's counselors versus three-quarters of the earlier group considered a 1 percent risk "low" or "very low." Rothman stressed that only three-fourths of her group thought 1 in 400 was low or very low. In the first decade of prenatal diagnosis, then, counselors' tolerance for genetic risk—the point at which they could justify intervention—diminished considerably.

Risk of Abnormality

We asked the thirty-one genetic counselors in our study a question that differed from Sorenson's 1973 question only in substituting the word "occurrence" for "recurrence": "If you were considering *only* the mathematical probability of occurrence of a genetic or chromosomal abnormality, how would you describe the following odds in your own mind?" The results are presented in Table 7.5.

Table 7.5 shows that the trend toward rating given levels of risk ever higher has continued. A 1 in 100 risk was rated as "low" by one-sixth of the respondents; as "moderate" by one-third; and as "high" or even "very high" by one-half. Responses to 1 in 200 continued to encompass all five categories. Only at the 1 in *500* level (a risk too low for inclusion in earlier studies) did all counselors feel there was no longer a high risk of abnormality. Even so, one-third considered this "moderate." Over 40 percent of counselors said that no presented risk category was "very low." When prompted for a definition of "low," two counselors answered "1 in 10,000," and one said, "1 in 40,000." All three smiled broadly at this point, in a nonverbal acknowledgment that these levels were not attainable in real life.

A counselor who called a 1 in 1,000 risk "moderate" continued by calling

Table 7.5

Counselors' Interpretations of Selected Levels of Numeric Risk for "Genetic or Chromosomal Abnormality" (N=31)

NUMERIC RISK, AS REPORTED BY COUNSELOR	RISK INTERPRETATION (%)				
	VERY LOW N %	LOW N %	MODER. N %	HIGH N %	VERY HIGH N %
1/1000	18 (58.1)	9 (29.0)	4 (12.9)		
1/500	8 (25.8)	13 (41.9)	10 (32.2)		
1/200	1 (03.2)	12 (38.7)	13 (41.9)	4 (12.9)	1 (03.2)
1/100		5 (16.1)	11 (35.5)	12 (38.7)	3 (09.7)
1/10		1 (03.2)	1 (03.2)	15 (48.4)	14 (45.2)
1/4				5 (16.1)	25 (80.6)
1/2				2 (06.4)	29 (93.5)

1 in 500 "sort of high." As for 1 in 200: "Everything else as far as I'm concerned is high; I have no objectivity left. If it's going to be one person in 200, it's going to be me." Once again, for risk-averse individuals a risk level lower than that provided by real life is subjectively felt as both high and personally threatening, perhaps because they have seen that 1 in 100 or 1 in 1,000 occurrences (*availability*). This is the reverse of the "magic thinking" used by teenagers who feel immune to the possible consequences of risk-taking behavior.

The greatest variations in interpretation over time or at any point in time occur for the moderate risk levels that most accord with reality. Responses for the 1 percent genetic risk range from low to very high. Only one-sixth of our group considered a 1 percent risk "low" compared to nearly half of Rothman's and three-quarters of Sorenson's. Clearly, this is the level of client risk that has seen the greatest increase in utilization in the past decade: from the 1 percent Down's syndrome risk for the age 40 woman to the 0.25 percent risk for the age 35 woman. The counselors are responding to the shifting *anchoring* of this risk.

The genetic counseling profession is grounded in an ethos of nondirectiveness (see Chapter 3). All counselors stated they would never try to influence clients' decisions as to whether to have prenatal testing or, if so, which test to have. In their personal lives, however, they use different criteria. A third of them would be more directive toward their own female relatives, perhaps raising the issue of counseling at a younger age than what they recommend for clients.

Five counselors were adamant in stating they would act differently toward female relatives, urging them to seek counseling, at the very least.

- I'd be more directive than with a patient; I'd put in my own two cents. I'd send or encourage her to seek real medical counseling.
- My sister-in-law was pregnant. She was only 24, and I was very nervous that she had no test.

Regardless of their personal views, counselors uniformly refuse to offer interpretation to clients who beseech them, "Would you consider a 1 in *n* risk high or low?"

- A patient asked me, "Is it comparable to this risk of being struck by lightning?" I said, "I couldn't interpret it for you; I can only give you numerical risk."
- A one-in-four risk seems very high to me, but to a patient I'd still say, "You have a 3 in 4 chance of having a normal baby". . . . When I talk to a patient, a 1 percent risk is significant though low; it's still 99 percent OK. But as professionals, we see the 1 in 20,000 instances.

Risk of Procedure

As stated above, all counselors were familiar with the rule that a patient should be offered prenatal diagnosis "when the risk of defect equals or exceeds the risk to the pregnancy of the procedure itself." The currently accepted procedural risks are about one-half percent for amnio and 1 percent for CVS—although several of our respondents worked in centers with procedural risks half the above or less. In practice, the main risk that concerns counselors and clients is that of miscarriage.

We asked the counselors, "How would you describe the same odds [as for genetic abnormalities] for the risk of procedural complications?," offering them the same five-point scale from "very low" to "very high." The results are presented in Table 7.6. Only thirty counselors answered this question. One counselor objected to the artificiality of the enforced choice: "No procedural risk is higher than one in 100 in real life. If I were at real risk of having a defective child, I'd take a one in two risk! But I wouldn't work for a place which caused miscarriages."

In general, counselors showed much greater agreement on what a given level represented for procedural risk than for genetic risks and were able to tolerate much higher levels of the procedural. All respondents found 1 in 1,000 a "low" or "very low" risk, and all but one found this so for 1 in 500 as well. Nearly 75 percent still considered 1 in 200 "low" compared to 42 percent who considered a comparable genetic risk "low." Even for 1 in 100, twice as many counselors answered "low" as for the comparable genetic risk. However, this level generated the first responses of "high," 31 percent of respondents calling

Table 7.6

Counselors' Interpretation of Selected Levels of Numeric Risk for "Procedural Complications" (N=30)

NUMERIC RISK, AS REPORTED BY COUNSELOR	RISK INTERPRETATION (%)				
	VERY LOW N %	LOW N %	MODER. N %	HIGH N %	VERY HIGH N %
1/1000	21 (70.0)	9 (30.0)			
1/500	14 (46.7)	15 (50.0)	1 (03.3)		
1/200	1 (03.3)	21 (70.0)	8 (26.7)		
1/100		10 (33.3)	11 (36.7)	9 (30.9)	
1/10			3 (10.0)	15 (50.0)	12 (40.0)
1/4				6 (20.0)	24 (80.0)
1/2				4 (13.3)	26 (86.7)

it such versus 48 percent for genetic risk. At some hypothetical point, respondents could no longer justify the procedure. At a risk level of 1 in 10, "You'd be nuts: no procedure would have this risk except maybe for a brain tumor!"

Three-quarters experienced procedural risks as subjectively lower on average than genetic risks. From their comments, counselors better tolerated procedural risk not because the client can control exposure to this danger (voluntariness) but because the consequences of the two are very different (severity). The repercussions of having an affected child are perceived as more severe and long lasting than those of having a procedurally associated miscarriage. The miscarriage, though devastating, does not create a lifetime burden.

Six counselors rated both kinds of risk identically, one commenting, "if you're *only* considering mathematical probability, then odds of the risk [of complications] remain the same [as for abnormality]."

At any given time, counselors' risk interpretations vary greatly, especially for genetic risk. Fewer than half the counselors rate a given genetic risk identically, except for the most extreme levels. However, for both kinds of risk they display a greater consensus on what is "very high" than for what is "very low."

The majority of counselors do not assess levels of genetic and of procedural risk against linear scales. Rather, they evaluate these risks against known background levels and against the risk for Down's syndrome at the prevailing boundary age for recommended use of the procedure (anchoring).

Perhaps the physician/geneticist counselors of earlier decades tolerated higher risk levels because they routinely counseled parents who had already borne an affected child. These parents faced a much higher risk of abnormality in a subsequent birth—typically, 1 in 4 or 1 in 2. Today's prenatal counselors, by contrast, see predominantly those women whose only known risk factor is maternal age. A substantial proportion of counselors view that risk as "high," that is, justifying medical intervention. The regularity of the shifts suggests that counselors are responding to a changed environment.

Counselors appear to base their assessment of *procedural* risk on the quoted miscarriage rate for CVS, the riskier of the two invasive procedures. In the future, the risk level for prenatal testing will decrease dramatically as tests extracting fetal cells from the maternal bloodstream become available. When non-invasive tests become routine (as with MSAFP and ultrasound), society may come to perceive all levels of genetic risk as intolerably high since genetic abnormality will be "controllable"—regardless of the cost to women. The changing risk interpretations of genetic counselors may be a harbinger of change in societal attitudes.

Medical knowledge is greatly valued in American culture: it is regarded as a good in its own right. Genetic counseling, perhaps more than other health fields, is predicated on the notion that information empowers. Our analysis, like earlier studies, suggests that the knowledge imparted to clients is inevitably shaped by the structure, history, and prevailing ideology of the profession as well as by the values of individual health care givers. At the same time, clients construe the meanings of this knowledge and its application to reproductive decisions in light of the personal and social context of their lives.

8

Attitudes about Abortion

Debbie's Story: "As a Mother, the Whole Concept of Termination Changes"

Debbie, a full-time homemaker, has four children, including 11-month-old twins. Debbie has had three abortions. The first took place in the 1960s, before the *Roe v. Wade* decision legalized abortion. Debbie, then a college student, traveled to Mexico to obtain the abortion, an experience that she wouldn't want her daughters to repeat. Debbie is committed to freedom of reproductive choice: "I think women should have the right to have an abortion for any reason," she says.

At age 39, after giving birth to a boy and a girl, Debbie found herself unexpectedly pregnant. "I am terrible about planning pregnancies," she says. "But I really did want another child. . . . Maybe it was unconsciously planned." Her husband, David, a businessman who has two college-age children from his first marriage, didn't want more children. Although David was "very unhappy," Debbie was determined to have this baby.

At 9 weeks' gestational age Debbie made an appointment for CVS. This was when she found out she was carrying twins. "The ultrasound technician said, 'We see two little bodies in there.' At first it didn't get through to me. She finally said, 'Look at the screen,' and I saw them. I think I fainted. . . . Really, for about five seconds, I blacked out. We had been debating whether or not we wanted a third child. Really, it was such a conflict. . . . And then to find out that there were two! I felt very bad at the time because it would have been David's fifth and sixth kid. I really wanted it, but I didn't know whether he could take two more. So I cried. I was so upset."

The clinic staff told her that amniocentesis would be a better choice than CVS because there was a possibility that one twin's sample might contaminate the other. They suggested that she go home and think about this since she was too emotionally wrought to make decisions. Debbie "stumbled out of there in a total daze." She called her husband at work and told him to come home right away. At the kitchen table she told him what had happened. "Then we just started laughing hysterically. It was a great cosmic moment. . . . It was so funny to us after the intense debate we had had that there should then be *two*. It was settled at that point that we were going to go ahead, presuming that everything was going to be O.K. . . . They [pointing to the babies in her lap] settled it for us by being two."

Despite the conflict with her husband, from the start of the pregnancy Debbie wouldn't consider an abortion. "As a mother who has had children the whole concept of termination changes. It becomes so unacceptable. When I was young and hadn't had children it was very much easier for me to even think about it. Having known what children are, I really could not [have an abortion]—It would have been a major trauma for me from which I probably would have never recovered. . . . I never want to have an abortion again, now that I know what being a mother is like. That's why I had my tubes tied."

THE SOCIAL CONSTRUCTION OF ABORTION: THEORETICAL CONSIDERATIONS

Abortion, like pregnancy, is socially constructed. Women's feelings about abortion reflect their experiences, roles, and identities. The meaning of terminating a specific pregnancy is constructed in the context of the pregnancy's place in a woman's life, her goals and her ongoing relationships. As Rothman (1989, pp. 107, 124) writes, "It is the meaning of a pregnancy for a woman that shapes the meaning an abortion holds for her. . . . For one woman, in one pregnancy, an abortion is a minor inconvenience . . . and for another woman, or for the same woman in another pregnancy, an abortion is the death of a baby."

A pregnant woman must sort out the meaning of the pregnancy. A first pregnancy, particularly an unplanned one, "presents a woman with a basic identity decision: whether or not to become a mother now, and by this man" (Benderly, 1984, p. 22). Subsequent pregnancies, too, involve identity and role decisions—whether or not to interrupt a career or delay reentry into one, whether or not to prolong full-time mothering, whether or not to stay in a crumbling marriage. Debbie's partner in her first pregnancy was unacceptable as a husband; she had no trouble deciding on the abortion. Years later, now in a secure and loving marriage, Debbie knew that having another child meant delaying her reentry into the job market. It meant as well additional childcare and financial responsibilities for her already overburdened husband. Debbie is aware of the irony that after fiercely debating whether to have a third child, the sonographic image of *two* more children made termination emotionally impossible. The knowledge that there were twins endowed them with a personhood; from that moment they were accepted as part of the family.

Sociologist Mary Zimmerman (1977) studied the abortion decision shortly after the passage of *Roe v. Wade*. She points out that a woman will have an easier time clarifying the implications of her pregnancy and deciding about abortion if she is "affiliated," that is, firmly attached to her social world, settled in her relationships, and clear about her "obligations, expectations, and future" (p. 56). Being secure in her role network and adult identity gives the woman "a sense of the 'right' time to have a baby" (p. 147). By contrast, women with poorly defined adult identities and tenuous role relationships search more frantically for meaning and help.

In the United States and other Western countries, first pregnancies are much more likely to be terminated than are subsequent pregnancies. Following the seminal work of theorist Robert K. Merton (1968), sociologist Joanne Badagliacco (1989) used the concepts of status and role to explain the different abortion rates for first and subsequent pregnancies. According to Merton's theory, *status* refers to any position in the social structure, such as mother, wife, teacher, or lawyer. Each status consists of several *roles* or patterned relationships. A professor has the roles of teacher to her classroom students, advisor to students who come to her office, colleague to other faculty members, boss to her research assistants, and employee to the university's administration. In each of these roles the person interacts with different role partners. Together, the roles constitute the *role set* that forms a particular status.

Using these concepts, Badagliacco has found that motherhood status is an important factor in the decision whether to have an abortion: "Women who are mothers at the time of their pregnancy are much less likely than nonmothers to abort" (p. 22). This is because a first pregnancy, if carried to term, involves the acquisition of a new status, motherhood, which will profoundly affect the woman's educational and career plans, relationships, and identities. Women who are already mothers do not acquire a new status with the birth of a subsequent child, but rather add *role partners*, a less drastic change. The abortion decision is constructed in the context of motherhood—present and future. This is why Debbie, who had three abortions, could not countenance another one now that she was a mother, although the birth of twins immensely complicated her life and that of her husband's.

Attitudes about abortion also reflect ideological world views. Sociologist Kristin Luker (1984) argues that participants in the abortion debate "are defending a *world view*—a notion of what they see as sacred and important—as well as a view of the embryo" (p. 7). Whichever side of the debate they support, individuals try to fit their views on abortion into this world view.

Leaders of both the pro-life and pro-choice movements hold world views that are well articulated, coherent, and mutually irreconcilable. These world views encompass beliefs about morality as well as about gender roles, the meaning of parenthood, and human nature. Pro-life activists accept moral codes as absolute and divinely inspired. They perceive motherhood as a woman's highest calling, disapprove of "artificial" contraception and sex outside marriage, and are disturbed by the notion of a woman controlling her fertility in order to accommodate career and financial goals. Pro-choice activists, by contrast, value women's control over reproduction as "essential for women to live up to their full human potential" (p. 176). They believe that childbearing should be carefully planned so as to give children the best possible economic and psychological chances. They also view ethics as situational and personal, with individuals morally empowered to make their own decisions. Pro-life activists hold a God-centered world view; pro-choice activists possess a world view centered on human beings, their capacity for reason, and their right to happiness.

In the public controversy surrounding abortion, the dilemma is often portrayed as a conflict between competing *rights*—the rights of the mother versus the rights of the fetus. Psychologist Carol Gilligan (1982), however, points out that women tend to make decisions on the basis of conflicting *responsibilities* rather than rights: "The abortion dilemma magnifies the issues of responsibility and care that derive from the fact of relationship" (p. 108). For women the abortion decision is not a matter of abstract balancing of the "rights" of the fetus versus those of the mother. Rather, women who confront this decision are attempting to untangle incompatible obligations incurred by existing relationships. These include, first, obligations to spouse and to living children, and, second, the anticipated commitment to the unborn child. Obligations to oneself, we might add, cannot be neglected; a woman who does not nurture herself cannot nurture others. And, as women increasingly participate in the labor force, they are obligated to fulfill the expectations of the workplace. Rights are unvarying; responsibilities change from one situation to the next, from one pregnancy to another.

Attitudes toward abortion, though grounded in ideological world views, are also shaped by women's reproductive histories and role relationships. Most women who use prenatal diagnosis are prepared (at least intellectually) to terminate the pregnancy should an abnormality be found. Our respondents strongly favor abortion rights. At the same time, these women are deeply committed to motherhood and are disturbed by the possibility of losing *this* pregnancy, or by any suggestion that abortion might be taken lightly.

ATTITUDES TOWARD ABORTION

The most extensive annual survey on abortion attitudes in the United States is done by the National Opinion Research Center's General Social Survey (GSS). Every year since 1972, GSS workers have interviewed a representative sample of English-speaking persons 18 years of age or older living in the continental United States. Between 1,500 and 2,000 individuals are interviewed. The average interview lasts about one hour and covers topics ranging from political attitudes and work satisfaction to religious beliefs and views about abortion.

The GSS asks whether, in the respondent's opinion, a woman should be able to obtain a legal abortion for different reasons. The reasons include the following: if there is a strong chance of a serious defect in the baby, if the pregnancy endangers the woman's health, if the pregnancy resulted from rape, if the parents cannot afford another child or do not want more children, or if the woman is unmarried. (See Appendix C for the GSS question on abortion.)

In order to compare the attitudes of our sample with those of the American population as a whole, we adapted the GSS questions (see Appendix A, questions 31 and 32). Our questionnaire differed from the GSS in several respects. In addition to asking about abortion rights in general, we asked whether the respondent herself would have an abortion under the specified circumstances; we asked how far in the pregnancy she would allow abortion for others as well as for herself; and we added questions on special issues raised by prenatal diagnosis, including different types of fetal abnormality and fetal sex. Altogether, we used two sets of twelve items. An item analysis of each set of questions yielded excellent Cronbach's alphas: Alpha = 0.92 for general abortion attitudes, and alpha = 0.90 for attitudes on abortion for oneself.[1]

We asked our respondents to indicate their agreement or disagreement with the statement that "*In general*, women should have the right to have an abortion for each of the following reasons." Using the same list, we also asked, "Under what circumstances would you consider an abortion *for yourself*?" The hypothetical reasons included a pregnancy resulting from rape or incest, a pregnancy endangering the mother's life or health, fetal abnormalities of differing severities and likelihoods, out-of-wedlock pregnancy, completed childbearing, wrong timing, inability to afford additional children, and sex selection. The results are reported in Table 8.1.

As Table 8.1 shows, nearly all women in our sample supported the freedom of choice to terminate a pregnancy that seriously endangered the mother's health, that posed a high chance that the baby had a serious defect, or that resulted from rape or incest. Nearly all our respondents indicated that they would consider an abortion for themselves in such circumstances. Over four-fifths of our respondents also supported abortion rights in the case of an out-of-wedlock pregnancy or when the family could not afford any more children, did not want a child at this time, or did not want any more children.

The overwhelmingly pro-choice position of our respondents contrasts with the lukewarm support of the American population as a whole. The gap is particularly noteworthy in attitudes toward "elective" abortions, those for economic or social reasons. While most Americans support the right to abortion in extreme circumstances, they are much less likely to approve of terminations viewed as elective. By contrast, our respondents strongly favored abortion rights in all circumstances except "wrong sex" (see Chapter 10).

When asked what they themselves would do in such situations, however, our

Table 8.1
Attitudes Toward Abortion: Comparison of CVS and Amniocentesis Users and the General Social Survey

	CVS AND AMNIOCENTESIS USERS (n=120)		GENERAL SOCIAL SURVEY (1987)	
PERCENT WHO BELIEVE A WOMAN SHOULD BE ABLE TO OBTAIN AN ABORTION FOR THE FOLLOWING REASONS:	IN GENERAL WOMEN SHOULD HAVE RIGHT TO ABORTION %	WOULD CONSIDER ABORTION FOR SELF %	IT SHOULD BE POSSIBLE TO OBTAIN LEGAL ABORTION: TOTAL (n=1819) %	WOMEN 18-44 (n=557) %
a. Pregnancy seriously endangers mother's health	100.0	98.1	88.3	90.3
b. Pregnancy resulted from rape or incest	98.2	97.2	80.4	82.0
c. Strong chance of serious birth defect	99.1	100.0	78.3	81.3
d. Low income, can't afford more children	86.7	61.2	44.9	46.8
e. Married, doesn't want more children	81.3	52.5	41.2	44.0
f. Single, doesn't want a child	88.5	74.5	40.0	42.3
g. Married, doesn't want child at this time	82.3	54.1	Not asked	Not asked
h. Doesn't want child of this sex	19.2	5.3	Not asked	Not asked

Note: This table reports the attitudes of all women in our sample. There was no significant difference between the attitudes of those aged under 34 and those 34 and older. For the exact wording of the questions on abortion attitudes see Appendixes A and C.

respondents were more hesitant. Only 53 to 61 percent said they would consider an abortion if they conceived out of wedlock, if they could not afford another child, if the pregnancy were mistimed, or if they did not want more children. The disparity between attitudes toward abortion "in general" and "for themselves" suggests that these women, strongly committed to freedom of reproductive choice, are aware of the difficulty of personal decisions on this matter.

Do the attitude differences between our respondents and other Americans reflect different personal stakes in abortion rights? We thought that women of childbearing age would be more likely than other groups to uphold the right to abortion. These women are vulnerable to an unwanted pregnancy and aware of its potential to disrupt their lives. Many, as we have seen, have personally experienced one or more abortions.

This is not what we found (Table 8.1). Women aged 18–44 among the GSS respondents support abortion rights only slightly more strongly than does the population as a whole: differences range from one and a half to three percentage points. Contrary to our expectation, then, a personal stake (as inferred from gender and age) does not significantly affect one's position on this issue. Abortion may not be a "woman's issue" after all.

A better predictor of pro-choice attitudes among GSS respondents is socioeconomic status. However, analyzing the effect of income in the GSS is difficult because that survey groups together all persons with an annual income of $25,000 and above. In 1987 nearly half the population fell into this category. In the following analysis we therefore used education as an indicator of socioeconomic status.

Whatever the reason given, more highly educated people are more likely to support women's rights to abortion. (Chi-square levels of significance vary from 0.05 to 0.001 or better.) This finding is confirmed by other polls.

The attitudes of GSS respondents also vary among different religious groups. Jews and persons with no religion are the most likely to back abortion rights in all situations. The favorable response among Jews ranges from 90 percent in case the couple does not want or cannot afford more children to 100 percent in other circumstances. People with no religion are somewhat less supportive, with approval ranging from 71 to 98 percent. Among the rest of the population, approval ranges from a low of approximately 40 percent for reasons of low income, not wanting more children, and out-of-wedlock pregnancy to a high of 80 to 90 percent in cases of rape, health risks, or fetal abnormality. Catholics and Protestants hold similar views.

Table 8.2 gives a more detailed breakdown of attitudes toward abortion in our sample. This table compares the views of women with different demographic backgrounds as well as those of amnio and CVS users. Noteworthy is the relative uniformity of views on the "hard-core" cases. Nearly all of our respondents, regardless of education, income, religion, place of residence, type of procedure used, and previous experience with abortion, support a woman's right to terminate a pregnancy in cases of danger to the mother's health, rape or incest, and fetal abnormality. A large majority also endorsed abortion for reasons often interpreted as less "compelling," such as out-of-wedlock pregnancy and insufficient family income. It is only with respect to these items that demographic variations made a difference: women with higher educations and incomes, Jews, those living on the East Coast, those who had CVS, and those who had had previous abortions were more likely to support a woman's right to "elective" abortion. Few of the differences were statistically significant.

Table 8.2
Attitudes Toward Abortion by Socioeconomic Characteristics (N=120)

% who believe that in general women should have right to abortion for the following reasons:	Woman's life is endangered by the pregnancy	Woman's health is endangered by the pregnancy	Certainty of fatal birth defect	1 in 2 chance of fatal birth defect	Certainty of nonfatal birth defect	1 in 2 chance of nonfatal birth defect
Region: East (n=60)	96.6	96.6	98.3[a]	86.4	91.5	88.1[a]
West (n=60)	96.6	94.8	91.4[a]	81.0	84.5	69.0[a]
Procedure: Amnio (n=72)	95.7	95.7	92.8	81.2	87.0	75.4
CVS (n=48)	97.9	95.8	97.9	87.5	89.6	83.3
Previous abortions: None (n=62)	96.7	93.3	93.3	80.0	86.7	76.7
One or more (n=34)	97.1	100.0	100.0	88.2	97.1	91.1
Education: H.S. (12 years or less) (n=10)	90.0	90.0	80.0	60.0[b]	90.0	60.0
College (13-16 yrs) (n=50)	97.9	97.9	97.9	93.8[b]	87.5	72.9

Grad. school (17+ yrs) (n=59)	96.6	94.8	94.8	81.0[b]	89.7	87.9
Income:						
$ 0-20,000 (n=7)	83.3	83.3	66.7	66.7	66.7	66.7
$20-40,000 (n=26)	100.0	100.0	96.0	72.0	84.0	64.0
$40-60,000 (n=34)	94.1	94.1	94.1	88.2	91.2	82.4
$60-80,000 (n=20)	94.7	94.7	97.4	84.2	89.5	84.2
$80,000 + (n=31)	100.0	96.7	100.0	90.0	90.0	83.3
Religion: None (n=16)	100.0	100.0	100.0	100.0	100.0	100.0
Protestant (n=57)	97.0	92.5	95.5	83.6	83.6	76.1
Catholic (n=27)	96.3	100.0	88.9	74.1	88.9	66.7
Jewish (n=7)	85.7	100.0	100.0	85.7	100.0	100.0

Table 8.2 (Continued)

% who believe that in general women should have right to abortion for the following reasons:	Pregnancy resulted from rape or incest	Unmarried and doesn't want baby	Low income; can't afford child	Doesn't want more children	Doesn't want child at this time	Doesn't want child of this sex
Region: East (n=60)	93.2	88.1[a]	84.7[b]	76.3	75.9	17.0
West (n=60)	91.2	69.0[a]	60.3[b]	56.9	60.3	15.5
Procedure: Amnio (n=72)	89.7	72.5	65.2	59.4	63.2	15.9
CVS (n=48)	95.8	87.5	83.3	77.1	75.0	16.7
Previous abortions: None (n=62)	93.3	76.7	73.3	66.7	65.0	16.7
One or more (n=34)	97.1	94.1	88.2	85.2	84.8	14.7
Education: H.S. (12 years or less) (n=10)	70.0[a]	70.0	60.0	50.0	50.0	0.
College (13-16 yrs) (n=50)	93.8[a]	70.8	70.8	58.3	60.4	16.7

Grad school (17+yrs) (n=59)	94.7[a]	86.2	75.9	75.9	77.2	20.0
Income:						
$ 0-20,000 (n=7)	66.7	50.0	16.7[b]	33.3[a]	33.3[a]	0.
$20-40,000 (n=26)	92.0	72.0	80.0[b]	68.0[a]	68.0[a]	20.4
$40-60,000 (n=34)	91.2	76.5	64.7[b]	58.8[a]	64.7[a]	11.8
$60-80,000 (n=20)	94.7	89.5	89.5[b]	84.2[a]	78.9[a]	31.6
$80,000+ (n=31)	96.6	86.7	76.6[b]	70.0[a]	72.4[a]	13.3
Religion: **None** (n=16)	100.0	93.8	100.0	93.8	81.3	31.2
Protestant (n=57)	92.4	74.6	65.7	61.2	59.7	11.9
Catholic (n=27)	88.9	74.1	66.7	59.3	76.9	22.2
Jewish (n=7)	85.7	100.0	100.0	85.7	85.7	0.

[a] $p < .05$
[b] $p < .01$

ABORTION AND MOTHERHOOD

The women in our study have had the same number of children, pregnancies, and abortions as other American women (albeit at a later age). They are by no means typical in their views on abortion, however. Their liberal views cannot be explained by their relatively high position in the socioeconomic scale. Rather, it appears that those who pursue prenatal diagnosis are a self-selected group. For the most part, only women who accept abortion (at least in principle) will have their pregnancies screened.

Prenatal diagnosis users are unique in other ways, however, ways that have to do with the very meaning of motherhood. These women are at a point in their lives when motherhood is especially poignant. Some are expecting their first baby or have recently borne that baby, while others have older children, a few of whom have disabilities. Still others have previously terminated a pregnancy because of a fetal abnormality. For all, this pregnancy is a wanted one; in some cases, it has been achieved after years of frustration. All had their pregnancies screened for fetal abnormality, an experience that focused their attention on the prospect of losing the baby. These experiences and their intense commitment to motherhood color their perceptions of abortion.

Women who undergo prenatal diagnosis have a stake in the availability of legal abortion for fetal abnormalities. However, our findings suggest that these women support the right to abortion even outside the context of extreme situations. The majority, those whose only reason for having the procedure is maternal age, may have postponed childbearing for professional or personal reasons. For these women, freedom from the consequences of unwanted pregnancy is central to their lives and identities. As writer Katha Pollitt (1988) points out,

There is another thing we [middle-class women now approaching age 40] have in common: no one had a baby before she was ready, wild to be a mother. And birth control being what it is, that means that many of the women . . . had had abortions. . . .

Here are some reasons why friends of mine had abortions: They were in college and wanted to graduate. They were in graduate school or professional training and wanted to finish. They could not care for a child and keep their jobs. They were not in a relationship that could sustain parenthood at that time. They were not, in short, ready or able to be good mothers yet, although those who have children are good mothers now.

The commitment to abortion rights was underscored by those of our respondents who cut short our interview questions on their attitudes toward abortion for different reasons. They said simply, "I think women should have the right to have an abortion for any reason." Yet the experience of a wanted pregnancy on which they had lavished considerable attention and anxiety put the personal decision on abortion in a different light. Our respondents wrote the following comments in the survey questionnaires:

- I would try to avoid abortion myself—but I believe it is up to the individual to choose—it's the woman's right.

- I feel as though a woman should have the right over her body. I would find having an abortion very traumatic now after delivering a wonderful baby.

- My own acceptance of an abortion has changed since having my child. It would be much more difficult now to terminate a pregnancy.

- [A woman who is pregnant for the first time after trying to conceive for nine years] I always believed in abortion until my sonogram when it really hit home that there was a "real life" inside of me.

Does this reluctance to abort "now that they know what being a mother is like" extend to abnormal pregnancies? The answer depends on what meaning not only abortion, but also a handicapped child has for the woman (see also Chapter 9).

In her novel *The Fifth Child*, author Doris Lessing (1988) writes about the impact of Benjamin, an extremely demanding, abnormal "demon-child," on his loving and closely knit family. In that novel the family is all but destroyed, not only because of Benjamin's destructive behavior, but also because his unrelenting claims on the mother's attention prevent her from tending to her other children and to her husband. Yet once the commitment to that child is made, the mother cannot abrogate it. In the wrenching climactic scene, the mother rescues Benjamin from an institution where he is slowly being killed by the staff. She knows that bringing him home will devastate the rest of the family; yet she cannot do otherwise.

Women who have had a handicapped child construct the hypothetical abortion decision in terms of obligations to all their children, the living and the unborn. Some who have come to accept and love their affected children and have learned to cope with the demands of caring for them feel they could do so again. Others, having seen the suffering of the affected child and the disruption of the family's life, believe that they would terminate another such pregnancy. One of our respondents, a mother who after several normal children had borne a child with a genetic defect, described the care obligations for the handicapped child. Those obligations, which included travel to weekly medical and therapy appointments, were more time- and energy-consuming than she had anticipated; they precluded any regular paid employment. Yet she decided to have another baby because she wanted her older children to see a normally developing child. She said that she would not have attempted this pregnancy without the existence of CVS and the possibility of early abortion. She thus modified her moral commitment to any unborn child because of the possible effects on the existing children.

Another respondent said that she would contemplate having an abortion if she were carrying a child with an abnormality or if her health were endangered because "now there are other children to consider; [I couldn't] deprive them of a mother.'' The couple's age, too, was a factor. They were both in their mid-40s and thus would be unable to care for a child with an abnormality when that child reached adulthood.

WHEN WOULD GENETIC COUNSELORS UTILIZE ABORTION?

Being pro-choice comes with the territory.
—Harriet Hirschfeld, a genetic counselor

Prenatal genetic counselors are overwhelmingly pro-choice; those who oppose abortion simply do not enter this profession. However, despite their technical knowledge, familiarity with the implications of specific syndromes, and daily observations of clients struggling with how best to deal with a diagnosis of abnormality, the counselors we interviewed were far from having achieved closure on whether they themselves would utilize abortion for a specific abnormality.

We asked genetic counselors what fetal abnormalities would lead them to abort their own pregnancy. Of the thirty-four who answered, eleven or one-third would abort for any detectable abnormality. Another five would probably abort for any anomaly, although they offered a few examples of conditions for which this decision would be hard. Thirteen would abort selectively, generally for the more severe disorders but not for sex chromosomal disorders or those with ambiguous prognoses. Finally, although they were clear that they would not accept all anomalies, five more responded that they simply did not know for which disorders they would terminate.

Those who would abort for any abnormality sounded very much alike:

- I of course would have an abortion, but I don't think it's relevant to my counseling. If I'm going to bother to do prenatal testing, I'd do it for everything.
- I am a Catholic and would terminate for all congenital malformations, especially if they lead to mental retardation.
- I believe I would abort for almost any fetal abnormality detected by routine amniocentesis or ultrasound, especially if there were the possibility of mental retardation.

Five respondents who would abort for essentially any detected condition indicated they would do so either more reluctantly than the above group or would spare those fetuses who were likely to be phenotypically normal. Two of the five counselors commented about the probable effects of a child with abnormalities on their or their families' lives.

- [stumbles] I think I probably would [abort]—but having had a child or a pregnancy, I think you're a little less likely to say yes unthinkingly. But knowing the effect of even a normal child on one's life, I probably would. For Trisomy 13 and 18 definitely;

for 21 I'm a little less sure. For sex chromosome abnormalities I would probably terminate.

- Yes. Most—because of what I've seen of the impact on families. Mosaicism I'd waiver on, but a straightforward sex chromosome abnormality I would terminate.
- Yes, almost all. A balanced translocation, where the kid would be normal, I wouldn't abort for.

The greatest number of counselors simply said they would abort for some conditions and not for others. Their choices and conflicts mirror those of their clients. They would terminate pregnancies with clearcut diagnoses of severe malformations or mental retardation; they would continue pregnancies with sex chromosomal anomalies or more ambiguous or lesser physical expression. Nine of the thirteen respondents in this category explicitly mentioned sex chromosomal abnormalities as the most troubling cases.

- It would depend. The variable ones are the hardest. I wouldn't hesitate with Trisomy 13 and 18. Down's, I don't know. That's why I have no trouble with nondirective counseling!
- Definitely where there is a known risk for a lethal genetic disease. Down's syndrome—probably. Neural tube defect—probably. If they could ascertain where it is in the neural tube—if the child is likely to be unable to walk . . . I wouldn't continue. As for sex chromosome abnormalities: I'd definitely struggle with deciding. I am empathizing with patients having difficult deciding!
- The mid-range—spina bifida, Down's syndrome—I personally would elect termination, but what would we as a couple do? My wife is from a different background. For sex chromosome abnormalities—the next level in severity—I find myself going back and forth. What I'd view as minor—cleft lip and palate—I'd not abort for, but we've had cleft lip and palate clients come in determined to abort if their fetus has cleft lip and palate.

A cleft lip is largely cosmetic, but a cleft palate may be associated with other problems of varying severities. Cleft lip and palate may be repaired surgically but may require several operations. In some cases, these operations cannot be done until the child is five or older. The operations frequently result in only partial repair; absent nerves or cardiac conditions cannot respond to surgery. Other problems associated with this condition, such as speech impairment, hearing loss, chronic respiratory and ear infections, and emotional and social maladjustment, may remain. Despite these problems, in our study four counselors explicitly exempted cleft lip and palate as conditions they would abort for. Possibly, they viewed these conditions as either purely cosmetic or correctable.

Perhaps the most convincing indication of the wrenching difficulty of the abortion decision is that, despite their familiarity with this dilemma from both training and experience, five of thirty-four counselors said simply that they did not know for which problems they would abort. These five were by no means junior or inexperienced counselors. Note also how fifteen or more years after the *Roe v. Wade* decision legalizing abortion, the stigma of deviance lingers:

- I think I would abort. I don't even know which ones. . . . Down's syndrome and spina bifida I would, but I don't know. . . . I think when you're brought up in a climate in which abortions were illegal and unthinkable, it's very hard for me to tell you.

- Lethal abnormalities—yes. Others, I don't know. Being a counselor doesn't help resolve this. I think that until you're put on the spot, you can't know how you'd decide.

- Probably would abort for Down's. But with a sex chromosome abnormality I am not sure what I'd do. It's more borderline in that case. With mosaicism It's even worse. I don't know.

- I am 37; would go for CVS. What I would do with the results, I don't know.

Prenatal genetic counselors hold pro-choice views by definition. Among women who utilize genetic testing, whatever their social class and religion, support for abortion rights is nearly universal.

As long as fetal therapy for most conditions remains a dream, the *raison d'être* of prenatal testing rests on the availability of legal abortion. Both counselors and clients are aware of this. However, both groups, despite giving much thought to terminating an abnormal pregnancy, are also aware that they would find it harrowingly difficult to do so. In the next chapter we turn to the actual experience of termination.

NOTE

1. Cronbach's alpha is a statistic that measures the reliability or internal consistency of a set of items. Alpha ranges from zero (no internal consistency) to one (perfect consistency). The higher the value, the more confident we can be that the items are reliably measuring the same underlying construct—in this case, pro-choice attitudes.

9

Abnormal Diagnosis and Termination

Peggy's Story: "All We Could See Was the Down's Syndrome"

Peggy and Craig, both college dropouts, decided to get married and have children right away because they didn't want to be "old parents" like their own parents. Peggy was 25 when her first child, Jennifer, was born with Down's syndrome.

Peggy speaks in a soft voice without bitterness. "When my daughter was born I thought there was something really lacking in the type and the amount of information we received at the time. Some of it was inadequate, some of it was out-of-date . . . I think everyone who came in contact with us was doing the best they could. It just seemed to me that they were lacking skills in dealing with new parents [of Down's syndrome babies] . . . It was more of a hindrance than a help."

Things did not get better. During the first few months of Jennifer's life, she had unnecessary heart surgery due to a misdiagnosis—as it turned out, there was nothing wrong with her heart—and then three eye surgeries. The family refused a fourth. "[The heart surgery] kind of made us distrustful," Peggy remembers. "That's what I call the dark side of medicine: we go through things we shouldn't have to."

Peggy joined a group of mothers of handicapped children. The leader, a social worker, lacked the skills to deal with the pain of these mothers, all of whom had dying or profoundly handicapped children. Insensitively, she kept mentioning her own healthy children and asking embarrassing questions. "I noticed that everyone came out feeling worse than before they went in. . . . It was just very upsetting." After quitting the group, Peggy located a suitable program of infant stimulation for Jennifer. It offered consultations with an array of specialists and one-on-one therapy. Jennifer's development finally turned around, and so did her parents' outlook.

However, the medical bills during the first year of Jennifer's life "were more than $6,000 above and beyond what the health insurance paid. For us, that was a lot of money. That was a blow, a drain." Not only was Peggy unable to return to work as planned, but she and Craig sold their townhouse and rented low-income housing so they could afford the private therapy and the travel to the clinic.

With Jennifer about to start public school and Peggy out of therapy, the parents began to plan for a new baby. "I think that if we didn't have prenatal testing available we wouldn't have taken that chance." Inexplicably, when Peggy got pregnant again she delayed seeing her obstetrician for twelve weeks. "Before Jennifer was born I had always thought things like that just happened to other people. Now I don't think that any more. [When I got pregnant with Andy] I had that lurking fear in the back of my mind that it was very possible that something could be wrong. I didn't want to face it or deal with it. I don't think Craig wanted to either because he never pushed the issue." Even with the delay, Peggy was able to have CVS. The results, which came that same afternoon, indicated no abnormality. Despite their misgivings about possible diagnostic errors, they were unable to contain their joy. "Gee, it was like Christmas. It was great. We were very happy."

In retrospect, Peggy says, "having a second child was a big part of the recovery" from their ordeal with the first. "I didn't realize it until after I had the second child, but it gave us a different aspect to life. We were so used to always thinking about abnormal child development. When we had Andy, it kind of balanced that out and gave us a more positive outlook on life."

Peggy, a Methodist, describes herself as liberal on abortion rights. Yet, had she known in her first pregnancy that the fetus was affected with Down's syndrome, would she have terminated the pregnancy? "It's a terrible question. I probably would have aborted her because I didn't know anything about retarded people. I'd never been around them. I grew up in a period in history when they didn't have them in the public schools. I'd only remembered seeing one person with Down's syndrome—a very obese little girl whose grandmother used to push her around in the grocery store in a cart. That's what came to my mind when I heard Down's syndrome. . . . So I probably would have aborted her. Now looking back, that's terrible, but that would have been the case out of ignorance."

Had the CVS in the second pregnancy resulted in an abnormal diagnosis, "We might have had an abortion or we might have kept him. I really don't know for sure. Craig was more for the abortion, but I don't think he was definitely committed." Their reasons were different this time. "I think with the first child I would have aborted because of the mental retardation. With the second child I knew that so many Down's syndrome children have other physical problems. [We would have to decide:] Do you want to give birth to a child that you know is going to suffer a lot and might not live? From our experience with the medical profession and observing other [severely handicapped or dying] children, that was something that I would have had to weigh too. So if we did decide to abort, it wouldn't be because of the mental retardation; that we definitely could live with. . . . But if there was a physical health problem—I don't know. That was something that we never did come to terms with, whether we would abort for that reason or not.''

Would Peggy have terminated her first pregnancy knowing what she knows now? "Now I don't know. Our feelings have changed since my daughter was born. . . . Now she is a person and we see her as a person. When she was first born, all we could see was the Down's syndrome. . . . Now we go for weeks without even seeing the Down's syndrome."

At the time of the interview Jennifer, 8, was doing well in a special education class, and Andy, 3, was delighting his parents. Craig, who had started out as an unskilled construction worker, had a new job as a foreman. They had bought a new house, and Peggy was back in college studying to be a teacher. Their debts paid, their life was back on track.

Elaine's Story: "The Rejection Lasted One Day"

Elaine was 28 when she and Tim had a baby with severe Down's syndrome. Elaine recalls, "Five hours post-partum my husband and I were told the child had Down's syndrome. Reactions: Disbelief, felt they misdiagnosed. Anger—why me? Rejection of the child. Fear of the unknown. Hopelessness, not knowing what to do. . . . The rejection lasted one day. I wanted to give Heather up for adoption. My husband disagreed and couldn't understand my rejection. We did take her home. I said I'd decide later—and I ended up getting attached to her."

Heather died after unsuccessful heart surgery at seven months. Elaine began to consult experts about the chances of her having another child with Down's syndrome. Disconcertingly, she received conflicting information: "I was told different things. Sometimes I was told one in 100; from other people, one in 2000 for age 28."

Two years later, the couple was ready to try again. They discussed CVS before conceiving. "My husband felt more strongly about aborting the fetus if there were a problem. I wasn't sure what I would do." At the CVS clinic, Elaine found the pre-procedural counseling "very helpful. . . . I was very nervous; I had been nervous since discovering I was pregnant." The test results indicated a healthy boy.

Elaine felt "fantastic when I discovered the baby was normal. I'd never had a normal child before. Thrilled is not the word." As for the sex, "I did not want a 'replacement child' [of the same sex as the one who died], and my husband had a hard time dealing with our daughter's death, so [having a boy this time] made it easier."

Elaine was totally unprepared for her first, affected child. She believes that "women should be advised at a much earlier age of the risk of genetic defects. Even though I have a B.A. in biology, I did not know what Down's syndrome was. I just assumed everything would be fine and was shocked. Perhaps there should be a pamphlet for newly pregnant women to read, cautioning them. . . . Today all [sic] women giving birth to babies with Down's syndrome are below age 35.'' However, she acknowledges that before she had Heather, she was not ready for such information: she would have shrugged it off as irrelevant. Her sense of invulnerability is gone now.

Elaine, who had an elective abortion before she was married, is clear about what circumstances would lead her to terminate another pregnancy. She would have no qualms about an abortion, even a late one if necessary, if the pregnancy endangered her own health or if the fetus had a severe abnormality. But she does not put Down's syndrome in this category. Rather, she considers this condition an intermediate hardship, on a par with an out-of-wedlock pregnancy, for which she would abort only if she could do so in the first trimester. If an early abortion were not possible, she would carry the pregnancy to term "even after having had the previous child. Seeing the baby suffer from the heart defect has affected us. But [children with Down's syndrome] are wonderful children.'' She would not abort for financial reasons, rape or incest but believes other women should be able to do so.

Elaine and Tim plan on one more pregnancy. CVS will definitely be used.

The *raison d'être* of prenatal diagnosis is to help people like Peggy and Craig, Elaine and Tim to avoid additional suffering by giving them a chance to have a healthy child. Yet, as their stories show, decisions about terminating an abnormal pregnancy are never easy. The worst aspect of Peggy and Craig's experience was not their child's Down's syndrome; it was the mistakes and insensitivity of the professional community, the unnecessary pain that they and their child underwent, and the financial devastation that Jennifer's condition wreaked on the family. Both Peggy and Elaine were surprised to find themselves capable of mothering an affected child. As Elaine says, "they are wonderful children.'' For both mothers, the decision to terminate another affected pregnancy would be based on different considerations from those they had initially imagined: the physical suffering in store for the baby and society's unintentional cruelty rather than the mental retardation itself.

In the rest of this chapter, we explore the experiences of women who have had to terminate a pregnancy following a diagnosis of abnormality with either amniocentesis or CVS. Because a finding of severe abnormality is statistically rare, only a few women who participated in our study had this experience. We supplemented their stories with published accounts and with the accounts of genetic counselors who have seen couples through this tragedy.

DIAGNOSIS OF ABNORMALITY

About two percent of all women who have prenatal testing will receive a diagnosis of a serious abnormality. Most, but not all, will choose abortion. The more severe the perceived abnormality, the more likely the pregnant woman is to terminate the pregnancy. When the fetus is diagnosed with a fatal condition such as Tay-Sachs or anencephaly, the pregnancy is nearly always terminated. With an anomaly involving severe mental retardation (an extra chromosome 13, 18, or 21), 94 to 97 percent of the women terminate the pregnancy (Golbus et al., 1979). About three-fifths choose abortion for sex chromosomal abnormalities not involving retardation (Faden et al., 1987). Fewer terminate for physical disabilities.

Wertz and her colleagues (1991) studied 271 parents who had a child with cystic fibrosis (CF), a disorder that carries progressive disability and a reduced life expectancy. Half of all persons with CF now die before they are out of their 20s, although new therapies may soon change this statistic. The authors found that only 20 percent would abort a subsequent pregnancy in which the fetus was found to have CF. Half of the parents, however, chose to be surgically sterilized.

Physician Thomas Elkins and his colleagues (1986) have found that among 101 mothers of children with Down's syndrome only about one-fourth indicated they would terminate another pregnancy with the same diagnosis. But participants in this study were not representative of all parents of children with Down's syndrome: they were members of advocacy groups, who by definition were committed to supporting the rights of the disabled and opposed to abortion for that reason. They were also disproportionately white, two-parent, middle-class families, those best able to cope with a disabled child. The very fact that their children were still alive indicates these children were not among those most profoundly affected with multiple anomalies.

Aborting an affected pregnancy is devastating. Pediatricians Bernard Adler and Theodore Kushnick (1982) describe fifteen couples who received a diagnosis of Trisomy 18 or 21. Fourteen chose to terminate the pregnancy; in one case the diagnosis was followed by spontaneous abortion. No couple regretted the termination. All believed that through prenatal testing and abortion they had averted the greater tragedy of having a severely affected child. Yet the grief that followed the termination was similar to the process of bereavement surrounding stillbirth or the death of a baby. One woman, with a thirteen-year history of infertility, felt a lingering bitterness toward couples who had normal children. Unable to conceive again, she questioned her femininity and feared she had missed her last chance to have a family. "How could God do this to us?" she asked twelve months after the termination. All the couples reported bitterness, anguish, doubts about their ability to have normal children, and impaired self-image.

A diagnosis of fetal abnormality is one of the cruelest blows life may deliver. Until recently, such a diagnosis came only at midpregnancy, when signs of fetal life were unmistakable and the mother's attachment to the baby strong. Terminating the pregnancy at this time is a wrenching experience. When CVS became available, many physicians believed that abortion for abnormality would become not only physically easier but also emotionally pain-free. However, we have found that first-trimester abortions for abnormality carry a burden of their own. This burden is largely unrecognized by caregivers and society at large. Couples who face such terminations are unprepared for the severity of the trauma and must endure it without emotional and social support.

A caveat is necessary. The women we interviewed expressed their concern that in the current political atmosphere surrounding abortion rights, discussion of the suffering entailed by "genetic" abortions might be used to advocate further restrictions on these rights. Our respondents stressed that they would make the same choice again in similar circumstances; genetic counselors confirmed this. In telling the stories of these women, we are attempting to give a voice to their suffering and to raise issues about public recognition and professional care.

Women who seek genetic counseling are rarely aware of the differences between first- and second-trimester terminations. Yet they must choose between diagnostic procedures on the basis not only of the risks but also of the different consequences of each procedure in case of abnormality. Genetic counselors seldom discuss the mechanics of abortion prior to the test and the diagnosis. Among the counselors we interviewed, of the twenty-three who worked at centers where clients had a choice between amniocentesis and CVS, eleven said they never discussed the abortion before the procedure and five said they discussed this only when asked. Only three counselors covered it routinely, and four usually asked if the client wanted to know about the abortion procedures (see Chapter 4).

The reasons for the omission vary. Some counselors simply state, "It's not part of my spiel." Some avoid the subject because it is politically charged and might be exploited by anti-abortion activists. Others feel that a detailed discussion of abortion at this point will cause unnecessary anxiety since only a few clients will need to face this dilemma (Larsen and MacMillin, 1989, p. 41). Clients, for their part, rarely bring up the subject of abortion. This reinforces the counselor's perception that there is no need to discuss it. The following excerpt is from an interview with a physician who both counsels clients and performs CVS and amniocentesis:

Most patients come with a fairly clear idea what the abortion alternatives are so it's not something we have to address specifically. . . . They know that abortion following CVS usually involves a D & C dilation and curettage. Very rarely am I asked questions about it because part of the knowledge of people who come here is that they have looked into that issue. That is part of the decision for the CVS vs. the amnio. They usually come having known that in the first place.

Our interviews with clients suggest that failure to ask the proper questions reflects not knowledge but ignorance about what questions to ask. Except for those who have already experienced such terminations, few pregnant women possess more than a general idea about the different procedures used in first- and second-trimester abortions.

Wendy, a 36-year-old professor of art history, had suffered two miscarriages and had a D & C (a procedure that involves dilating the cervix and scraping the lining of the uterus in order to diagnose or treat uterine problems) prior to the present pregnancy. Although Wendy knew about CVS, she chose to have amniocentesis because she believed it carried a lower risk to the fetus. Like many women, she was unaware that it would entail much greater suffering should an abnormality be found: "I suppose I would have been knocked out. When I had the D & C I didn't have any anesthesia and I was awake the whole time. But that was a different situation. I assume that I would not have been conscious. I don't think I would have wanted to be conscious. That's all I know." In fact, unless the abortion is done by D & E (dilation and evacuation), the woman is usually conscious during a second-trimester termination. Wendy's decision, then, could not have been a truly informed choice.

ABORTION FOLLOWING AMNIOCENTESIS

Second-trimester abortions may be done by one of three methods: saline or urea injection, prostaglandin induction, D & E (dilation and evacuation), or a combination of methods. The first method involves injecting saline solution or urea into the amniotic fluid, which causes the death of the fetus. The woman then goes into labor and delivers the dead fetus. In the second method a drug, prostaglandin, is used to induce labor. In the third method, D & E, the cervix is dilated, the woman is sedated, and the fetus is removed in pieces. Although the third procedure is easiest on the woman since it is fast and performed under anesthesia, it is rarely used because it is highly distasteful to physicians (Benderly, 1984; Hern, 1984; Hern and Corrigan, 1980).

Second-trimester abortions entail a higher rate of maternal complications than earlier procedures. The death rate is 0.5 per 100,000 procedures up through week 12 of the pregnancy; it is 5.8 per 100,000 procedures—nearly twelve times higher—after week 16. Abortions performed after 16 weeks, although a small fraction of all terminations, are responsible for half of all abortion-related maternal deaths. Death may occur from infection, amniotic fluid in the woman's bloodstream, or hemorrhage (Atrash et al., 1987; Grimes, 1992).

When it is necessary to terminate the pregnancy, couples are unprepared for the severity of the pain and grief. Unlike first-trimester abortions, second-trimester abortions usually take place in hospital maternity wards. The hospital staff may also underestimate the physical and emotional pain, for they are used to dealing with births, not abortions. This was the experience of Carol, who had an abortion following an amniocentesis finding of Tay-Sachs:

It was psychologically and physically horrible. I checked into University Hospital. They put in laminaria [sea weeds used especially for this purpose] to soften the cervix and then gave me the saline solution. The doctor said the whole thing would take no longer than three hours and the pain wouldn't be any worse than a normal period. Then he just disappeared.

He had lied to me! It was much, much worse than he had led me to expect. It lasted thirteen hours and the pain was very intense. They induced the labor with pitocin, and induced labor is always very painful. They wouldn't give me any anesthesia even though I asked for it because they didn't want to slow down the labor. . . . After the baby came out they did a D & C to remove the remaining parts of the placenta. I felt the D & C very cruelly. It hurt like hell. I don't know why they wouldn't give me the anesthesia. I wasn't going anywhere anyway. I was staying in the hospital overnight and I wasn't going to be breastfeeding, so they didn't have to worry about messing up my body with drugs.

The abortion is especially cruel when the baby is born alive. Cheryl, who had an abortion following a diagnosis of Down's syndrome with amniocentesis, describes her experience:

It's just inescapable that you are going to go through labor, a full normal labor, and give birth to a dead child. In my case he died after he was born. I had prostaglandins without salines. If you use just the prostaglandins, the child is still alive and will die after birth.

It's silly to call it an abortion. . . . To say that I am going to have an abortion negates the fact that it's a child and that I have attachments to it and I have bonded with it and that I have to give birth to it in order for it to die. . . .

I think that the healing with a second-trimester abortion is complicated by the fact that you have gone through a delivery and your body is adjusting normally. Some women have milk that comes in and that's very painful to deal with. There are all the normal hormonal changes and the bleeding. There are physical reminders that you've just had a labor and delivery but you have no child. Not only is there the tremendous grief of having a child die but there are physical reminders also. That has to be taken into account.

When the fetus is born alive, the staff suffers its own anguish. Obstetrician Morton Stenchever writes:

I recall a second-trimester abortion of an anencephalic infant that was live-born and survived in a newborn intensive care unit for 10 days. This caused severe anguish for the couple and their families, for the physicians involved, and for the nursing staff. In fact, one nurse had an emotional breakdown while caring for the infant. (1992, p. 300)

Regardless of the abortion method, the grieving is more intense and lasts longer than most people anticipate. "Rose Green" (a pseudonym), a 40-year-old scientist with two children, terminated a pregnancy at 20 weeks' gestational age following amniocentesis and a diagnosis of Down's syndrome. The D & E procedure took about 15 minutes and, with general anesthesia, was painless. Yet her grief was overwhelming:

All of my wanted pregnancies have knitted themselves into every nook and cranny of my awareness and my body. . . . Somewhere in my consciousness there was this little song: "I am pregnant (tra-la-la)". . . .

Now this pregnancy has been wrenched and torn out of all these same nooks and crannies, and it *hurts*. I'm a big open wound, dripping torn tissue and blood all over. (Green, 1992, pp. 62, 68)

Much of the trauma is caused by the lateness of the procedure and by the undeniability at this stage of both the life and the death of the fetus. Yet, earlier abortions, though easier in many ways, are by no means emotionally painless.

ABORTION FOLLOWING CVS

The promise of CVS—the reason why it was hailed as a great advance—is that it is performed during the first trimester of the pregnancy. First-trimester abortions are usually done by suction as an outpatient procedure in a freestanding abortion clinic. Physically, this procedure is simpler, cheaper, and safer for the woman than later terminations. Socially, in the first trimester it is possible to hide the pregnancy from selected others, for example, office mates who disapprove of abortion or relatives who would not be able to control their own grief. Ethically and legally, a first-trimester abortion is less controversial.

First-trimester diagnosis may be more acceptable from a religious point of view as well. While no religion favors abortion, some religions tolerate it early in the pregnancy under special circumstances. Although the Catholic Church now condemns abortion from conception, Saint Augustine (A.D. 354–430), the theologian whose writings shaped Catholic dogma, believed that the fetus formed only after 40 days' gestation for a male and 80 for a female. In ancient and medieval times, Christians disagreed on whether early abortion—when the embryo was "unformed"—was in fact murder (Luker, 1984, pp. 12–13). Muslim law, the Shari'ah, similarly states that the soul enters the body 120 days after conception or at about 18 weeks gestational age. In the first forty days, the fetus is a seed (*nutfa*) and is not protected by laws about the taking of a life (Abdallah, 1982; Modell, 1986, p. 272). Orthodox Jews have similar beliefs about gestation. Both Muslims and Jews hold relatively lenient views about very early abortion. For orthodox Muslim and Jewish women, amniocentesis comes too late in the pregnancy. While the results of CVS are not available within the permissible time period, a determined woman can still hide her pregnancy and have an abortion if her physician cooperates.

Psychologically, however, abortion following CVS may be no less traumatic than one following amniocentesis. Social work professor Rita Black (1989) studied 121 women who had suffered pregnancy loss following CVS or amniocentesis. Of these, seventy had terminated an abnormal pregnancy and fifty-one had miscarried. Black found that even after six months, the participants experienced depression, reduction in social activity and work performance, decline in sexual satisfaction, and marital stress. There were no clear-cut differences in the intensity of grief between those who had amniocentesis and CVS. Black concludes that women who lose pregnancies after prenatal testing, whether the loss is spontaneous or induced, and whether it occurs in the first or second trimester, experience similar patterns of grief. All these women have lost an intensely, even desperately wanted baby whose existence had been made poignantly real through the ultrasound. All needed a great deal of social support to cope with their grief, but received little.

In Detroit, physician Arie Drugan and his colleagues (1990) studied eighty patients who received a diagnosis of fetal abnormality. Of these, fifty-eight had been diagnosed by amniocentesis and twenty-two by CVS. The major determinant of the decision to terminate the pregnancy was not the timing in the pregnancy but the severity of the diagnosed condition. Among patients who received a diagnosis of a severe anomaly in the fetus, for example, an extra chromosome 13, 18, or 21—conditions that lead to severe mental retardation and in some cases to early death—93 percent chose abortion. Among those who received a "questionable" prognosis—sex chromosomal abnormalities or balanced translocations, that is, a transfer of segments between chromosomes without changing the total amount of genetic material—only 27 percent terminated.

Did CVS make it easier to decide on abortion in case of an abnormality? Drugan and his colleagues found that this was not the case. In fact, the same proportion of women opted for abortion after both procedures. The authors conclude that "contrary to previous apprehensions, the increased utilization of first-trimester prenatal diagnosis procedures in recent years does not cause a shift in parental decisions to interrupt pregnancies affected by chromosome anomalies" (p. 490).

Most couples who opt for CVS and many caregivers expect the termination to be relatively untraumatic. When an abnormality does happen, the intensity of the grief comes as a shock. "Judy Brown" (a pseudonym), a pediatrician who had an abortion following CVS, writes: "It took several weeks to recover physically; emotional scars are still raw 2 years later" (1989, p. 2735). As one genetic counselor told us,

Quite honestly, if the results are abnormal, what I have seen in the families is that it is devastating whether it's in the first trimester or second. . . . The perception prior to doing the procedure is that it won't hurt as much if they do it in first trimester, that they don't feel as pregnant. But the fact turns out that if they have a child with an abnormality they are just as sad whether it's after CVS or after amnio. . . . Initially they *think* there is less bonding in the first trimester. But in reality it hurts just as much whether they are at 12 weeks or 18 weeks because they wanted that baby. In the end result, what people will say is, "I guess that's why I had the procedure." They wanted to have the procedure for that reason. But it hurts just as much.

Genetic counselors therefore believe it is wrong to anticipate less grief and to offer less support to clients following termination with CVS: "We do people a disservice if we don't tell them about post-termination morbidity."

The reasons for the trauma are independent of gestational age. If the pregnancy is a wanted one, bonding—emotional attachment to the unborn baby—starts even before conception. As one genetic counselor put it, "Most people are pregnant a year before they get pregnant." Couples often plan ahead for a baby, perhaps timing the conception and the birth to fit into the family life cycle. As Green (1992, p. 61) points out, "Morally, religiously, and politically I do not believe that a fetus is a full human being. However, I have been forced to recognize that emotionally, at least for me as a pregnant woman, I was carrying a *baby*, pretty much from the moment I confirmed I was pregnant."

Bonding grows as the pregnancy progresses. While fathers may not get emotionally involved until later, mothers experience physiological changes in their bodies almost immediately. Involvement is speeded up by recent technological advances that make possible very early detection of the pregnancy, often before a single menstrual period is missed.

Psychologically, it is quickening (the mother's perception of fetal activity) that makes abortion following amniocentesis so difficult. However, in some centers amniocentesis is performed early enough so that the results are available before quickening. With respect to the subjective awareness of fetal life, the difference between amniocentesis and CVS is narrowing.

Sonography also contributes to the shrinking of the difference. The ultrasound performed before the CVS underscores the baby's separate existence. "The visual images of fetal anatomy and movement serve to enrich the mother's preexisting mental imagery of the fetus. . . . It is not uncommon for a sonogram copy to be preserved and cherished as 'baby's first picture' " (Blumberg, 1984, p. 208). Paradoxically, then, the attention focused on the early pregnancy by the diagnostic procedures makes parents more intimately aware of the fetus as a separate being, highlights their hopes and fears, and enhances their bonding (Modell, 1986, p. 271).

Sonography may also have the opposite effect. Parents sometimes find it difficult to comprehend the implications of a fetal anomaly after viewing the karyotype (a photograph of the chromosomes arranged in pairs). However, visualizing the fetus on ultrasound has a considerable impact: the reality of the abnormality sinks in, clinching the decision to abort. Drugan and his colleagues (1990) conclude that in an age dominated by television, the visual image of anomalies has a major impact on the decision to interrupt the pregnancy.

Regardless of gestational age, the lost baby is felt as irreplaceable and its death is keenly mourned. As one genetic counselor put it, while all pregnancies are precious, some are more precious than others. Most women who undergo prenatal diagnosis are aged 35 or older; some are in their 40s. They may be aware that this is their last chance to have a child. Advanced parental age and previous infertility or pregnancy loss heighten the investment in the present pregnancy and sharpen the grief attending its loss.

THE GRIEVING PROCESS

Parents' response to abortion after CVS is similar to that following amniocentesis. The critical factor is wantedness, not gestational age. Elective abortion of an unwanted pregnancy, although often accompanied by some sadness, rarely evokes long-term psychological trauma (Luker, 1976; Zabin, Hirsch, and Emerson, 1989). The reaction is often in the realm of fantasy: "I wonder what the baby would have looked like." By contrast, the reaction to "genetic" abortion is akin to the grief response to perinatal death (Blumberg, 1984, p. 211).

The reactions include intense anger at the blind injustice of the genetic dice. According to nurse Joan Oustifine, who interviewed six women who had undergone "genetic" terminations, their "isolation and sense of unfairness stemmed from the fact that not one of the women . . . knew anyone else who had ever been through this. Therefore, they had no support system to rely on. . . . They were angry they had invested in their pregnancies in vain." As one woman said,

The question I had most was, "Why me?" And why [my husband]? And why us? You know, here we are, healthy, I was doing everything I was supposed to, everything the doctor told me to do. . . . I stopped drinking tonic, I didn't use salt, no fried food, I mean I just cut everything out. . . . I kept thinking I was just so good, I did everything. (Oustifine, 1990, n.p.)

Conversely, the parents may irrationally blame themselves for the genetic condition that caused the baby's abnormality. Science writer Beryl Lieff Benderly (1984, p. 151) points out that the couple feel they have done everything "right" in order to have a healthy baby, including taking the socially responsible step of prenatal diagnosis to assure the child's health. Nevertheless, "in their own eyes they may carry a profound guilt, seeing themselves as tainted . . . in their very being." Moreover, they are aware that a similar outcome is possible in future pregnancies. Abortion in such circumstances shakes the foundations of self-worth because self-worth depends in part on the unconscious faith in "the ability to create a normal, healthy family" (Blumberg, Golbus, and Hanson, 1975, p. 806).

When it is not the fetus but the parent who is diagnosed as a carrier of a potential lethal condition, the guilt may be equally devastating. Peter, whose wife Joyce had had repeated miscarriages, broke down and could not leave the counselor's office when he learned he was carrying a balanced chromosome translocation. In the words of their genetic counselor, "he was looking at himself as if he were a monster."

A balanced chromosomal translocation involves a transfer of parts of one chromosome to another; one chromosome will be shortened while the recipient chromosome, which may be part of a different pair, will be lengthened. If the number of chromosomes and the total amount of genetic material is not changed, the person will be normal. Some offspring of such parents will inherit healthy chromosomes; others will inherit the balanced translocation, meaning that they are normal but their own children will be at risk. An unbalanced chromosome translocation (that is, where only one of the two defective chromosomes is inherited, creating a change in total genetic material) may be incompatible with life. This is what killed Peter and Joyce's babies in utero. Carriers of balanced translocations, like carriers of the Tay-Sachs gene or the gene for Huntington's disease, may view themselves as flawed at the very center of their being.[1]

Cheryl, the mother of a healthy toddler, who in her second pregnancy had an abortion after a diagnosis of Down's syndrome, says, "It shakes up your self image as a kind mother or a kind father. I needed to have people confirm that I was a good mother."

Unlike other perinatal losses, in this case the parents must take active steps to bring about the death of their baby; they "play God." Judy Brown (1989, p. 2735) reports that being presented with a "choice" to terminate the pregnancy or give birth to an affected child only makes things worse: "The semblance of control and the heart-wrenching options magnified the pain many times over. . . . The real tragedy was the loss of a healthy child, and *that* I had *not* had a choice about."

The guilt over having "killed" the baby may echo the parent's personal history. Women who previously have had an elective abortion may feel they are being "punished." Women who were unwanted or abused children may, in the words of one genetic counselor, "feel that they are abusive parents because they decided to terminate. Also their own sense of being an unwanted child will resurface at this point because they have just at some level said that they don't want their child. These issues can potentially resurface in very powerful ways. It complicates the grieving."

The guilt is inevitably compounded by the hostility to abortion in parts of our society. Couples who have prenatal diagnosis often support the principle of freedom of choice on abortion; those who oppose abortion probably avoid prenatal diagnosis in the first place (see Chapter 8). Yet, however strongly they feel their decision was right, the bereaved parents worry about being criticized by others for "killing" their baby. They may avoid telling acquaintances, coworkers, or relatives who might say, "You should not have had the abortion" or, in the case of parents who are known carriers of serious genetic abnormalities such as Duchenne's muscular dystrophy, "You should not have gotten pregnant."

A genetic counselor who leads a support group for people who have terminated abnormal pregnancies finds that feelings of guilt need to be aired so that they can be put to rest:

That's something that's really central: the political climate about abortion today. . . . In today's cultural climate nobody feels good about abortion; no one goes through an abortion without feeling very upset about it. . . . So some parents think, Are you a murderer because you have taken this child's life? A large number of people initially come in and say, "I feel like I killed my child". . . . People need to talk about that. Once they talk about it, though, they feel better.

While the guilt disappears if the couple receives enough support, the grieving goes on and on. In Cheryl's words,

You get disoriented. You have a sense that the foundation has been pulled out from under you. You value life and have wanted a child, yet you have taken this child's life. It shakes you up. . . .

You are feeling very exposed. Your emotions are exposed. It's comparable to what people would feel after a sudden death of someone: that they are not in this world, that their consciousness is outside the normal rhythm of everyday life.

The duration of the mourning surprises many parents and increases their isolation. Family and friends, even husbands, tend to be supportive at first, but after a month or so they feel that the woman should put the experience behind her and move on. Carol reports that her mother told her after four or five weeks, "That's enough crying, honey." Her husband, too, felt she was "overreacting." The experience drove a wedge between her and her parents and caused enough bitterness in the marriage to lead, ultimately, to a divorce.

Men and women grieve differently. Sociologist Kathleen Gilbert (1988) interviewed twenty-seven married couples who had experienced a fetal or infant death. While this situation differs from "genetic" abortions, the grieving follows the same patterns. When a baby dies during pregnancy or near birth, "each parent experiences a different symbolic loss, and it is this symbolic loss with which they must cope" (p. 4). The mother, who carried the baby in her body, developed a stronger attachment to it and a greater sense of its personhood. For the father the loss is more ambiguous. A genetic counselor in our study confirmed this difference.

I think parental sex makes a really big difference. Women call it their child and fathers identify it as a fetus. I think part of that is the truth of the experience. The mother has already lived with this child . . . and she has already bonded with it. The father hasn't at that point. . . . Men and women react differently to grief. Men's concern initially seems to be much more for their wives and the care of their wives.

While the wife is overwhelmed by the loss of the baby, the husband's overriding concern may be with his wife's recovery. She may view his attitude as insensitive; her grieving may seem to him excessive.

Society allows fathers even less leeway to grieve than it allows mothers. While women are still at home recuperating, men must deal with "the stress of maintaining the family, facing financial worries, going to work and being expected to 'produce one hundred percent' while at the same time . . . serving as the only support for their wives. A stressor commonly reported by men was their feeling of complete isolation in their efforts to cope with their own grief while supporting their wife in hers'' (Gilbert, 1988, p. 5). Men who are trying to support their wives may get very little attention for their own grief.

Couples differ not only in the social construction of the loss they endured and in the grieving process, but also there is often a disparity in the speed with which they resolve their grief. Recovery usually takes years, not weeks or months; and when the recovery proceeds at different rates, the relationship is further strained.

Paradoxically, a factor that facilitates healing is parental bonding with the baby, the perception that the loss is one of a real son or daughter rather than of a vaguely acknowledged fetus. The following account by a genetic counselor describes the experience of a couple, both in the mid-40s, who fully accepted the reality of their dead baby and insisted that their support system—friends and relatives—do the same:

[This couple] fully recognized their child. They knew that their child had some severe abnormalities. They were very clear about having an abortion, and they treated this child as a full child all the way through the process. They announced to their support system that they were going to have the abortion and that they wanted to have a funeral and that they wanted people to participate in it as much as they would if it had been a stillborn child or a child that had been born alive and died shortly after birth. They located a funeral parlor that gave them a coffin and they had a funeral ceremony and they named the child. . . . They even asked of people who were making things for the baby to finish them and give them to the parents. . . . [That couple] gave the child the full benefit of being their child. . . . They dealt with their own grief as fully as they could.

In this case, the counselor believes, the couple's slim chance of conceiving to begin with helped them to make this a real child; probably this was the only child they would ever have.

Parents who did not have a chance during the abortion to see and hold the baby, and who have neither memories nor mementos such as a photograph, may find it more difficult to let go. Some blame the hospital staff for inadequate counseling on this matter. Cheryl, whose baby was born alive, now regrets that she never said goodbye:

We didn't look at my son. At that point I was just too terrorized. I was in such deep trauma that I couldn't bear the thought of seeing him die in front of me. That just was too horrible. . . . [The hospital staff] wanted to know if I wanted to hold him and be with him. It's just that my husband and I couldn't do it. I never saw [the baby]. And it was very difficult for me to heal because of that. I had a sense at least for a year that I couldn't find him, that he was present but I couldn't grasp his reality. . . . My own fear of death was just enormous because it was such a traumatic type of death . . . something that is associated with birth. . . .

Part of my own healing is to grapple with the fact not only that he died but that I never bonded with him visually and with touch, so that I couldn't let him go. There was some way that I had to do that before I could let him die . . .

Our society has no rituals, no baptism or funeral, for babies who die in utero or shortly after birth (Herz, 1984). The bereaved couple sometimes improvises rituals. One woman who had an abortion following amniocentesis belatedly brought the mourning to a closure by naming her dead son and by holding a symbolic burial. In this way she was able to recapture him, make him real. Another woman had the baby's remains cremated and has kept the box in her basement. She, too, named the baby after the fact. She says she thinks about "my Sarah" every time she goes to the basement. Both of these women were finally able to say goodbye. Both went on to become pregnant again and gave birth to healthy children. Although grief and healing are experienced differently by different couples, as one genetic counselor told us, "How well a couple attends to making the child real by naming it and by looking at it is . . . correlated with healing afterwards."

While women who abort following CVS do not have to go through labor and delivery, the grieving, the guilt, and the feeling of irreplaceable loss are the same as with amniocentesis. In fact, an early abortion creates special problems. D & C and suction procedures are performed in clinics where the majority of clients are teenagers with unwanted pregnancies. The woman seeking an abortion, overwhelmed with her own grief, may have to brave the gauntlet of anti-abortion demonstrators outside. The clinic's staff may not be sensitive to the tragedy of losing a wanted child. Some abortion clinics require that all clients watch a film on fetal development and receive counseling on contraception. This further insults and hurts the parents. Friends and relatives, too, may be less supportive after an earlier abortion. A couple who terminated a pregnancy following CVS may be made to feel that they don't "deserve" to grieve as much as those who have had a later abortion. As a genetic counselor described it,

CVS patients are much less likely to go through the "proper" recovery period. They are likely to go right back to work, which is psychologically a mess. I called one woman, an investment banker, the day after the abortion [to follow up], and she is literally weeping over the phone. I said, "Why did you go back so soon?" Also, since the pregnancy has usually not been announced, they have no support network.

After all, the investment banker (and her partner) had made a rational decision to have CVS in order to avoid giving birth to a child with an abnormality. She proceeded to act on that decision rationally (and with her emotional defenses up). Why then, when she returned to work the very next day, should her psyche unexpectedly smite her with overwhelming grief? With a CVS rather than an amnio, the volcanic emotional sequelae of the abortion caught her unprepared.

Many communities have support groups for couples who have suffered pregnancy or perinatal loss. However, those who have terminated a pregnancy for abnormality usually cannot find solace in those groups. Ordinary miscarriage support groups are at worst hostile to those would-be parents and at best uncomprehending of the specific sources of their grief. "Genetic" terminations are so rare that it's almost impossible to find an ideal support system: a group of women or couples who have experienced the same type of loss at approximately the same time.

Big cities today have a pool of couples who have shared these losses over the years since prenatal diagnosis was introduced. But most couples pass through the initial stages of grieving rather quickly, so that they cannot share the acute shock of the initial mourner. In a year or two, many of these couples will have gone on to conceive and bear a healthy child. In any case, many may choose not to continue to expose this personal loss to strangers. The strength of a person's friendship network rather than "the kindness of strangers" seems to be the determinant of how much support a bereaved parent will receive.

˙ The loss of a wanted pregnancy, regardless of gestational age, is experienced more as a perinatal death than as an elective abortion. Unlike other pregnancy losses, however, "genetic" abortions are especially poignant because the parents take an active part in the baby's death.

The assertion that the pain of couples who have this experience deserves wider recognition should not be taken as an argument against prenatal diagnosis or against "genetic" abortions. Such abortions must be considered in the context of the alternatives. For couples at risk of having a child with chromosomal abnormalities, the other available choices may be even more dreadful: having an affected child or foregoing further childbearing. There is no evidence that couples who have experienced the turmoil associated with such abortion regret their decision. Most emphasize that for them it was the right decision.

Similarly, by emphasizing the distress that accompanies abortion following CVS, we are not denying the importance of this advance in prenatal diagnosis. However painful this experience is, the alternative—second-trimester abortion following amniocentesis—is far worse.

We wish to emphasize merely that society needs to be more aware of the emotional repercussions of this experience so that it can offer the couple better support. This is true for genetic counselors, medical staff, and the bereaved couple's informal networks. Couples undergoing prenatal diagnosis deserve more complete information about the consequences of the alternative procedures so that they can make truly informed decisions. Women having an abortion must be given candid information about the process and encouraged to bond with the baby before they let go. Couples need to be told to expect disparities in the grieving process; knowing that their reaction is normal may lessen the strain on the relationship. And finally, in the aftermath of the termination, the couple must be treated by society as the bereaved parents they are and allowed to mourn the death of their baby.

NOTE

1. Carrier status raises ethical questions about the obligation to tell relatives who might be affected. One woman we interviewed had several children, one afflicted with an unbalanced translocation and multiple handicaps including retardation. A second child (a male) inherited her balanced translocation, and the others inherited normal chromosomes. After completing the standard interview, we conversed informally at length, until we raised the question of when she was planning to inform the young son who had the balanced translocation. She first looked startled—apparently she had not heretofore considered this—then said vaguely, "Well, I guess before he gets married, or perhaps when he leaves for college." We then asked if she knew what percentage of the local high school students was sexually active. At that point, she realized that she had to discuss this sensitive topic with her son upon his attaining puberty. If she did not, then as soon as he became sexually active, he risked transmitting a disabling and potentially lethal genetic disorder to the offspring of an unsuspecting partner. Even more than other sexually active young men, this boy would have an obligation to use contraceptives. The parents had had extensive genetic counseling, but nothing had ever been said about the mother's obligation to inform him.

10

Fetal Sex Identification

KNOWLEDGE OF THE SEX OF THE FOETUS: If the woman remains always in good health from the time that her pregnancy is certain, if she preserves the good looks of her face and a clear complexion, if she does not become freckled, then it may be taken as a sign that the child will be a boy. The red colour of the nipples also point to a child of the male sex. The strong development of the breasts, and bleeding from the nose, if it comes from the right nostril, are signs of the same purport.

The signs pointing to the conception of a child of the female sex are numerous: frequent indisposition during pregnancy, pale complexion spots and freckles, pains in the matrix, frequent nightmares, blackness of the nipples, a heavy feeling on the left side, nasal hemorrhage on the same side.

—The Perfumed Garden of the Sheikh Nefzaoui,
a fourteenth-century Arabic marriage manual

Donna's Story: "I Still Really Want a Girl"

Donna and Eric, both 40-year-old professionals, were interviewed together at their home when Donna was nine months pregnant with their first child. For her, finding out through CVS that the baby was a boy was a major disappointment, one that she was only beginning to come to grips with.

Donna: I really wanted a girl and I was very upset. I think it's a good thing that I had that much time [6 months since the CVS] to get used to the idea that it's not a girl. . . .

The first time I can remember thinking and talking about this was when I was 18. From then on I assumed that I would adopt rather than have a natural child, not for any medical reasons but for political reasons, since there are enough children around . . . I assumed that I would adopt a little girl . . . It's still real hard for me. I still really want a girl . . . I never had taken any energy to get used to the idea that it wouldn't be a girl. I think I wanted a girl mainly because I can relate much more to a girl. . . . There is an unusually strong bond between my mother and myself. I think it's a healthy bond. . . . So I wanted to continue that. . . . Also, though I believe exceptions can be made, I think generally girls are much closer to their parents than boys are in later life as well, and I was looking forward to that. On a frivolous level, I was looking forward to the fun of dressing her up and that sort of thing. A lot of my friends have boys whom I love and enjoy, but I don't really love and enjoy them as much as I love the girls who are children of my friends. All of those combined—I really wanted a girl.

Eric: I didn't really care. I wanted to *have* a child. I didn't want to adopt. That's basically the reason that we did have our own child. I didn't have a [sex] preference.

Donna: He was really supportive of my wanting a girl. He knew how much I wanted one, so all along up until that time it was perfectly fine with him. I felt that he felt bad because I felt bad . . . [When I found out the CVS results] I was relieved that the baby was healthy, but I was hysterical for a few hours. I was really upset.

Donna and Eric don't expect any more children. This is in a real sense the end of Donna's life-long, deeply cherished dream of having a daughter. With the disclosure of the fetus's sex part of her identity thus died.

How much difference does the disclosure in utero of biological sex make? With amniocentesis or ultrasonography, this information is available at four or five months' gestational age; with CVS it may come as early as two months into the pregnancy. Many writers fear that CVS, by disclosing the fetus's sex so early, may make it easier to abort healthy fetuses of the "wrong" sex (Wertz and Fletcher, 1989a, 1989b). In the future even earlier, less invasive procedures may be used to find out the fetus's sex. Such technological advances may increase the temptation to abort for sex selection. Given the pressures of patriarchal societies, many fear that the aborted fetuses will be predominantly female and that sex selection will turn into "gendercide," a war against females in utero.

SEX PREFERENCE IN THE UNITED STATES

Historically, there has been a nearly universal preference for male children: "everyone wants an heir and a spare." King Henry VIII of England (1509–

1547) not only divorced or beheaded several wives, but tore England away from the Church of Rome, allegedly because of his obsession with siring a male heir.

Outside royal families, sons have been desired because they carry the family name, continue the family line, pray for dead ancestors, manage property, work in the fields, and support the parents in old age (Clark, 1985; Warren, 1985). In William Faulkner's 1935 novel *Absalom, Absalom,* a southern planter who loses his family and his fortune in the Civil War desperately tries to sire a (white) male heir in order to reestablish the family line. He courts a girl several decades his junior but will not marry her unless she first conceives and bears a male child. Indignant and humiliated, she refuses, and they are both doomed to loneliness, symbols of the decaying Old South.

In contemporary United States, any preference for children of one gender, if it exists, is mild. Most American studies show a preference for a sex-balanced family combined with a desire for a male first child. When only one child is desired, it is usually a son; when an odd number of children is wanted, ideally the number of sons exceeds the number of daughters. Sociologists Gerald Markle and Charles Nam (1971) surveyed Florida college students, asking about their ideal family size and the desired sex composition of their children. They found that 122 male children were desired for every 100 female children, a ratio of 6:5. The preference for sons is stronger among blacks than among whites. It is more pronounced among Catholics and Jews than among Protestants and those with no religious affiliation. Men and women, including women with feminist convictions share the same preference for sons over daughters (Coombs, 1977; Gilroy and Steinbacher, 1983; Westoff and Rindfuss, 1974).

There is some evidence that the traditional sex preference has turned around in recent years. Nursing professor Molly Walker (1992) found out that of 88 pregnant women who had a sex preference, those with one or more children usually wanted a child of the sex opposite to the existing child(ren). Among the twenty-two women who were having their first baby, fifteen (68 percent) wanted a daughter.

Until recently, the only way to have a given number of boys or girls was to continue having children until this goal was reached. Studies have found that families whose children are of one gender are somewhat more likely to have an additional child than are mixed-gender families. The likelihood of having another child is the same whether the existing composition is all female or all male.

Sociologists Richard Dixon and Diane Levy (1985), however, have found that in the United States the desire for small families outweighs the desire for a child of a specific sex. That is, most families will not have more children than they want in order to have a child of the desired sex. The authors conclude that "sex preferences are virtually unimportant factors in actual or intended fertility behavior in a low fertility population" (p. 263). Just as the "Far Side" cartoon shows, most American couples "don't care whether it's a boy or a girl—as long as it has ten fingers and ten toes."

THE FAR SIDE   By GARY LARSON

"Well, Frank's hoping for a male and I'd like a little female. . . . But, really, we'll both be content if it just has six eyes and eight legs."

If technology enabled people to have children of the sex they wanted and only when they wanted them, would they take advantage of this technology to achieve the desired sex and birth order composition of their families? The controversy over abortion illustrates that, although the technological capability exists to avoid having a child at an inopportune time, people may not use it. The ability to predetermine not only the number and timing, but also the sex of future children, may encounter even more serious ethical and pragmatic opposition. Dixon and Levy (1985) have found that only one-quarter to one-third of their respondents favor using *preconceptual* sex-selection methods such as separating the X- and the Y-sperm. However, as with any new technology, sheer availability will probably create the demand. If sperm separation becomes cheap and reliable, few couples will be able to resist the temptation to "custom-design'' the sex composition of their families, just as contraceptives have made it not only possible but nearly mandatory to control the number and spacing of offspring.

In Dixon and Levy's study, approval of sex determination dropped to 11 percent to 13 percent when the proposed method was abortion following prenatal disclosure of the sex of the fetus. Most Americans continue to find this practice abhorrent. Contrary to earlier fears, amniocentesis has not resulted in a wave of abortions for sex selection in the United States. Of course, no one knows how many procedures are done for sex selection alone, since women over 35 or those with an actual or fabricated family history of genetic defects may request testing for "legitimate" reasons and hide their intent to use it for sex selection.

Perhaps the first major debate on the use of prenatal diagnosis for sex choice appeared in the *Hastings Center Report* in 1980. In its lead article, ethicist John Fletcher publicly reversed an earlier stance condemning such usage. Reconsidering his opposition in light of his interpretation of the 1973 *Roe v. Wade* Supreme Court decision, Fletcher stated that supporting a woman's absolute right to abort necessitated accepting reasons society would judge trivial: "It is inconsistent to support an abortion law that protects the absolute right of women to decide and, at the same time, to block access to information about the fetus because one thinks an abortion may be foolishly sought on the basis of the information'' (1980, p. 16).

Margaret O'Brien Steinfels, the then-editor of the *Report,* challenged Fletcher's interpretation of *Roe* in her rejoinder. She noted that the right to privacy acknowledged in *Roe* was not absolute but only "broad enough to encompass a woman's decision whether or not to terminate her pregnancy." Furthermore, the "court specifically disagreed with the proposition 'that the woman's right is absolute and that she is entitled to terminate her pregnancy at whatever time, in whatever way, and for whatever reason she alone chooses' '' (1980, p. 20).

Both she and religion professor James Childress observed that, although a woman is not required to state a public reason for an abortion, the current rules permit an inquiry, notably by the physician, as to these reasons. They also stated that the physician's obligation to perform an abortion is not absolute. Childress distinguished between an individual's or patient's negative right, which is a justified claim to noninterference, and a positive right, which is a justified claim to someone's assistance.

Contributors to this forum voiced nearly every consideration expressed to this day as to good, sound, and perhaps sufficient reasons to oppose ethically and operationally sex-selective abortion. Fletcher himself recounted the four reasons supporting his original opposition:

• Prenatal diagnosis was developed to detect disease, and sex is not a disease.

• Sex-selective abortion in a male-preferring society could contribute to social inequality and bias against women.

• Sex choice is an ethically frivolous reason to abort.

• Amniocentesis [then the only available method] was a scarce resource that was not yet available to all women who had medical reasons to have it, and it was indefensible to use it for low-priority uses when higher ones went unmet. (p. 2)

Nine years later, writing with Dorothy Wertz (1989a, 1989c), Fletcher reverted to his original stance against sex selection. The proportion of U.S. physicians willing to perform prenatal diagnosis for this reason, or to refer patients to someone who would, had grown from 1 percent in 1972–1973 to 62 percent in 1985. Disconcerting, perhaps, was their finding that

Woman doctors, who constituted 35 percent of the survey respondents, were twice as likely as men to say that they would actually perform prenatal diagnosis for this couple. Apparently the feminist movement in the United States cuts two ways on the issue of sex selection. Belief in freedom of reproductive choice and a revolt against medical paternalism—both of which are keystones of the Women's Health Movement—may in practice override feminist views that sex choice is an evil. (1989c, pp. 2–3)

Fletcher apparently had reconsidered his stance again in response to the argument that permitting fetal selection on one nonmedical ground opens the way for future selection of fetuses for other nondisease characteristics, such as appearance and sports prowess. He and Wertz observed that

At the extreme, such prenatal tinkering with desired characteristics could lead to a redefinition of "normal". And . . . the power to make this definition will reside with those who can pay for non-medical prenatal diagnosis out-of-pocket. What happens now, with sex selection, will set the pattern for moral acceptance or rejection of such choices. . . . If . . . the (medical) profession were to adopt a moral code opposing sex selection through prenatal diagnosis, this could go a long way toward preventing its use for "cosmetic" purposes. (1989c, pp. 9–10)

In short, "gender is not a disease. Prenatal diagnosis for a nonmedical reason makes a mockery of medical ethics" (Wertz and Fletcher, 1989a, p. 24).

Finally, they examined the potential conflict between patient autonomy and "right-to-know" practices, and the specter of medical paternalism inherent in physicians' withholding of information. Wertz and Fletcher argue that the sex of the fetus is not medical information (except in instances of sex-linked diseases). They recommend that this information not be disclosed routinely, unless the couple specifically asks for it.

Given the serious cultural disapproval of this practice in the United States, couples who seek prenatal diagnosis and abortion for sex selection are motivated by much stronger needs than the typical desire for a sex-balanced family. Typically, they suffer considerable anguish and despair. Wertz and Fletcher (1989a) report the case of a couple who had three boys and the husband wanted no more children. When the wife unexpectedly became pregnant, he threatened to leave her. She wanted the child, whatever the sex, but also wanted to preserve the marriage. Finally, they struck a bargain: if the fetus was female she would carry it to term; otherwise she would abort. It was a girl, and she continued the pregnancy.

In Western societies, most couples who seek abortion for sex selection are immigrants or temporary residents from Third World societies with a paramount emphasis on sons. Pediatrician Haig Kazazian, Jr. (1980) observed that at Johns Hopkins University Hospital in Baltimore, nearly all the couples seeking amniocentesis for sex choice were Asian-born, frequently Indians desperate for a son after the birth of several daughters.

Although there is no statistical documentation, obstetricians and genetic counselors believe that aborting a fetus of the ''wrong'' sex has become more common with CVS (Kolata, 1988). At the gestational age of two or three months the pregnancy may still be private; neither the pregnancy nor the abortion needs to be known to anyone other than the woman. When information about the sex as well as the health of the fetus comes so early, the meaning of the pregnancy changes. As Rothman (1986, pp. 142–143) points out,

The problem with amnio results, the tragedy of amnio, is that results come at a time when it is so very hard to abort. The problem with earlier results may be that they come at a time when it is hard to continue. . . . Decisions will be phrased as timing issues, as not wanting a third child, and so on—I do not think that the decision will be consciously made or overtly stated to abort for the wrong sex. But there it is: the decision will be influenced by knowledge of sex. As everything is influenced by knowledge of sex.

In Western societies, the use of prenatal diagnosis and abortion for sex selection is not expected to have a major effect on the birth rate and the sex ratio of the population. If such practices became widespread, the major impact would be on birth order, with more first-born and only sons and more second-born and subsequent daughters.

Changes in the birth order of boys and girls may have important consequences. Research shows that birth order influences personality traits: first-born children are more assertive, independent, and achievement-oriented than subsequent children. Highly achieving women are often first-born children whose parents gave them the extra attention and stimulation parents tend to lavish on first-born or only children. Columnist Anna Quindlen writes of the special relationship she had with her father, a relationship that raised her aspirations and her achievements:

I was raised as my father's oldest son. I have always known how to fish, and I have always known how to talk back. . . . His motto was ''winners need not explain.'' He treated B's as if they were F's. He was fast and funny; if you couldn't keep up, you got left. I kept up. . . .

And then, not so many years ago, I realized that . . . his expectations for me had become my own. (*New York Times,* June 20, 1993, p. 17)

Some fear that a society in which most boys were first-born and most girls second-born would perpetuate the stereotyped view of women as more passive, weaker, and less achievement-oriented than men. Feminist medical student Liana Clark (1985, p. 4), though committed to freedom of reproductive choice, expresses her qualms about American parents' preference for first-born sons:

[The] preference for the male first-born is a function of the patriarchal society in which we live. Given a different social context, where women were empowered with a strong sense of selfhood, parents would be more inclined to choose female children over male ones. As it stands, men are more in control of the world, and parents want their firstborn to have the advantage of being able to compete on the best footing in society. . . . If sex preselection were allowed, women would indeed be relegated to a second class status.

The disclosure of the fetus's sex may contribute to gender stereotyping in other ways. Sex is a central aspect of personhood. Knowing that the fetus is a girl or a boy personalizes it: the "fetus" becomes a "baby," and the difference between "expecting" and "having" blurs. Knowing the sex of the fetus implies more than awareness of its chromosomal or anatomical makeup. It also implies images of personality and social role expectations: "not only what the fetus is, but what we expect the child to become" (Rothman, 1986, p. 127; Rubin, Provenzano, and Luria, 1974). With CVS, gender stereotyping may start in the first trimester of the pregnancy.

MALE PREFERENCE IN TRADITIONAL SOCIETIES

The stakes are higher in Third World countries. In many societies the preference for sons is overwhelming. The ideal sex ratio—the preferred number of sons divided by the preferred number of girls—goes as high as three to five boys for every girl among some segments of the population in India and North Africa. Paradoxically, the pressure to have a son often grows with economic development because governments apply disincentives against large families. Couples become less willing to accept large families but still hope to have the desired number of sons.

In India, urban middle-class couples who want a small family typically desire two sons and no daughters or one daughter. Many couples will seek sterilization after they have two sons. Poorer, less educated people may simply neglect "surplus" girls. A girl who is seriously ill is less likely than her brother to get medical attention; if food is in short supply, girls will get less than boys. The result is higher rates of mortality among girls. The sex ratio in India—the number of females for every 1,000 males—declined from 972 in 1901 to 933 in 1981. The state of Haryana in the north has the lowest sex ratio of any of India's states: 874 females for every 1,000 males (Gargan, 1991; Patel, 1991).

Amniocentesis, and more recently CVS and ultrasound, have widened this gap. Social scientist Roger Jeffery and his colleagues (1984, p. 1212) quote an

Indian hospital leaflet that advertises amniocentesis as a means of helping couples to have sons without unduly increasing the population and straining the family's resources by giving birth to more daughters. The leaflet indicates that if the family already has one or more living daughters sex determination will be done to keep "some check over the accelerating population as well as give relief to the couple requiring a male child."

Although several Indian states have outlawed sex determination, it still occurs widely. Ultrasound has lowered the cost of sex detection and spread its use to rural areas, where women are sometimes pressured by their husbands and relatives to undergo the test and to abort female fetuses. "No one wants girls" (quoted in Gargan, 1991, p. 1).

A similar situation exists in other Asian and African countries. In China, where governmental pressures for a one-child family are powerful, parents are "fearful of 'wasting' their quota on a girl." In this technology-poor country, the number of ultrasound scanners in 1990 was estimated at 100,000. "Chinese peasants use ultrasound to have sons" (Kristof, 1993b, p. A1, A6). The number of "missing" girls each year is estimated at between 900,000 and 1.2 million. These girls were either aborted before birth (often late in the pregnancy), allowed to die as newborns, or hidden away and not reported to the authorities so that the couple might be permitted to try again for a son (Kristof, 1993a, 1993b).

Governments everywhere frown on the preference for sons and promote the notion that daughters are equally desirable. However, the cultural preference for sons in Hindu, Muslim, and Confucianist cultures remains strong. According to all reports, the availability of CVS and ultrasound has increased the incidence of female feticide.

The potential social and demographic consequences of the use of abortion for sex selection are controversial. Some writers speculate that female abortion may have positive consequences, slowing down the rate of population increase because couples would be guaranteed the desired number of sons. A further decline in the birth rate would occur in the long run because fewer women would be available to bear children in the future. Another possible benefit is an improvement in the situation of women, both mothers and daughters. Women who produce desired sons would have security in their marriages and more prestige in their husbands' families. Fewer unwanted girls born may mean an improved treatment for those already alive, lowering the rate of female neglect and female mortality. Finally, to the extent that women are viewed as an economic commodity, scarcity may enhance their value and eventually eliminate gender inequality (Williamson, 1983).

Such speculation may be overly optimistic, however. At present there is no evidence that where women are in short supply they are treated better. Rather, in those societies women's status remains low, and patriarchal values remain well entrenched. Population growth, too, has not lessened significantly. There appears to be little reason to expect that the wider use of abortion for sex selection, made possible through ultrasound and CVS, will have desirable consequences for women or for the society (Jeffery, Jeffery, and Lyon, 1988; Patel, 1991; Powledge, 1983, 1984; Warren, 1985).

CLIENTS' SEX PREFERENCES

If fetal sex identification is a new moral battleground, the women who use prenatal diagnosis and their health care providers are at the front line. Confronted by choices many would rather not have, both clients and providers have been forced to come to grips with the meaning of gender in the context of parenthood and with the dilemma this raises—where do we draw the line on abortion?

We asked our survey respondents—users of prenatal diagnosis who had healthy babies—whether they found out the fetal sex at the time they received the results of the test and if so, what was their reaction and that of their husbands or partners. The father's reaction is given not through his own response but indirectly, through that of the mother.

Nationally about 10 percent of all couples choose not to be told of the baby's sex. In our sample the proportion was approximately 20 percent. Those who preferred not to know were more likely to be amniocentesis users, college or professional school graduates, and high-income couples. It takes some sophistication and strength of character, plus a determination to delight in the baby regardless of its sex, to resist one's curiosity. The following comment was written in the survey questionnaire by a woman who had amniocentesis:

I like the surprise after getting through labor. [My husband] feels the same—plus we already have one of each. Even if we had two of the same sex I don't believe we would want to know. We still like the element of surprise. Plus it is much harder to be disappointed when your [sic] looking at this new life you've just brought into the world.

As for those who opted to find out, previous studies had led us to expect a preference for boys, particularly among fathers. However, our respondents were more likely to be pleased with a girl than with a boy. Fully 73 percent of the women who found out they had a girl were pleased with the fetus's sex, compared to 44 percent of those pregnant with boys. More expectant mothers of boys than mothers of girls reported a disappointment with the baby's sex. Fathers, too, were reported by their wives to be happier with girls, albeit more mildly. The results were essentially the same whether the disclosure occurred at four or five months' gestational age, with amniocentesis, or at two and a half to three months, with CVS. We did not ask about the sex composition of our respondents' previous children. Nevertheless, the results are so skewed that we surmise that the desire for girls goes beyond the wish for a sex-balanced family.

What does being "pleased" with one sex or another mean? That the parents wanted a baby of this sex? Or merely that after the anxiety of waiting for the test results they would accept with pleasure whatever came along, as long as it was a healthy baby? Or that they were expressing a socially approved attitude, in some cases masking a disappointment? We don't know. It must be remembered that our respondents are not representative of the American population. Our findings therefore may or may not reflect a true decline in patriarchal attitudes. It appears, however, that in some segments of American society, women, freed from the opprobrium of the traditional desire to perpetuate the male line or to please their husbands and their own families by having a son, freely express their true wishes for a girl.

Whatever the baby's sex, acceptance by the parents varies with one's socio-economic status (SES). (We used the women's and men's educational attainment and their household income to measure SES; see Chapter 6.) About 10 percent of both the women and the men were disappointed. There were no statistically significant differences among women at different educational levels, but among men those with less education were slightly more likely to express a disappointment.

Income had a more pronounced effect: the lower the income, the more likely were both mothers and fathers to be disappointed by the fetal sex (Table 10.1). A third of the women whose household income was $20,000 per year or less, but only one-eighth of those in households making more than $80,000, reported disappointment. For men, the reported disappointment ranged from 40 percent of the lowest income group to 9.1 percent of those with the highest income. This pattern held regardless of the use of CVS or amniocentesis and in both the San Diego and Washington metropolitan areas.

Several writers have expressed concern that a baby of the desired sex, a "made-to-order child," may be construed as a luxury consumption item by couples "who have everything" (Clark, 1985; Kolata, 1988; Rothman, 1986). This fear, like the concerns about patriarchal preferences for a male child, was not borne out by our research. Affluent couples are *less* likely than those at the bottom of the economic scale to have a strong preference for the sex of their child. More than 90 percent of our sample are older couples who perhaps have postponed parenting to shore up their personal and professional lives; the remainder have a previous history of affected children or abnormal pregnancies. In this pregnancy all have confronted possible tragedy, whether through the birth of an affected child or through the possibility of losing the pregnancy. These parents are not particular about the baby's sex: they are grateful for a healthy child.

To measure the effects of infertility, we used the length of time it took to achieve this pregnancy. One year of "trying" is the accepted benchmark of infertility in the medical community—the point at which medical intervention is warranted. Those women in our sample who said that the present pregnancy was planned were divided into two categories: those who had taken less than twelve months and those who had taken twelve months or longer to get pregnant. We found that, indeed, women who had difficulty in conceiving were more likely to be pleased with the baby's sex. Among women who conceived in less

Table 10.1

Reaction to Baby's Sex, by Household Income (N=93)

| | MOTHER'S REACTION | | | | | |
| | ANNUAL HOUSEHOLD INCOME | | | | | |
	$20,000 OR LESS %	$21,000-40,000 %	$41,000-60,000 %	$61,000-80,000 %	$81,000 OR MORE %	ROW TOTAL %
PLEASED	16.7	66.7	47.6	66.7	56.5	55.1
NEUTRAL	50.0	20.8	47.6	25.0	30.4	32.2
DISAPPOINTED	33.3	12.5	4.8	8.3	13.0	12.6
TOTAL	100.00	100.00	100.00	100.00	100.00	100.0

p < .1

| | FATHER'S REACTION (AS REPORTED BY MOTHER) | | | | | |
| | ANNUAL HOUSEHOLD INCOME | | | | | |
	$20,000 OR LESS %	$21,000-40,000 %	$41,000-60,000 %	$61,000-80,000 %	$81,000 OR MORE %	ROW TOTAL %
NOT APPLICABLE	16.7	-	-	-	-	0.9
PLEASED	20.0	73.9	48.0	53.8	50.0	53.9
NEUTRAL	40.0	13.0	48.0	30.7	40.9	33.7
DISAPPOINTED	40.0	13.0	4.0	15.4	9.1	12.4
TOTAL	100.00	100.00	100.00	100.00	100.00	100.00

p < .1

Note: In analyzing the responses we combined the categories "very pleased" and "mildly pleased"; as well as the categories "very disappointed" and "mildly disappointed".

than one year, 43 percent were pleased with the baby's sex; among those who took longer than a year, the proportion was 64 percent. Women who most feared an abnormal diagnosis and hence the loss of the baby (those who rated their chances of having an affected pregnancy as high) were also more likely to be pleased with the baby's sex.

The great majority of our respondents made it clear that sex preference, if it exists at all, is mild. Most parents who indicated they are pleased with one sex would have been equally pleased with the other sex. The concern for what Walker (1992) terms the baby's "safe passage" overwhelms other considerations. As one woman wrote in the survey form, "We [already] have a boy and are thrilled to be having a girl though a healthy child is all that mattered." Another, who previously terminated an affected pregnancy after amniocentesis, wrote, "Very pleased it's a boy, since it was a boy that we lost and we have a 5-year-old girl, but we would have been happy with a girl, too!"

Sometimes each member of the family has a different preference. Laura, a nurse who has just had her third child, a boy, expresses the complexities of these wish/fantasies. Laura has two older children, a girl aged 7 and a boy aged 3.

[With the second child] I did probably want a boy, just to have one of each. But mostly I really wanted a normal child. That was 99% and the sex preference was 1%. . . . [Nevertheless], I was thrilled because we had a girl and now we were having a boy. That was really neat.

[With the third child] In the logistical sense, I thought a boy would be more convenient because of the way we have the rooms set up in our house. . . . Also, my mother and I are very close. With Abby being the only girl, it replicated my relationship with my mother. . . . My daughter was disappointed, though; she wanted a sister. There was a part of me that was going along with her because that's what she wanted.

Greg [Laura's husband] never had a preference either way. . . . Greg is not interested in football or anything like that. He is not "macho" in that way. He is just as happy with girls.

Ben and Martha, interviewed together toward the end of Martha's fourth pregnancy, also emphasized that they didn't have a preference. In fact, this couple, both observant Jews, with three older girls, clearly wanted a boy; they were thrilled to find out their fourth child would be a son. But in the interview they gave the socially approved answer—"it doesn't matter so long as it's a healthy baby." They had convinced themselves, too, to some extent, that it didn't matter.

Ben: I don't think we had a preference [for a boy or a girl]. We have three girls, so we thought a boy would be nice.

Martha: I was expecting another girl based on our track record. I wasn't going to be unhappy about it; I had prepared myself psychologically for that possibility.

Four other couples, however, readily admitted a strong preference. Unlike Donna and Eric, the couple portrayed in the beginning of this chapter, two of these couples indicated they would have considered an abortion for this reason. Danielle unexpectedly got pregnant four months after the birth of her third child, a girl (the first two children are from her previous marriage). She strongly considered an abortion. Without telling her husband about her pregnancy, she sought CVS, knowing that she might abort if it turned out to be another girl. Instead, she was "very relieved to find out it was a boy"—the first boy in her husband's family.

Cindy, a real estate broker, had always wanted a girl; she had picked out a name when she was 12. Cindy and her husband Ed, a lawyer, went further than most couples in "customizing" their family. After two boys, Cindy and Ed used sperm separation to conceive a girl. It worked. When Cindy had CVS, her primary motive was sex selection, although of course she did not tell the clinic. She received her preliminary results within a few days, but had to wait two more weeks for the sex chromosome results. In her words: "I was anxious every day to find out the sex. . . . [When the news finally came] it was overwhelming. It was the same feeling I had at the birth of my sons. I was speechless, overwhelmed. A chilling feeling all over your body. . . . I kept yelping—I just couldn't take it in."

Usually the news of the baby's sex comes together with the finding of "no abnormality." For most couples it is not the fetus's gender but its health that matters at this point. The disclosure of the fetal sex in this context is construed as "yes, you have a healthy (boy or girl)." Nevertheless, knowing the fetus's sex makes it more real, which is usually a pleasant side effect. Wendy, eight months pregnant with her first baby, pointed out: "It depends on the person. For me it's better because I can already bond to the fetus. I have a sense of a human being there that's easier for me to visualize. It's more personal. If you don't know the sex it's like an 'it'. "

Twenty years after the beginning of the women's liberation movement, gender stereotypes still play a role in the desire for a boy or a girl. Yet, there is also a desire among both men and women to replicate their own identity through having a child of the same gender.

COUNSELORS' VIEWS ON FETAL SEX

Would genetic counselors, if they or their wives were pregnant, want to know the fetal sex? Of the thirty who answered this question, eighteen answered "yes," twelve "no." Needless to say, sex selection did not prompt those who did or would request this information. Indeed, a sex preference was spontaneously offered by only two who wanted to know prenatal sex and one who did not: all three preferred a girl.

Those who wanted to know mentioned that they "hated surprises." Those who did not want to know gave as their reason their love of surprises. The second group said that knowing "takes away too much of the wonder," while learning the sex at time of birth represents "something mystical about going through all the pain and then [a reward]." Two counselors added that for a second or subsequent child, they might put practicality ahead of surprise and opt to know the sex early.

Those who did not want to know felt that early knowledge would not necessarily increase bonding. It would, on the other hand, lead to disappointment if the fetus's sex was not the one they wanted.

- I wanted to know. My husband didn't, so we didn't ask. I'm glad now because of how the delivery turned out. I felt I was going to have a boy, but I wanted a girl. I was ecstatic to get what I wanted.
- This is a hard one. Part [of me] says no—I would want one sex very badly and I'd be disappointed. If you don't know, I think there is less disappointment when you have the actual child. No sense in fantasizing if it were something else.

Such responses were balanced by those who would or did want to learn fetal sex:

- I didn't really care, but my husband really wanted a daughter and wanted time to adjust [to a boy]—and indeed, I think it did make a difference.
- I would like a little girl, but if it were a boy, it would be great. I'd have time to adjust, also for planning—clothes, names, baby showers.

Some counselors expressed the view that anything that further personalized the fetus and strengthened the parents' bonding with it was desirable. Indeed, one counselor who began by saying, "I don't attach a great deal of emotional significance to knowing the sex," concluded with "I find it objectionable to call a baby an 'it' during pregnancy. . . . I think sex stereotyping will occur before or after birth, so what's the difference?"

Whether preparing for a child whose sex is known before birth translates into a pernicious type of sex stereotyping is debatable. Genetic counselors are sensitized to this debate, yet our small sample behaved just like other women in their pleasure in being able to better personify the fetus by learning the fetal sex:

- You bond differently because you know a little more. . . . I don't go for "colors for males."
- I could name the baby ahead of time and plan the baby's room. I think this personalizes the pregnancy. [I thought] of the baby even more.

This group of highly educated, middle-class Americans clearly views knowledge of the fetal sex as an attribute that rounds out one's mental picture of the fetus, but that is irrelevant to the decision on whether or not to keep this particular pregnancy. What little sex preference was expressed was for girls.

CLIENTS' ATTITUDES TOWARD SEX SELECTION

It is a far cry from expressing a preference for a baby of one sex or another to contemplating the possibility of abortion for this reason. Yet the specter of widespread use of prenatal diagnosis for sex selection has haunted medical ethicists, genetic counselors, and feminist writers.

We asked our respondents to indicate up to what gestational age, in their opinion, abortions should be allowed for different reasons. One of the reasons was "if the couple does not want a child of the sex that was diagnosed before birth." Another question asked whether the respondent would consider an abortion *for herself* for this reason and if so, and up to what point in the pregnancy (Appendix A, questions 31 and 32; see Chapter 8 for a full discussion of attitudes toward abortion).

Although users of prenatal diagnosis are considerably more pro-choice than the population as a whole, we found a strong rejection of abortion for sex selection. The rejection was stronger among amniocentesis users (75 percent) than among CVS users (58 percent). Since the CVS group has a higher SES, its more pronounced pro-choice attitude may be an artifact of SES.

Socioeconomic status is normally a predictor of pro-choice attitudes: people with higher educational attainment and income are more likely than those with a lower SES to uphold a woman's right to have an abortion for any reason. Our data on attitudes toward abortion for sex selection follow this pattern (Table 10.2). Among respondents with only a high school education, 70 percent answered "never"; the remainder answered "not sure." No one gave an unqualified "yes." Among women with post-graduate education, 64 percent answered "never," while 17 percent answered "not sure" and 19 percent said "yes." Similarly, women with higher household incomes were slightly more likely to support the right to abortion for sex selection. Controlling for the diagnostic procedure or the geographic region did not alter these findings.

Table 10.2
Attitudes Toward Abortion for Sex Selection, by Education

Question 31. Please indicate whether you agree or disagree that in general, women should have the right to have an abortion for each of the following reasons. If you agree, indicate up to what point in the pregnancy abortion should be allowed for each reason.

(Item L.) The couple does not want a child of the sex that was diagnosed before birth.

HIGHEST LEVEL OF EDUCATION COMPLETED			
	HIGH SCHOOL (n=10)	**1-4 YEARS COLLEGE** (n=48)	**GRADUATE SCHOOL** (n=58)	**ROW TOTAL** (N=116)
NEVER	70.0	72.9	63.8	68.1
NOT SURE	30.0	10.4	17.2	15.5
YES	-	16.7	19.0	16.4
TOTAL	100.0	100.0	100.0	100.0

Note: The responses "yes--up to third month", "yes--up to sixth month", and "yes--any time" were collapsed into a single category, "yes."

Research has shown that members of churches that condemn abortion, such as Catholics and Baptists, are no less likely than other women to terminate their pregnancies or to support abortion rights (Henshaw and Silverman, 1988; Williams, 1982). Researchers have found that it is the degree of religiosity rather than religious affiliation that predicts attitudes toward abortion. People who are personally religious, regardless of affiliation, are more likely to hold a pro-life position.

Personal religiosity involves a complex system of beliefs about God, the afterlife, good and evil, and the purpose of humans on earth. We used a crude behavioral indicator to measure religiosity: the frequency of attending religious services. In our sample, neither religious affiliation nor personal religiosity mattered with respect to attitudes about abortion for sex selection. The distaste for this practice was equally strong—70 percent or more—among members of all religions and all levels of religiosity. There was one exception. Women who reported no religious affiliation or who did not attend services were less likely than others to reject abortion for sex selection.

Our data suggest that regardless of socioeconomic status or religious beliefs (with the possible exception of those without religious affiliation), women who seek prenatal diagnosis—and who support freedom of choice on abortion—draw the line at abortion for sex selection. Clearly, this practice is not merely a logical extension of abortion on demand. When it comes to sex selection, even pro-choice respondents see the fetus as a baby, not as an unwanted pregnancy, and the abortion as taking a life. The comments written in the survey questionnaires illustrate the depth of feeling on this issue:

- Each case is individual and it's hard to make general statements. But abortion should not be used to get rid of a child because of sex!
- Some of the reasons for which I answered [yes] are personally repugnant—but I believe in the general principle of personal choice.
- I think if they wanted a baby, they should be glad it's OK and except [sic] the sex as a 50/50 chance.
- [Abortion for sex selection] is a really objectionable question to me. If people answer other than "never" they should not be told the [fetus's] sex.

The women in our sample are either pregnant with a wanted baby or have recently given birth. For those still pregnant, prenatal testing has focused their attention on the possibility of losing the pregnancy and increased their awareness of the fetus and their emotional attachment to it. For all these women the experience of motherhood is at its most intense. Abortion for sex selection appears in this context not only as a trivialization of motherhood but as a violation of its sanctity.

Many who believe as a matter of principle that women should have the right to abortion under given circumstances, such as economic hardship, will not countenance terminating their own pregnancy for the same reasons (see Chapter 8). This is also true for sex selection. Regardless of the demographic or situational breakdown we used—amniocentesis versus CVS users, those with only a high school education versus those with college or graduate degrees, women at different income levels and different religious affiliations, and those who have little or much reason to fear losing this pregnancy to abnormality or miscarriage—close to 90 percent of our respondents said they would never abort for sex selection. Only six out of 120 (5 percent) said they might do so, and another six said they were "not sure."

Again, the written comments illustrate the distinction between ideological support for abortion rights and personal behavior: "Personally, we would not choose abortion for the wrong sex. However, [couples] should have the right to choose."

COUNSELORS' ATTITUDES TOWARD SEX SELECTION

As the gatekeepers who control access to prenatal diagnosis, genetic counselors increasingly encounter clients who request testing for reasons of sex selection. In most cases, the clients cover up their true motive, but when a pregnancy diagnosed as normal is subsequently terminated, the suspicion of sex selection is inescapable. Like most Americans, genetic counselors generally condemn this practice. Furthermore, since counselors are typically female, they must deal with an implicit devaluation of their own sex. Counselors experience great personal as well as professional stress in dealing with such clients.

How often do clients request prenatal diagnosis for sex selection? Of the thirty-four counselors who responded, five said, "plenty" or "all the time," or "it's happening everywhere but in small percentages." Another twelve counselors indicated that it was not rare to encounter such couples whether by phone or in person. Counselors pointed out that requests for sex selection came predominantly from Chinese, Indian, Arab, and Iranian couples; only one has heard this request from an American-born couple. Counselors felt that this practice has become more common since CVS became available.

Half, however, had encountered such couples rarely (12) or not at all (5). Typically, they might speak with couples making initial inquiries about sex diagnosis; only very rarely did they discover a suspicious abortion. These counselors were more likely to be in places with few immigrants or in centers that did not offer CVS.

Of all the questions that came up in our study, the counselors held common views on only two issues: they upheld the ideal of nondirective counseling and they condemned the use of prenatal diagnosis for sex-selection purposes. Clearly, the two principles conflict. Only one counselor claimed to be ethically neutral without qualifications, that is, to go along with client demands without attempting to influence them. All the others made it clear that they did not consider this practice "business as usual."

Using prenatal diagnosis for sex selection imposes a double burden of stress on counselors. They are outraged by the use of scarce medical resources for what they perceive as a frivolous reason at best, and a morally shoddy abuse of reproductive freedom at worst. The same counselors are simultaneously aware that their profession and the services they provide depend on a bedrock of legal elective abortion. Few people would seek invasive prenatal diagnosis if neither cure nor abortion were available when a fetal defect is discovered. Sex selection challenges counselors' pro-choice commitments.

Counselors are schooled in and ideologically committed to nondirective, non-judgmental counseling. Having such strong feelings aroused is clearly at variance with their usual professional detachment.

- I detest it. I feel it's disgusting, I don't understand how a female can terminate a female.

- I have difficulty because personally I would never terminate for sex. Professionally, I can't let my judgment intrude. I believe in the integrity of patients, so I have difficulty with withholding sex information until month seven, etc. . . . I'm still of mixed feelings. Having gone to [a top women's college] and being a feminist I find sex selection abhorrent. After all, they present fictitious family histories.

- I am uncomfortable with this. . . . I feel rotten, angry, very uncomfortable. I voice my objections to the couple. I feel I and my training are being misused and misapplied. I resent the misuse of these.

Counselors whose clients are largely Asian or Middle Eastern are well aware of the cultural clashes involved. They are torn between condemnation of those cultures' lesser valuation of women and sympathy with clients who are caught between their own native culture and that of the American mainstream.

- If I believe you have a right to abortion, why do I get so upset? . . . Why don't I understand that in these cultures they have a whole different mindset about what is culturally male and what is female?

- We certainly have Chinese couples with two, three or four girls who have aborted. I can understand people wanting to choose the sex; I'd rather they have a wanted pregnancy. If they're going to be miserable and mistreat the kid . . . I don't think it's so bad to have a kid you're happy with.

- I cannot judge them. One woman said, "I'll be beaten if I have another girl". . . . Sometimes they're angry at me, the bearer of bad news [a female fetus].

Although counselors occasionally encounter native-born middle-class couples who are tempted by sex selection, the sex preference of Americans (or Europeans) is less predictable. Two counselors reported encountering women with three sons who wanted girls. One terminated a healthy male fetus; the other, who would have done the same thing, was relieved to find out she was carrying a girl. The counselor said, "I wasn't as hostile with her." Such comments suggest that counselors might not find sex-selective abortion quite so offensive if it were balanced between the sexes or if it were carried out by people with similar cultural views to their own.

About two-thirds of our respondents work at institutions with a strict policy against performing CVS or amniocentesis without a valid medical indication, such as a familial history or advanced maternal age. But in practice these policies tend to be increasingly meaningless. By the time these couples have had several children of one sex, the wife is frequently 35 or older and hence eligible on age grounds alone.

Furthermore, although centers still insist on a documented *bona fide* higher risk for women seeking CVS, the higher risk procedure, the boundary age for either procedure has crept steadily downward. Most centers now offer amniocentesis to any client who is insistent enough. This is due partly to the recognition that a woman at any age can bear a genetically affected child (and sue her health care providers) and partly to the decreasing risk posed by both procedures as doctors become more skilled. One clinic loosened its rules after it reluctantly performed an amniocentesis for a highly anxious woman in her late 20s—whose fetus turned out to have a lethal trisomy.

Therefore, both counselors and clients have made an accommodation of sorts. A third of our counselors discussed the role of cover stories. To spare other staff members discomfort, two counselors actually suggested to clients interested in sex selection that they give a more acceptable cover story. As one counselor said, the fiction that they're anxious or of late maternal age is a social lubricant. A third admitted, "If they had lied or embellished a true story, we could have offered it."

Others have learned not to probe: "Whatever story they give, I go with it. If there's a medical indication, they're entitled." Counselors point out that the staff usually cannot check a reported familial history. A half-dozen counselors noted that clients who have resided in the United States for any reasonable length of time have become sophisticated enough to offer an acceptable reason for seeking prenatal diagnosis. "[Those seeking sex selection] have all been Indian. The *modus operandi* is, 'There's a relative with Down's Syndrome in the old country.' There's a joke going around in the program about these relatives in the old country."

Counselors cope by redefining the issues. The counselor who eventually saw a fetus of the wrong sex as being another subcategory of the broader category of "unwanted pregnancy" used one such mechanism. Three noted the relativity of cultural values. Resignation through an appeal to the pro-choice philosophy was the most common response among our respondents:

- If you believe in pro-choice, there's only so much probing you can do. CVS does make [sex selection] easier.

- I don't feel it's an appropriate reason to run the risk of the procedure. If you're pro-choice, though, you can't weigh reasons. And on the other hand, we offer it to those who are age 30 and anxious. There's a shade of difference: fear of abnormality vs. fear of wrong sex.

• This is a difficult issue. Given that women can terminate any pregnancy without a medical indication up to 20–24 weeks' gestation, it may not be right to not allow sex selection with the idea of perhaps preventing a termination. However, as a feminist it would be difficult for me to be involved with a woman terminating a female because it was "the wrong sex."

In several interviews, we asked counselors what they thought of the Canadian practice of not releasing information on the sex of the fetus until the seventh month of pregnancy, when it is too late to abort. Responses varied little among counselors:

• I think that is more comfortable—but my boss would stress patient autonomy and right to know. I foresee that if we all said we would not release sex information, they'd go to some doctor who would.

• We report the results as soon as we get them; we feel it's our legal obligation. I understand that legally the patient has the right to all test information. I think that's right: if you start making exceptions, it can get out of hand.

• [Aborting for sex] makes me a little nauseous, but I still stick by my original thing that anyone who wants that information should be allowed to have it. There are people who say you cannot have this. . . . It's really hard because nobody likes it on any level: the nurses don't like it; the physicians don't like it; the lab staff don't like it. And of course it's up to every clinic, but I still stick by the fact that on a broad level people should be able to have that information if they want it. . . . I'm not here to make judgments.

Of twenty-four responses that addressed policy issues, five called for outright prohibition of sex selection or stated in strong terms they could not counsel such clients. Six more approved current or past practices in which their clinic could turn down or discourage such clients. Seven counselors believed that the pro-choice ethos of the *Roe v. Wade* decision precluded holding a client seeking sex selection to a different standard than other abortion seekers, however much the counselor disapproved of the practice. Finally, six counselors raised the issue of a patient's right to the information. Two backed this right without reservation; one had not resolved her conflicts. Three felt torn between the attraction of the Canadian practice of withholding information and the sense that their own or their clinic director's commitment to patient autonomy would not countenance this practice.

Our study, together with other available data, suggests that for the near future, fears of the widespread use of abortions for sex selection in the United States are unfounded. This practice is widely condemned by those closest to it—genetic counselors as well as women who seek prenatal diagnosis. For the large majority of parents, a preference for a boy or a girl will not be translated into selective abortion. Nevertheless, most professionals in this field believe that with earlier and safer diagnostic procedures, such abortions will become more common.

The implications are far-reaching. On one hand, this practice may make it possible for people to realize the family of their dreams, down to sex composition and birth order. On the other hand, it may distort the birth order of males and females and fuel existing gender stereotypes. It may also open the way to abortion for other "undesirable" characteristics not related to health and eventually threaten the availability of abortion for any reason.

Like most women who use prenatal diagnosis, genetic counselors are vehement in their own conviction that prenatal testing should not be used for sex-selection purposes. They view this practice as a misuse of scarce medical resources. Furthermore, they are outraged on behalf of their own sex, and they condemn the cultural values that create so strong a sex preference that parents are willing to abort a healthy fetus of the "wrong" sex.

Cognitive dissonance is created on several fronts. Genetic counselors' training stresses the supremacy of nondirective counseling. Therefore, a counselor internally feels she is compromising this value when she condemns sex selection. Moreover, in a profession that is predicated on the existence of legal abortion, counselors are self-selected as well as socialized to be pro-choice. The inconsistency of maintaining that a woman need not provide a reason to abort while condemning some reasons as unacceptable is not lost on this group.

Counselors reject the paternalism that characterized the (overwhelmingly male) medical profession in the past and emphasize the importance of patients' autonomy. A final, unrecognized source of stress for many stems from their own awareness that knowledge of the fetal sex can add materially to the psychological pleasure parents receive from a pregnancy. Three-fifths of our respondents felt that knowledge of sex personalizes the fetus and strengthens bonding.

The stress from these inner conflicts is heightened by the fact that counselors lack the power to set the medical protocol guiding their own practice. It is unclear what empowering counselors would change in this realm, however. They are as divided on what constitutes desirable social policy about sex selection as they are united in personally condemning the practice. It will not be easy to achieve societal consensus on sex-selection practices, given both the complicated rights that must be balanced and the fervor of the abortion debate. After all, what is a frivolous reason to abort for one woman is a serious, legitimate reason for another.

11

Knowledge for What? Prenatal Testing and Competing Social Goals

To know is to predict; to predict is to control.

—Comte, 1896, pp. 20–21

Auguste Comte (1798–1857), the "father" of sociology, professed unlimited faith in the power of knowledge. Knowledge achieved through science, he believed, would give people control over their lives and pave the way toward a society free of human suffering, a new age of reason and happiness.

As a result of the Human Genome Project, knowledge of the genetic basis of disease has been exploding. Hopes run high for understanding the mechanisms that cause genetic diseases and eventually for treatments or even cures. This promise, however, still lies in the remote future. For the present and the near future, the new genetic knowledge will be applied in the medical field primarily through prenatal diagnosis and selective abortion.

Prenatal testing carries undeniable benefits. For expectant parents it offers improved chances of having healthy offspring, provides some reassurance of fetal health during pregnancy, and increases women's bonding with the "child-in-the-making." It offers the medical profession a technique if not a treatment to assist parents, albeit imperfectly, in reaching their goal of a healthy child. It offers society the promise of reducing the incidence of some genetic disorders.

Yet in the real world the elusive goal of achieving a healthy baby raises pragmatic and ethical questions. Some of these questions relate to how the process of prenatal testing should be carried out; others relate to the propriety of the goals of testing and under what circumstances it should be employed. Like all "advances," the new knowledge and technology will entail costs—some foreseeable and others doubtlessly not—and behavioral and attitudinal changes—some foreseeable and others, perhaps the majority, unintended and unforeseen. (Consider the social effects of the telephone and the automobile.) Using the technology wisely—controlling it lest it control us or cause unintentional or unnecessary harm—requires that all of those involved contemplate both the process and its possible consequences. Much of this book has examined the generally underestimated psychological demands prenatal testing imposes on both parents and counselors. We will briefly recount a few of these demands. In addition, all parties involved—prospective parents, health care workers, and society—must comprehend both costs as well as gains in the broader social context. Ultimately, we must decide what constitutes responsible use of this knowledge and what constitutes misuse.

THE PARENTS' PERSPECTIVE: THE ILLUSION OF CONTROL

> The husband of one woman expecting their first child turned to me and asked, "What can I do to be absolutely sure of not having a child with a defect?" I replied, "Abort this pregnancy and have a vasectomy: then I can guarantee you'll never have a child with a problem."
>
> —Shirley Weinstein, a genetic counselor

Pregnancy entails risk-taking. Prospective parents have always sought to minimize these risks, whether by making offerings to the gods or by utilizing modern prenatal diagnostic tests. Ideally, the quest for a risk-free pregnancy with a guaranteed healthy outcome would entail neither physical nor psychological costs to the parents.

Prenatal testing imposes both. The very existence of the procedures has imposed a burden of decision making on prospective parents in the late twentieth-century Western medical system. Each in this series of decisions frequently carries its own high psychological cost.

Clients learn to their disappointment, and even anger, that prenatal diagnosis offers only the illusion of control. It can never banish the specters of undetected defects in the fetus or of birth trauma, and ordinarily it cannot turn an affected fetus into a healthy baby. Like Ulysses, expectant parents may find themselves forced to choose between the lesser of two evils, not once but several times. They must choose between

- testing, with its risk of accidentally losing the pregnancy and with the possibility of a bad diagnosis, compelling yet another decision, or

- rejecting a test and renouncing the option of minimizing the risk of abnormality.

If the parents are well informed and come for prenatal care early enough in the pregnancy, they then must choose which procedure to have. On the basis of testing (often a series of tests), the following outcomes are possible:

- Obtaining a negative (i.e., good) test result and feeling reassured. If there is an eventual problem, the parents will be unprepared.

- Obtaining a positive (i.e., bad) result and having to decide whether to abort the fetus or to bear a child certain to have some degree of impairment.

- Obtaining an ambiguous result (an outcome whose effect on the child is mild, delayed, or unknown) and having to make decisions without knowing what the future might bring.

The pioneers of CVS assumed that the risk parents were willing to accept in order to increase their chances of having healthy children depended at least partly on timing in the pregnancy; that early testing would greatly increase utilization. As social scientists, we suspected that things were more complicated—that neither risk perceptions nor attachment (or lack of it) to the unborn child were one-dimensional, quantifiable entities subject to a simple tradeoff. Nevertheless, we believed that a comparison of the two principal invasive technologies, CVS and amniocentesis, would bring into sharp focus the ethical and social issues surrounding prenatal diagnosis.

Our research has shown that, contrary to speculation, early prenatal diagnosis is not a panacea. To be sure, it is a significant improvement over mid-trimester testing. Yet even early in the pregnancy the fetus is real enough to the mother that its loss—even the contemplation of such a loss—is dreadful.

Knowledge does not always empower; instead, it may confuse and paralyze. Prospective parents may have to contend with perhaps the most unforeseen consequence of all: too much information, that is, information they never realized the testing might yield and information they are not emotionally equipped to handle. At present, certain kinds of genetic testing, namely, that for late-onset diseases such as Huntington's or Alzheimer's (if a familial marker has been identified), are not conducted for an individual unless he or she expressly requests it and understands the import of what is being requested. Prospective parents, especially those who somehow assume that any identified fetal anomalies will be restricted to the fetus, are frequently ill equipped for the discovery that one is a bearer of an abnormal gene or a chromosomal translocation and, indeed, may have already passed it on to one or more children. Even those who know they carry a recessive gene for Tay-Sachs or sickle cell, or have a Fragile X chromosome (a condition that involves mental retardation) may not have considered that this knowledge carries with it the moral obligation to inform one's children, siblings, and possibly cousins. Genetic service providers, too, are torn between the need to protect the client's privacy and the imperative to inform others who might be at risk.

THE PROBLEM OF ACCESS

For whosoever hath, to him shall be given.

—Matthew 12:13

The "Matthew principle," (as sociologist Robert Merton has called it) is a well-known paradox in sociology: those who already possess considerable resources are the most likely to obtain coveted rewards. All studies of prenatal care, including ours, document that "those who have, get"; that is, the more advantaged in education and income utilize prenatal diagnostic services to a greater extent than their less advantaged sisters. The very people with the greatest access to resources for helping a handicapped child are increasingly able to avert the birth of one, if they so wish. Taken to the extreme, some observers (for example, Wertz and Fletcher, 1988) have argued that only the children of the poor will evidence syndromes or traits that the better off classes will have selected out from their own liveborn children.

There is widespread awareness of the inequalities in the American health care system and a growing societal determination to rectify these inequalities. Undoubtedly, if financial and logistical barriers were removed, prenatal testing would become more widespread. Today, while utilization rates in the United States vary by state, they are unlikely to exceed 50 percent of all eligible women in any state.

Yet access is only one part of the equation. Our findings corroborate those of other studies, namely, that equalizing access to health resources will not produce identical levels of utilization among women of all incomes, levels of education, and ethnic backgrounds. Just as there are profound differences in the cognitive "maps" of literate and illiterate women, so to a lesser degree there appear to exist persistent differences in how women with greater or lesser degrees of formal education approach decision making. They subjectively evaluate identical risk levels differently; they are more or less fearful of the pain associated with the procedure; and if results of other studies hold in this context, they have different degrees of trust in the objectivity and ends of the health care provider. These differences in turn account for much of the difference in the utilization rates of these procedures.

Economists might provide yet another rationale for the skewed utilization rates: that the different propensity of high-earning professional women and those less educated and less well-to-do to use prenatal diagnosis may accurately reflect the differences in "opportunity costs" (the value of alternatives foregone) between the time of these two groups. In our opinion, this rationale smacks of the same condescension as shown by those who argue that the quest for a healthy child is an artifact of social class and culture and that middle-class professionals should not impose their own standards of "perfect children" on working-class parents or those from minority groups.

Is it only, in fact, cultural relativism and "opportunity costs" that motivate some groups and not others to avail themselves of a technology that diminishes somewhat (albeit at a price) the uncertainty associated with childbearing? We assert that no individual or couple, given the choice between bearing a healthy child or bearing an affected one, would opt for the unhealthy one. But unless mere wishing accomplishes this end, parents will differ about the rightness of interfering with the natural order of things and about the acceptability of the physical and psychological costs of intervention.

Human beings are diverse, and their beliefs, especially in a pluralistic society, are frequently irreconcilable. The profound ethnic and religious and ideological schisms among Americans make it highly unlikely that women of all backgrounds will ever utilize prenatal diagnosis to an identical extent. Public policy in an open society requires that we aim at equality of knowledge and equality of access. We then must learn from genetic counselors to define success as achieving a well-informed client rather than sameness of outcome.

Having said this, should we be content with an overall 50 percent utilization rate or less? In countries with universal health coverage, the rates are much higher. In some parts of Denmark 80 to 85 percent of all pregnant women aged 35 and over are screened (Fuhrmann, 1989). But Denmark differs from the United States in more than its national health care system. Denmark is economically more egalitarian, ethnically more homogeneous, and geographically far more compact than is the United States. The United States can never resemble Denmark in the last two attributes, but it can work to reduce the extreme inequalities of wealth, education, and ability to control a person's life chances—the inequalities that form the bedrock of the American stratification system. Only when we have assured true equality of access ought we to accept group differences in utilization rates.

THE COUNSELORS' PERSPECTIVE: NONDIRECTIVENESS, ETHICAL NEUTRALITY, AND INFORMATION GIVING

> My job is just to give the information until I am comfortable that they really understand what's going on. Their job is to make the decision.
> —Norma Watson, a genetic counselor

Nondirective counseling is the pervasive ethos of the genetic counseling profession. The nondirective counselor is committed to helping clients make a well-informed decision. This goal requires that clients receive as full information as time constraints and their own comprehension permit and that clients be encouraged to explore their values and "gut feeling" about what feels right for them.

But nondirectiveness is not the same as value neutrality. The stress of clinical genetics on nondirectiveness originated partly from a desire to repudiate the abuses of the eugenics movement. Eugenicists, who enjoyed widespread respectability in Western countries until after World War II, had sought to persuade individuals to make reproductive decisions for the good of society; where persuasion failed, coercive measures were applied. The most notorious of these measures were mass sterilization and the killing of those deemed unworthy to live. As bioethicist Arthur Caplan points out (1993, p. 161), "Few areas of science have had to live with the historical legacy of abuse that haunts clinical genetics. . . . As a result, few areas of science or medicine have been so keen to restrict or confine the role played by professionals to matters of fact, not value, as genetic counselors."

Genetic counseling went beyond repudiating the abuses of eugenics. Grounded in an unbounded faith in the capacity of human beings to make enlightened decisions on the basis of knowledge, it has regarded as its primary role educating the client—imparting full and unbiased information while carefully avoiding influencing the client's decision. Paradoxically, this ceding of all decision-making authority to the parents runs counter to the trends in neonatology, where medical intervention carries its own momentum and parents' wishes are often ignored.

Yet value neutrality is nearly impossible to attain in practice. Sorenson, the chronicler of the genetic counseling profession, states, "To apply knowledge requires making decisions about what to inform people, when to inform them, and how to inform them. These decisions are influenced by values. . . . Genetic counseling probably has never been nor ever will be value neutral" (1993, p. 3). Genetic counseling by its very nature implies value judgments. Even using words like "abnormality," "defect," and "recurrence risk" in connection with a given trait connotes a value stance (Nance, 1993).

Exclusive of nondirectiveness, Sorenson identifies the following value preferences that have shaped the practice of genetic counseling:

- Informed decision-making is better than non-informed.
- The individual or couple, rather than the community or society, is the proper "client" of genetic counseling services.
- The measure of genetic counseling's success is its utility to individuals and couples rather than to society. The manifest goal is to enhance parents' autonomy rather than to reduce the rate of birth defects in a given population. (1993, p. 12)

The related question is whether value neutrality is even desirable. Wertz and Fletcher (1988) condemn the touted practice of supporting *any* client decision, a practice that "implies total moral relativism" (p. 593). Caplan (1993, p. 163–164) concurs, arguing that "value neutrality is no longer healthy for the practice of clinical genetics." Insistence on value neutrality leaves counselors "powerless in the face of what may be immoral requests on the part of clients," such as a decision to abort for sex, for a minor medical condition, or for a nonmedical trait. Caplan concludes that "An ethic of value neutrality provides no foundation for counselors to try and dissuade parents from making choices that are frivolous, silly, or malicious."

Caplan also relates this ethic to the counselor's moral obligation to take a stance on public policy issues:

Value neutrality discourages those in the field from coming to grips with the central ethical question that now confronts the field—how to define genetic disease and disorder in order to lay out appropriate targets for testing and counseling.... With a mountain of new information about the human genome looming in the not so distant future, genetic counseling can no longer afford to ignore the question of what sort of disorders and diseases it wishes to discover, why, and what exactly it wants to say about them. (1993, p. 163)

On the basis of both the clients' and the counselors' accounts we heard, we have singled out four practices or issues that need to be better addressed. A fifth, the issue of fetal sex selection, is addressed later, in the next section.

The first is discussing the specifics of abortion, in particular the implications of first-trimester abortion versus those of a later one. Maternal mortality resulting from procedures performed in the sixteenth week of pregnancy or later is eleven times higher than that of procedures performed in the first twelve weeks; the emotional trauma is also much greater (see Chapter 9). Yet, our study shows widespread ignorance on this topic among women who have prenatal testing. We ask, how is it possible to make an informed decision about which test to use without taking into account the consequences of later versus earlier abortion? We urge that this information be imparted to all women who confront this choice.

A second problem area is how to compare the risk of procedurally induced miscarriage to that of having an affected child. As we know, there is no good way of comparing risks for such different outcomes. Counselors frequently grapple with this dilemma by reminding patients that the procedural risk is compressed into a moment of time ("a one-time shot"), while an abnormality, if present, entails potentially a lifetime burden on the family as well as on the affected child. We believe this comparison, however well intentioned, deals too cavalierly with the psychological costs of losing a wanted pregnancy through a procedure that the mother freely chooses.

A more honest description of the comparative costs would have to acknowledge that, although pregnancy loss as a result of the procedure is rare (but with miscarriage risks of 1 in 100 or 200, not *that* rare), the grief experienced by the woman who does lose her pregnancy in this manner—like that experienced by the woman who aborts an affected fetus—will be long lasting. The grief will persist even if she has another pregnancy (and perhaps more so if she never conceives again). Furthermore, the mourning will differ in intensity, duration, and overt manifestations between mothers and fathers; this is normal.

This forewarning about the emotional costs of pregnancy loss should be balanced by a discussion of the full consequences for an affected child of living (or dying) with a disability. The discussion should also include the commitments and responsibilities a woman already has, and how these would be affected by the burden of caring for a sick child.

A third underaddressed counseling problem is how to provide emotional support to couples who have either suffered a procedurally induced miscarriage or who have terminated a pregnancy with an abnormal fetus. Support groups for this type of loss are rare (see Chapter 9). Other than referring to one-on-one psychotherapy, counselors can do little but continue their present informal practice of putting each individual client in contact with another woman who has recently experienced this sort of loss. We are left with the industrialized society's solution to the cry for help: books and films for this small but well-defined audience.

A fourth challenge to counselors stems from the results of research identifying which counselor/client characteristics facilitate communication between these two parties. Research shows that counselors and clients communicate best when counselors are trained in interviewing techniques and when clients have high levels of education and income and low levels of risk: in short, when they resemble each other demographically. Trends in the training of counselors in the past twenty years have produced practitioners who are better trained in psychotherapeutic interview techniques than were their more research-oriented predecessors. This bodes well for the outcome of a counseling session.

The opposite trend is at work in the changing composition of women seeking prenatal genetic counseling. The growing use of prenatal diagnosis (particularly of so-called noninvasive techniques) has resulted in the influx of clients who represent a demographically more diverse group than was the case in the early years of amniocentesis. The new clients, especially in such major immigrant destinations as New York City and Los Angeles, are likely to have less formal education and perhaps different concepts of health behavior and etiology than the early amniocentesis clients. The democratization of access and utilization has magnified communication problems between counselors and clients. We received vivid descriptions of the difficulties in both collecting and conveying essential data. Continuing demographic changes in the composition of the U.S. population will place demands on training programs to increase the sensitivity of counselors to cross-cultural differences in meanings and their skills in cross-cultural interviewing techniques.

FETAL SEX SELECTION

Americans from a Western cultural tradition do not express an overwhelming preference for a child of one sex over the other. Large national surveys as well as the small select group we interviewed indicate a near-total rejection of sex selection through abortion. At the same time, there is widespread preference for a male first child followed by a female second child. Many are willing to consider preconceptual sex-selection techniques (such as sperm separation) to achieve the desired sex composition and order, without recognizing that such practices carry serious social outcomes.

By contrast, families in some segments of Chinese, Indian, and Muslim societies have a strong preference for sons. As prenatal screening technologies, particularly ultrasound, proliferate in these countries, the rate of abortions of female fetuses will grow. Although politicians publicly disapprove of such practices, as do human rights advocates, most agree that the spread of these technologies cannot be stopped.

In the United States the stakes are different. Here, even newcomers from traditional societies generally do not seek to practice sex selection until they have already had two, three, or four daughters. Thus, sex selection would not have an effect on the birth order of boys and girls. Since couples who have sons presumably stop at a smaller number of children than those who have daughters, sex selection will encourage smaller family size. This will increase the resources available for each daughter as well as each son.

As social scientists and feminists, we feel strong peer pressure to condemn the practice of sex selection, and at the beginning of our study we did. However, during the course of our research, to our surprise we have become more sympathetic to this practice rather than more outraged by it. We stipulate utilizing preconceptual but not postconceptual methods.

What considerations have prompted us to change our minds? In the United States there is little likelihood that sex selection would result in a strong sex imbalance. Furthermore, attaining sex balance within a family is considered desirable by nearly all cultures except the three mentioned above. Couples everywhere want the experience of rearing "a boy for you, a girl for me." Given a desired family size of two children, we must admit to agreeing with the counselor who said, "Is it such a terrible thing to want a child of each sex?" Our main objection is that this would forevermore deprive people of a sibling of the same sex, and society of the kinds of friendships that this configuration produces. Another objection revolves around birth order. We would wish to persuade American couples that if they want to select the sex of their child, they not practice this on a first pregnancy.

We are alarmed enough about population growth in the United States as well as worldwide to endorse almost any voluntary means of reducing fertility. If choosing the sex of one's second child will curtail the overall number of children born, we believe the societal benefits will outweigh any disadvantages.

Indeed, the major problems with sex selection will occur in societies that promote one-child families, like China. Here is where a strong preference for males will be translated into an overwhelmingly imbalanced sex ratio. And here is where the government and all social institutions should be—must be—enlisted to refashion the cultural values and security nets that underlie this compulsion to have a male child.

We must also point out that no government can recall the several technologies that facilitate sex selection. Sperm separation techniques require widely available electromagnetic charge devices and centrifuges; ultrasound scanners are too valuable in detecting and treating physical anomalies to be banned. Moreover, the vast majority of the counselors we interviewed do not endorse a paternalistic use of medical authority ("we decide which information we will or will not impart to you") and therefore will not withhold information that has been gathered through invasive prenatal diagnosis. We are left with trying to devise policies and public education that promote equal valuing of females and males. The decision of whether to allow sex selection has been permanently placed in the hands of the consumer.

SOCIETY'S PERSPECTIVE: PARENTAL AUTONOMY AND RESOURCE ALLOCATION

> Have you heard the old folk story about the woman with a healthy chicken and a sick chicken? She killed the healthy chicken to make soup for the sick.
>
> —Estelle Duncan, a genetic counselor

Prenatal testing—or rather, the uses to which it is put—is caught in a tug-of-war between the rights and autonomy of parents, the needs of the community, and ethical concerns. Although balancing these claims will be very difficult, we cannot afford to focus on one side only while discounting the others. Feminists who object to intrusive measures being employed on women's bodies; bioethicists who defend the autonomy of individuals in the face of societal pressures; policy framers for neonatal treatment; anti-abortion activists; disability rights advocates; and health economists who argue that genetic screening is justified as long as it saves money for society: all present conflicting claims about the uses and abuses of testing. All except the last implicitly posit a society with unlimited resources. Possibly these claims cannot be reconciled, but they must be acknowledged.

Clinical geneticists distinguish between genetic testing, which is recommended for individuals at high risk of a certain abnormality, and screening, which is routinely used on an entire population. Screening makes sense only if the procedures are cheap, easily administered, and detect a high enough number of abnormalities to offset the economic cost. As we know, however, the psychological toll—the price clients pay in anxiety while waiting for the results or when receiving false positive results—is rarely entered into the equation.

Mass screening for most heritable conditions is not feasible for several reasons. For rare conditions mass screening would detect too few cases to be economically justified. Accurate and cheap-to-administer screening tests are as yet available for very few genetic anomalies. For cystic fibrosis, the most common birth defect in the United States, physicians Benjamin Wilfond and Norman Fost (1992) have calculated that the cost of screening most pregnancies would be staggering. To screen 3 million women each year (three-quarters of all those carrying pregnancies to term in the United States), even if each session lasted only ten minutes, counseling alone would consume 638,000 hours annually. This would equal one-quarter of the workload of all clinical geneticists and genetic counselors. Even with this effort, many cases would escape undetected given the test's current capabilities. Wilfond and Fost suggest that cheaper alternatives such as brochures, videos, and community-based programs be used to educate and inform patients.

Despite the low sensitivity of many tests and the price women pay for inaccurate or inconclusive results, prenatal screening is expanding rapidly. Whether through so-called noninvasive methods or through invasive techniques, more and more conditions are now detectable. Initially, the avowed purpose of amniocentesis was to detect, and abort, fetuses with major chromosomal defects. As genetic knowledge increases, however, ever-milder conditions may come to be defined as unacceptable. In addition, as the genetic risk level for which medical guidelines justify "intervention" (that is, invasive testing) has decreased, so has the level of risk for abnormality considered high by genetic counselors, a knowledgeable group. If the public follows suit and comes to perceive ever-lower and ultimately all levels of genetic risk as (intolerably) high, an increasing proportion of pregnant women will find themselves defined as at "high" risk of having an abnormal fetus. As testing procedures become safer and are available earlier, the pressure on women to have the tests will grow.

Society currently condemns a mother who bears a child with fetal alcohol syndrome, drug addiction, or any condition attributable to maternal behavior known to be harmful to a fetus. In a culture that prizes "control" over "fate," a "que sera, sera" (what will be, will be) attitude is seen as an abnegation of individual responsibility. Refusal to be tested or to terminate an affected pregnancy may be placed in the same category. Societal norms may soon affix on parents the responsibility for bearing a child with a prenatally identifiable genetic or developmental defect. The unfortunate public condemnation of the childbearing decisions of broadcaster Bree Walker and columnist Anna Quindlen, mentioned in Chapter 1, reveals that this is not an idle threat.

What about a woman's right to make her own decision whether or not to abort? Whose baby is this anyway? Biologist Ruth Hubbard, after stating her firm support for women's right to abortion for any reason, warns about subtle (and unsubtle) societal pressures to abort "for the good of society"—thereby raising the specter of eugenics:

Once a technique exists to identify a fetus that will be born with a particular disability, individual women and families become responsible for acting out these prejudices. If a test is available and a woman doesn't use it, or completes the pregnancy although she has been told that her child will have a disability, the child's disability is no longer an act of fate. She is now responsible; it has become her fault. In this liberal and individualistic society, there may be no need for eugenic legislation. Physicians and scientists need merely provide the techniques that make individual women, and parents, responsible for implementing the society's prejudices, so to speak, by choice. . . . And once the means to avoid bearing a child with a particular disability are available, women who have medical and financial access to that so-called choice may not feel entitled to refuse. (1988, pp. 232–233)

Pressures may come from opposite directions. Some in the pro-life movement, and their supporters in the federal and state governments, oppose a woman's right to abortion for any reason, including abnormality. British philosopher Agneta Sutton (1990, p. 123) holds that a fetus, no matter what its physical condition or gestational age, is a person whose life cannot be taken for any reason: "Consequently, the supposed right to a healthy child cannot be invoked in order to justify the abortion and killing of a defective fetus." She, too, invokes the specter of eugenics, but she draws opposite conclusions—that prenatal diagnosis is never justified if abortion is a possible alternative.

As a means of avoiding the birth of children affected by genetic illnesses or malformations, prenatal diagnosis constitutes a way of identifying children thought to be socially undesirable. As such, then, it is a tool for weeding out prospective lives which are regarded as not worth living. Both those who provide and those who make use of it with a view to selective termination of pregnancy reflect the influence of negative eugenics on present-day attitudes to unborn life. . . . It is a form of elitism of the fit and healthy . . . eugenic elitism. . . . Such elitism is the antithesis of that compassion and humility which are prerequisites of civilized society. (Sutton, 1990, pp. 61, 124, 125)

In Sutton's view the rights of the fetus are absolute; they should never be superseded by those of the mother, other family members, or society.

Both of these antithetical views ignore the changed reality for the child with a defect, her family, and the medical profession wrought by the antibiotic era. The introduction of the drug sulfa circa 1935, followed in rapid succession by antibiotic drugs, has altered the course of many disabilities. With each advance in medicine and pharmacology has come a prolongation of life expectancy for individuals born with such genetic diseases as Down's syndrome and cystic fibrosis. Each advance has entailed a significant cost in resources but (to date) no eradication of the underlying disease.

In the pre-sulfa era, a majority of Down's syndrome children succumbed by age 5 to heart defects, respiratory disease, and other infectious diseases. Today, 90 percent of Down's children survive to age 5 (Fryers, 1984; Thase, 1982). The life expectancy of persons with cystic fibrosis rose from less than 3 years in 1953 to 28 years by 1991 (Cystic Fibrosis Foundation, 1991). In 1992 a federal panel approved a research proposal to treat cystic fibrosis by inserting new genes into the patient's airway tissue. There are as yet no cost estimates for this highly experimental and uncertain treatment awaited by the 30,000 persons currently alive who have cystic fibrosis.

Another genetic disease, Gaucher's, a fat-storage disease found primarily among Jews, may provide insight into the cost of treatment for genetic disorders.

Unlike sufferers from other genetic diseases, many persons with Gaucher's lead a nearly normal life; others will do so only if they receive treatment. Annual costs for enzyme replacement therapy range upward of $50,000 per person, with $300,000 charges being common. If we assume that one-third of the approximately 15,000 patients, Jewish and non-Jewish, in the United States are affected severely enough to require treatment, the national treatment cost would exceed $1 billion a year. Even a more economical drug regimen would cost $250 million per year for drug costs alone (Beutler, 1992).

With the increasing flow of knowledge from the Human Genome Project, more and more genetic conditions are being identified. Should we then screen for the deleterious ones? Abort identified fetuses? Prolong the lives of those with the disease by using incredibly expensive therapies? And who is to decide?

The ultimate goal of genetic testing, of course, is therapy for diagnosed disorders; many see abortion as merely an interim step. Yet for most disorders cure is many years away. In the interim, such treatment as is available may be frightfully expensive. As a society, can we afford the treatment? And in the absence of complete cure, what would be the quality of life of those who survive with major disabilities? How would the caretaking responsibilities and costs affect the lives of those around them?

Two paradoxes are inherent in this controversy. The first is the discrepancy between the availability of genetic testing and the pressures on women to make use of it, and the erosion of abortion rights. In the absence of public funding and in the face of mounting pressures from right-to-life groups, abortion for any reason is increasingly difficult to obtain. This is particularly true for poor women and those living outside metropolitan areas. When abortion rights are threatened, so is the *raison d'etre* of genetic services.

The second paradox is the inconsistency between our collective (un)-willingness to pay for chronic disease and the policies that create more victims of these diseases. Recently, a health maintenance organization (HMO) denied coverage to a child born with cystic fibrosis. The condition had been diagnosed before birth, and the parents had chosen to have the child. The HMO eventually backed down, but other instances have been reported of the discriminatory uses of genetic tests by employers and insurance companies (Billings et al., 1992; Natowicz, Alper, and Alper, 1992). Clearly, as long as there is no national health insurance in the United States, both insurers and employers will balk at paying for the high cost of treatment for those born with genetic disabilities or with genotypes that make them susceptible to other diseases.

Health policy analysts Neil Holtzman and Mark Rothstein point out that we must confront the reality of the cost of treatment if we are to avoid eugenic pressures on individuals:

A universal entitlement to health care could eliminate the potential for denying (whether for genetic or other reasons) people and their children access to health care. . . . The public's health would be better served by assuring access to care for everyone, rather than by compelling the relatively small number of people who would choose to have children with serious disabilities not to do so. (1992, pp. 457–458)

Even a national health care system, however, would be vulnerable to economic pressures. A comprehensive health care plan would protect individuals from arbitrary exclusion, but it would not solve the problem of resource constraints. The most expensive therapies would still need to be rationed.

Insurance and employment discrimination based on the abuse of genetic information appears to fuel fears that prenatal testing will erode society's willingness to accept persons with disabilities (Fuhrmann, 1989; Hubbard, 1988). However, it is not clear whether this intolerance is new or merely masquerading in new forms. No one has any way of knowing whether people of previous generations accepted disabled persons out of a sense of kinship and generosity of because they had no way of avoiding life's afflictions. Certainly, the widespread use of euthanasia of sick newborns, the high natural mortality rate for many victims, and the always inadequately funded support services for disabled persons cast a doubt that society has ever assumed a burden of care and acceptance of the afflicted more generous than it has today.

The conflict between society's unwillingness to pay for costly treatments and policies that create more victims is also played out between the aims of clinical genetics and those of neonatology.

The point of view of genetic counseling is that families count. Genetic counselors believe that a couple cannot make a well-informed decision without considering the effect of this decision on the family system. Always the "client" is viewed as the entire family. Many clients we interviewed echoed the notion that decisions must be made in the context of conflicting responsibilities to existing family members and to themselves. In making treatment decisions about sick newborns, however, governmental guidelines strictly enjoin physicians from taking either the family or the societal context into consideration. Federal and state regulations also instruct hospital staffs to ignore considerations of the child's quality of life and the cost of medical care. This policy was first formulated during the Reagan administration in the wake of two highly publicized cases in which the parents of infants with genetically caused disabilities requested that medical treatment be withheld. In the words of the President's Commission for the Study of Ethical Problems in Medicine and Biomedical and Behavioral Research:

Such permanent handicaps justify a decision not to provide life-sustaining treatment only when they are so severe that continued existence would not be a net benefit to the infant. ... This is a very strict standard in that it excludes from consideration the negative effects of an impaired child's life on other persons, including parents, siblings, and society. (President's Commission, 1983, p. 219)

These regulations were challenged by the American Medical Association and others and were eventually overturned by the Supreme Court. They were re-

placed by the Child Abuse Amendments, which placed responsibility for regulating life-and-death decisions with state child welfare agencies. State laws
forbid doctors to withhold medical treatment, food, and water from disabled or
critically ill infants unless doing so is in "the child's best interests." This is an
"infant-centered standard": the completely helpless newborn, whose life depends entirely on those responsible for its care, is designated as the sole client
on whom all resources must be focused. The interests of family members and
society are excluded from consideration.

In practice, decisions on withdrawing treatment in neonatal intensive care
units vary greatly, depending on the physician, the nursery, and the hospital.
However, despite the concern of the federal and state governments about medical
neglect of disabled infants, overtreatment is in fact more common than under-
treatment (Anspach, 1993; Guillemin and Holmstrom, 1986). The United States
historically has initiated aggressive treatments of very premature or sick newborns sooner, and discontinued it later, than other Western countries (Rhoden,
1986). In the wake of the governmental regulations of the 1980s, aggressive
interventions became even more common. At the same time, the social services
necessary to support disabled children who survive because of these interventions have been drastically reduced.

After the birth of a severely disabled baby, the mother may no longer have
any control over his or her fate, not even to the extent of letting nature take its
own course. A woman's only defense against misguided medical intervention
after birth may well be to screen her pregnancy and abort an affected fetus.

In our opinion, existing governmental regulations as well as the norm of
aggressive treatment ignore the fairness question—the legitimate interests of
family members as well as the child's quality of life. The regulation and norms
have also sidestepped the implications of these policies for resource allocation.
We may choose to ignore but we cannot nullify the reality that all societies with
finite resources must confront the results of allocative decisions.

The United States to date is paralyzed in its fight to control health care spending partly because Americans dislike all schemes that make rationing decisions
explicit. We have yet to reconcile the paramount importance we place on parental autonomy in reproductive decisions with the reality that society cannot
afford to offer life-enhancing treatment to very many persons with genetic disease. We cannot continue to "kill the healthy chicken" to save the sick. Only
by accepting the reality of limited health resources, together with the adoption
of a universal health care system, will the United States be able to frame a
consistent care policy that avoids the charges of coercion and abuse.

SAFEGUARDING REPRODUCTIVE AUTONOMY: GUIDELINES FOR
FUTURE PRACTICE AND RESEARCH

In 1991 the Human Genome Project's Division of Ethical, Legal, and Social
Issues convened a conference entitled Reproductive Genetic Testing: Impact
Upon Women. Meeting at the National Institutes of Health in Bethesda, Mar-

yland, the conference issued guidelines for future policy and research in reproductive genetic services. The guidelines are summarized below. Note, however,
that "removing social, legal and economic constraints on reproductive genetic
services" does not eliminate constraints on the availability of treatment for genetic conditions.

- "Reproductive genetic services should not be used to pursue 'eugenic' goals but should
  be aimed at increasing individuals' control over their own reproductive lives. . . . Reproductive genetic services must ultimately serve personal—not public—interests."
  Whenever the primary goal of genetic services becomes the prevention (for society's
  benefit) of the birth of children with birth defects, parental self-determination is
  threatened.

- "Reproductive genetic services should be meticulously voluntary." Testing should
  never be so routinized that women are railroaded into compliance without fully understanding the implications and without having a genuine opportunity to refuse. To
  assure that clients' consent is truly an informed one, counselors must provide clients
  with adequate information about the procedures' "benefits and risks, including those
  beyond biology."

- "Reproductive genetic services should be value sensitive." Providers must be sensitive
  to clients' cultural and ethnic differences as well as to those rooted in their personal
  circumstances. Providers also need to be aware of their own values and biases.

- "Standards of care for reproductive genetic services should emphasize genetic information, education, and counseling rather than testing procedures alone." Services
  should be custom-tailored to the individual client's needs and interests, but should
  include adequate information about the disorders for which the test is done and their
  implications.

- "Social, legal, and economic constraints on reproductive genetic services should be
  removed." In other words, no woman should be denied access to prenatal services
  because of inability to pay, lack of insurance coverage, or other, noneconomic barriers.

- Care should be taken that the growing use of prenatal testing does not stigmatize
  individuals with disabilities. (NIH Workshop Statement, 1992, pp. 1161–1163)

WHEN DOES THE PERSONAL BECOME POLITICAL?

The research described in this book was conducted on relatively small numbers of respondents who answered a written survey or spoke about their own
experiences. Although our sample was necessarily biased, these respondents are
in many ways representative of the people who use prenatal diagnosis and of
those who counsel about it. On the basis of our data analysis, we have explored
new ways of understanding the implications of prenatal testing and suggested
some ways of improving the delivery of these services. Many of our recommendations echo those of the NIH conference above.

Despite its obvious benefits to would-be parents, prenatal testing is no "magic
bullet" that potentially could eliminate serious birth disorders. Improvements in

genetic knowledge and in diagnostic technology have led us to focus on those conditions that can be diagnosed in utero. But as we know, prenatal testing detects only a small proportion of all serious disorders. Many more disabilities result from the birth process; others are the product of poverty and inadequate prenatal care. The often-cited "background risk" of birth defects, 2 or 3 percent, pales beside the incidence of premature and low-birthweight babies born to the 25 percent of pregnant American women who receive inadequate or no prenatal care.

If our goal is healthy babies, focusing on the relatively small number of disabilities that can be screened genetically is myopic as well as opening the door to abuse. A far better policy—one that is more cost-effective as well—would provide all women with adequate prenatal care, improved nutrition, and freedom to end an unwanted pregnancy for whatever reasons. Research shows that women with wanted pregnancies obtain better prenatal care than those with unwanted ones (Institute of Medicine, 1989). As long as this country has the highest proportion of unwanted pregnancies of any industrialized nation, we cannot expect to have the healthiest babies.

The United States devotes sizable resources to high-tech methods that enable a few individual women to avert bearing a tiny number of affected babies. At the same time, it starves the low-tech social and medical programs essential to minimizing the far larger number of sick babies whose problems could have been avoided. While recognizing the importance of prenatal testing, we would like to add our voice to those who would like to see these priorities change.

Appendixes

Appendix A
Survey Questionnaire for Women Who Had CVS

Note: The questionnaire for amniocentesis users was identical except for questions 12 and 13. For amnio users, the word "amniocentesis" was used instead of "CVS".

COVER SHEET AND CONSENT AGREEMENT

This study is being conducted by the _____ Institute in cooperation with the Sociology and Anthropology Department at George Mason University in order to find out more about the complex social and psychological factors involved in CVS and amniocentesis. The study has been approved by the Human Subjects Review Board at George Mason University. This questionnaire is voluntary and confidential. Respondents will not be identified in any way. The information will be used for statistical purposes only.

If you agree to participate in the study, please sign the consent form below and tear it off. You may either hand it in at the office or mail it back separately from the questionnaire to ensure anonymity. Two stamped, self-addressed envelopes have been provided for your convenience, one for the consent form and one for the questionnaire.

If you have any questions about the study, or would like a summary of the results when they are available, please call Dr. Kolker.

DIRECTIONS

We prefer that you answer all questions. However, feel free to omit any questions if you would rather not answer them. In some questions more than one answer appears possible. Try to circle only the single "best" answer. Some questions call for information about your husband or partner. If you are not married or in a relationship please circle "not applicable," when answering these questions. If you need more space for comments, or do not understand any question, please write your answer on the back and indicate to which question you are referring. Please return the completed questionnaire in the supplied postage-paid envelope.

Completing the questionnaire usually takes between 20 and 45 minutes.

A.   Deciding to Have CVS

    1.   How did you first find out about CVS?

       a.   From OB/GYN or family doctor
       b.   From a friend or a relative
       c.   From a newspaper or magazine (name of paper or
           magazine_____)
       d.   From a radio or TV report (channel or
           program_____)
       e.   From another source (explain _____)

  2.   What was the most important reason why you decided to have prenatal
     diagnosis?

       a.   You were 35 or older
       b.   You had previously had a child with Down's syndrome or another
           disorder (which disorder? _____)
       c.   You had previously had an abnormal pregnancy which resulted in a
           miscarriage or abortion (please explain _____)
       d.   You or your husband are known to carry a chromosomal or genetic
           disorder such as Tay-Sachs (which disorder? _____)
       e.   Other (specify _____)

  3.   How would you describe your husband/partner's attitude toward your having
     the test?

       a.   Not applicable
       b.   He was strongly in favor
       c.   He had hesitations but was generally in favor
       d.   He had no opinion or felt the decision was up to you or your doctor
       e.   He strongly disapproved
       f.   Other (specify_____)

  4.   How would you describe your OB/GYN or family doctor's attitude toward
     your having the test?

       a.   In favor and encouraging
       b.   Neutral
       c.   Not in favor or discouraging
       d.   Never heard of test

    e.   Didn't discuss it with him/her

    f.   Other (explain_____)

5.   As far as you know, given your age and genetic history, what were the approximate chances of your pregnancy resulting in a child with a chromosomal abnormality such as Down's syndrome?

    a.   1 in 1000 or less

    b.   1 in 500

    c.   1 in 200

    d.   1 in 100

    e.   1 in 10

    f.   1 in 4

    g.   1 in 2

    h.   Don't know

6.   How would you describe this chance?

    a.   Very low chance

    b.   Moderately low chance

    c.   Moderately high chance

    d.   Very high chance

    e.   Don't know

7.   Please describe how much different types of abnormalities would concern you if you had a child with these problems. For each type of abnormality please circle the number that best describes your feelings [Response categories for each item include "very concerned," "somewhat concerned," "not sure," and "not concerned."]

    a.   Facial or bodily features that look abormal

    b.   Defects resulting in early death

    c.   Severe mental retardation

    d.   Physical handicaps which intefere with normal activities

    e.   Mild mental retardataion

    f.   Defects resulting in prolonged illness and death

    g.   Other (explain_____)

8. As far as you know, what are the approximate chances of the CVS resulting in a miscarriage or in damage to the fetus?

    a. 1 in 1000 or less
    b. 1 in 500
    c. 1 in 200
    d. 1 in 100
    e. 1 in 10
    f. 1 in 4
    g. 1 in 2
    h. Don't know

9. How would you describe this chance?

    a. Very low chance
    b. Moderately low chance
    c. Moderately high chance
    d. Very high chance
    e. Don't know

10. As far as you know, what are the approximate chances of the CVS resulting in a serious complication to yourself?

    a. 1 in 1000 or less
    b. 1 in 500
    c. 1 in 200
    d. 1 in 100
    e. 1 in 10
    f. 1 in 4
    g. 1 in 2
    h. Don't know

11. How would you describe this chance?

    a. Very low chance
    b. Moderately low chance
    c. Moderately high chance
    d. Very high chance
    e. Don't know

12. As far as you know, how does the risk of complications as a result of CVS compare with that of amniocentesis?

    a.   CVS carries a much lower risk than amniocentesis
    b.   CVS carries a slightly lower risk than amniocentesis
    c.   CVS carries about the same risk as amniocentesis
    d.   CVS carries a slightly higher risk than amniocentesis
    e.   CVS carries a much higher risk than amniocentesis
    f.   Nobody knows for sure

[Question 12 for amniocentesis users: When you decided to have amniocentesis, did you know about CVS?

    1. Yes
    2. No]

13. What were the reasons why you chose CVS instead of amniocentesis? For each reason below please circle the number that best describes your feeling [Response categories for each item include "very important," "somewhat important," "not important."]

    a.   Earlier testing means earlier reassurance that everything is O.K.
    b.   Earlier testing of possible abnormalities would make it easier to have an abortion should one be decided upon.
    c.   Earlier diagnosis of possible abnormalities would make it easier to carry the pregnancy to term and plan for a child with an abnormality.
    d.   Earlier diagnosis of the sex would make it easier to plan for a boy or a girl.

[Question 13 for amniocentesis users: If yes, what was the most important reason why you decided to have amniocentesis rather than CVS?

    a.   It was too late in the pregnancy for CVS.
    b.   The risks of CVS are potentially higher than the risks of amniocentesis
    c.   Other. Explain _____]

B.   The Procedure and the Results

14. How would you describe your concerns <u>before</u> the CVS? For each statement please circle the number that best expresses your feelings [Response categories include "strong," "mild," "none."]

    a.   Concern about possible miscarriage
    b.   Concern about damage to the fetus
    c.   Concern about pain or discomfort
    d.   Concern about the diagnosis
    e.   Concern about having to decide on abortion
    f.   Concern about the test's unknown aspects
    g.   Other (Explain _____)

15. How would you describe your concerns <u>during</u> the procedure? For each statement please circle the number that applies [Response categories include "strong," "mild," "none."]

    a.   Physical pain or discomfort
    b.   Concern about possible miscarriage
    c.   Concern about possible damage to the fetus
    d.   Concern about the diagnosis
    e.   Concern about having to repeat the procedure if not enough cells are obtained
    f.   Other (Explain _____)

16. How would you describe your reaction to the sonogram?

    a.   Happy to see the fetus for the first time
    b.   Concerned that something might be wrong with the fetus
       (Explain _____)
    c.   No particular reaction
    d.   Other (Explain _____)

17. Did your husband/partner accompany you during the procedure?

    a.   Not applicable (go to question 19)
    b.   Yes (answer question 18)
    c.   No (go to question 19)

18. If your husband/partner accompanied you, what were his reactions? [Response categories include "strong," "mild," "none."]

    a. Concern about possible miscarriage
    b. Concern about possible damage to the fetus
    c. Concern about your own pain or discomfort
    d. Concern about the diagnosis
    e. Other (Explain _____)

19. How would you describe the counseling you received at the ____ Institute before the procedure?

    a. Very useful (Explain _____)
    b. Moderately useful (Explain _____)
    c. Not useful (Explain _____)

20. How long did you have to wait for the results of the CVS? ____days

21. How would you describe your feelings during the waiting period? For each statement please circle the number that best describes your feelings. [Response categories include "strong," "mild," "none."]

    a. Concern about possible miscarriage as a result of the procedure
    b. Concern about damage to the fetus as a result of the procedure
    c. Concern about the diagnosis
    d. Concern about having to decide on abortion
    e. Other (Explain _____)

22. What were the results of the CVS?

    a. Normal fetus, everything is O.K. (please go to question 28)
    b. Down's syndrome
    c. Another disorder or abnormality. Please specify

    _____

IF THE RESULTS SHOWED AN ABNORMALITY, PLEASE ANSWER
QUESTIONS 23-27

23. What did you decide to do about the pregnancy?

a. Have an abortion
b. Carry the pregnancy to term

24. How long did it take you to arrive at the decision after finding out the
results?

_____weeks _____days _____hours

25. If you had an abortion, how far along was the pregnancy when you had it?

_____weeks

26. How would you describe the reaction of people with whom you have
discussed the abortion decision? [Response categories for each item include,
"favored abortion," "thought decision should be up to you," "favored keeping
the pregnancy," "didn't discuss," "not applicable."]

a. Your husband/partner
b. Other relatives
c. Your friends
d. Your clergyperson
e. Your doctor
f. Your genetic counselor
g. Other (specify _____)

27. Did you consult any books, articles, or other written information before
arriving at the decision?

a. Yes   b. No

(Please skip to question 31)

IF THE RESULTS WERE NORMAL, PLEASE ANSWER QUESTIONS 28-30

28. Did you find out the baby's sex at the time you received the results of the CVS?

   a. Yes--a girl
   b. Yes--a boy
   c. No

29. What was your reaction to the news about the baby's sex?

   a. Very pleased about the baby's sex
   b. Mildly pleased about the baby's sex
   c. It didn't make any difference
   d. Mildly disappointed about the baby's sex
   e. Very disappointed about the baby's sex
   f. Was not told
   g. Other (Explain _____)

30. What was your husband/partner's reaction?

   a. Not applicable
   b. Very pleased about the baby's sex
   c. Mildly pleased about the baby's sex
   d. It didn't make any difference
   e. Mildly disappointed about the baby's sex
   f. Very disappointed about the baby's sex
   g. Was not told
   h. Other (Explain _____)

C. Feelings about Abortion

31. How would you describe your feelings about the abortion rights controversy? Please indicate whether you agree or disagree that in general, women should have the right to have an abortion for each of the reasons below. If you agree, please indicate up to what point in the pregnancy abortion should be allowed for each reason. [Response categories for each item include, "yes--any time in the pregnancy," "yes--up to the 6th month," "yes--up to the 3rd month," "not sure," "never"].

A woman should be able to have an abortion if:

a. She is unmarried and doesn't want to have a baby.
b. Her health is endangered by the pregnancy.
c. There is a certainty of a fatal birth defect such as Tay-Sachs.
d. There is a 1 in 2 chance of a fatal birth defect.
e. There is certainty of a nonfatal birth defect such as Down's syndrome.
f. There is a 1 in 2 chance of a nonfatal birth defect.
g. She is married but doesn't want to have a child at this time.
h. Her life is endangered by the pregnancy.
i. The family has a low income and can't afford any more children.
j. She is married but doesn't want any more children.
k. The pregnancy resulted from rape or incest.
l. The couple does not want a child of sex that was diagnosed before birth.

Comments_____

32. Under what circumstances would you consider an abortion <u>for yourself</u>?
    Please circle the appropriate number for each reason. [Same items as in
    Question 31, substituting "you were" for "she is." Same response categories.]

33. Do your religious beliefs have any influence on your views about abortion?

    a. No
    b. Yes (Explain _____)

D. <u>Background Questions</u>

34. What was your age at the time of the CVS? ____

35. In what month of the pregnancy are you now? ____

36. Was this pregnancy planned or unplanned?

    a. Unplanned.
    b. Planned. How long did it take you to get pregnant? ___years ___mos.

37. How many pregnancies have you had prior to this one? ____

38. How many living children do you have? ____

39. How many unsuccessful pregnancies (that is, pregnancies not resulting in living children) did you have prior to this one? _____

40. If you have had unsuccessful pregnancies, how many times have you had the following outcomes:

    a. Spontaneous abortion (miscarriage) ____ times
    b. Therapeutic abortion (abortion for reasons of health or fetal abnormality) ____ times (Explain _____)
    c. Elective abortion (abortion for a reason other than health or abnormality) ____ times
    d. Stillbirth or infant death ____ times

41. Have you ever had amniocentesis before?

    a. No
    b. Yes. How many times? ____

42. If you have had amniocentesis before, what were the results?

    a. Normal results ____ times
    b. Abnormal results ____ times (Please explain _____)

43. Have you ever had CVS before?

    a. No
    b. Yes.

44. If you have had CVS before, what were the results?

    a. Normal results
    b. Abnormal results (Please explain _____)

45. Are you currently employed for pay?

    a. No
    b. Yes, part time (approximately how many hours per week? ____)
    c. Yes, full time (approximately how many hours per week? ____)

46. a.   If you are currently employed, what is your job? _____
    b.   If you are not currently employed, what was your last job?

    _____

47. What is your husband/partner's job? _____

48. What is the highest level of education you have completed?

    a.   Some elementary school (less than 8 years)
    b.   Completed elementary school (8 years)
    c.   Some high school (9 to 11 years)
    d.   Completed high school (12 years)
    e.   Some college (1-3 years)
    f.   Completed college (4 years)
    g.   Some graduate or professional school
    h.   Completed graduate or professional school. Degrees awarded_____

49. What is the highest level of education your husband/partner has completed?

    a.   Not applicable
    b.   Some elementary school (less than 8 years)
    c.   Completed elementary school (8 years)
    d.   Some high school (9 to 11 years)
    e.   Completed high school (12 years)
    f.   Some college (1-3 years)
    g.   Completed college (4 years)
    h.   Some graduate or professional school
    i.   Completed graduate or professional school. Degrees awarded_____

50. What is your current religious preference or affiliation?

    a.   None
    b.   Protestant. What denomination? _____
    c.   Roman Catholic
    d.   Greek Orthodox
    e.   Jewish
    f.   Moslem
    g.   Other_____

51. How often do you attend religious services?

    a. Never
    b. Less than once a year
    c. About once or twice a year
    d. Several times a year
    e. About once a month
    f. Two or three times a month
    g. Nearly every week
    h. Every week
    i. Several times a week

52. What is your current household income?

    a. Less than $10,000 per year
    b. $11-20,000 per year
    c. $21-40,000 per year
    d. $41-60,000 per year
    e. $61-80,000 per year
    f. $81-100,000 per year
    g. More than $100,000 per year

53. Did your medical insurance pay for the CVS?

    a. No
    b. Partly. How much did you have to pay? _____
    c. Yes--the whole amount
    d. Don't know yet

54. Are you planning to have any more children?

    a. No
    b. Not sure
    c. Yes. How many? _____

55. If you become pregnant again, would you want to have CVS or amniocentesis?

    a. Neither CVS nor amniocentesis (Please explain why

    _____)

    b. Probably CVS (Please explain why _____)

c.   Probably amniocentesis (Please explain why_____)

****

You have now completed the questionnaire. Please take a moment to answer some questions about the questionnaire itself. Use the back if you need more space.

A.   Were any questions hard to understand? Please tell us which ones.

B.   Did any questions make you uncomfortable when answering them? Please tell us which ones.

C.   Did answering the questions benefit you in any way? Again, please tell us which ones.

D.   Have we left out anything that is important to you? If so, what?

THANK YOU VERY MUCH FOR YOUR COOPERATION! IF YOU HAVE ANY QUESTIONS ABOUT THE STUDY, OR WOULD LIKE A SUMMARY OF THE RESULTS WHEN THEY ARE AVAILABLE, PLEASE CALL DR. KOLKER.

Appendix B
Interview Guide for Genetic Counselors

1. Do you do both amniocentesis and CVS at this center? Approximately how many CVS's have you done? Do clients come here specifically for the purpose of having one or the other or do they make a choice after counseling?

2. If a client showed no preference, would you recommend CVS or amnio? Why?

3. At what point in the pregnancy do you do CVS? What about amniocentesis? How long is the waiting period for the results with each?

4. Approximately what is the refusal rate here for both amnio and CVS? I.e., how many clients decline any prenatal diagnosis after counseling? What reasons do they give? How do you feel about these reasons, i.e., are there "good" and "bad" reasons for declining prenatal diagnosis?

5. In an ordinary prenatal diagnosis session for maternal age, what points do you think most important to cover? Do you cover the following points usually, sometimes, rarely, or never:

   a. What amnio feels like
   b. What CVS feels like
   c. The need for AFP following CVS
   d. The rate of false positives with AFP
   e. The rate of false positives with CVS (mosaicisms)
   f. The rate of complications following CVS and amnio
   g. What Down's syndrome is like
   h. What other genetic conditions are like (are there any that you name?)
   i. Sex chromosome abnormalities
   j. Neural tube abnormalities
   k. Risk rates for Down's syndrome at various ages
   l. Risk rates for other abnormalities
   m. Family genetic history
   n. What are their choices if abnormalities are found (Do you raise the issue of termination or do you wait for them to?)

o.   How an abortion would be done

p.   What sonograms are

6. How often do people bring up religious objections to abortion? How do you handle this?

7. Do you discuss the possible effect of a disorder on the child's or the family's life? What about the economic burden of the disorder?

8. In counseling sessions, do you sometimes see disagreements between spouses about either the test or the abortion decision?

9. What makes for a good counseling session? A bad session? What do you look for in a client?

10. Some counselors try very hard to be nondirective and others feel more directive counseling is appropriate under some circumstances. Where would you say you fall on this continuum? Under what circumstances do you find you are most directive in your counseling? Least directive?

11. Please tell me about the bad results you have had to report. How many cases of Down's syndrome? Neural tube defects? Other abnormalities? How many have terminated the pregnancy? Of those who choose not to terminate, what reasons do they give? How important is follow-up counseling? Are there any support groups for therapeutic abortion?

12. I understand that with CVS, sometimes the sonogram reveals a nonviable pregnancy. How often does this happen? What happens at this point? How do you handle it?

13. In your experience have you encountered couples who want prenatal diagnosis just to find out the fetal sex? Do you know of any abortions of a healthy fetus with the "wrong" sex? Does CVS, with its earlier timing, make a difference in these cases? How do you feel about people who come in for this reason?

14. If you were considering only the mathematical probability of occurrence of a genetic or chromosomal abnormality, how would you describe the following odds in your own mind? (very low, low, moderate, high, very high)

    a.   1 in 1000 or less
    b.   1 in 500
    c.   1 in 200
    d.   1 in 100
    e.   1 in 10
    f.   1 in 4
    g.   1 in 2

15. How would you describe the same odds for the risk of procedural complications?

16. In your opinion what's the ideal age at which to start doing CVS or amnio?

17. If you or your daughter or sister were pregnant, would you have or advise her to have CVS or amnio? At what age would you start?

18. If (when) you were pregnant, would you have wanted to know the sex? Why or why not?

19. Would you personally have an abortion for fetal abnormalities? Which conditions would you abort (not abort) for?

20. Have you had any personal experience with birth defects? (self, children, other people close to you).

21. Tell me about your education, including training for genetic counseling (degrees and majors or fields).

22. Why did you decide to go into genetic counseling?

23. Do you see yourself doing genetic counseling in 5 years?

Thanks very much for your help!

Appendix C
Questions about Abortion Attitudes in the General Social Survey

Please tell me whether or not *you* think it should be possible for a pregnant woman to obtain a *legal* abortion if . . . [Possible answers: yes, no, don't know]

A. If there is a strong chance of serious defect in the baby?

B. If she is married and does not want any more children?

C. If the woman's own health is seriously endangered by the pregnancy?

D. If the family has a very low income and cannot afford any more children?

E. If she became pregnant as a result of rape?

F. If she is not married and does not want to marry the man?

G. The woman wants it for any reason?

Appendix D
Occupational Prestige and Socioeconomic Status

A commonly used measure of social inequality is the index of socio-economic status, composed of the respondent's income, education, and occupational prestige. To understand our respondents' socio-economic status we asked about their income, education, and occupation. Since we were interested in the characteristics of both parents, we asked about the education and occupation of the respondent's husband or partner as well.

Our measures of occupation turned out to be not useful. We used the scale of occupational prestige developed by the National Opinion Research Center (NORC) in Chicago (Hodge, Siegel, and Rossi, 1966). This scale assigns a prestige score, from a high of 100 to a low of 20, to various occupations. There are nearly 1,000 occupations for which prestige scores are available in the *General Social Survey of the United States* (GSS).

Yet, when we coded our respondents' occupations and those of their partners, we found out that many of these occupations were not listed in the GSS. Our respondents and their spouses, residents of the Washington, D.C. and San Diego metropolitan areas, were employed mostly in professional and managerial fields; many were in the military, the civil service, or the not-for-profit sector. No standard occupational codes and prestige rankings have been devised for such jobs as defense contractor, grants coordinator, military officer, and executive officer of a health group. We had to assign these occupations to the catch-all categories, "Professional, Technical and Kindred" and "Managers and Administrators—Not Elsewhere Classified." These "other" categories rank in the middle of the prestige scale (NORC scores 50 and 51 out of 100). Nearly a quarter of our respondents fell into these categories. The result was that the prestige scores of our sample did not adequately reflect their true occupational prestige.

The mean occupational prestige for our respondents was 52.6; that of their husbands, 57.2. The mean score for the U.S. population is 40.2 (*General Social Survey,* 1985). There was almost no difference between the scores of amniocentesis and CVS users. Because of the relative lack of sensitivity of this measure, we decided not to use it in our analysis.

We therefore used the other two variables, education and income, to indicate the respondent's socio-economic status.

References

Abdallah, A. A. 1982. "Shari'ah Point of View on Abortion." Paper presented at the Faculty of Law Seminar, Bayero University, Kano, Nigeria, February 24.

Adler, Bernard, and Theodore Kushnick. 1982. "Genetic Counseling in Prenatally Diagnosed Trisomy 18 and 21: Psychosocial Aspects." *Pediatrics* 69: 94–99.

American College of Obstetricians and Gynecologists (ACOG). 1985. "Professional Liability Implications of AFP Tests." *DPL ALERT,* May.

American Society of Human Genetics (ASHG). 1987. "Policy Statement for Maternal Serum Alpha-Fetoprotein Screening Programs." *American Journal of Human Genetics* 40: 75–82.

Anspach, Renee. 1993. *Deciding Who Lives: Fateful Choices in the Intensive Care Nursery.* Berkeley: University of California Press.

Ashton, Jean. 1976. "Amniocentesis: Safe But Still Ambiguous." *Hastings Center Report* 6(1): 5-6.

Atrash, Hani K., H. T. MacKay, Nancy J. Binkin, and Carol J. R. Hogue. 1987. "Legal Abortion Mortality in the United States: 1972 to 1982." *American Journal of Obstetrics and Gynecology* 156: 605–612.

Badagliacco, Joanne M. 1989. "Does Motherhood Matter in Abortion Choice Among American Women?" Paper presented at the Meetings of the American Sociological Association, San Francisco, California.

Barela, Alicia I., Gary Kleinman, Ira M. Golditch, David J. Menke, W. Allen Hogge, and Mitchell S. Golbus. 1986. "Septic Shock with Renal Failure after Chorionic Villus Sampling." *American Journal of Obstetrics and Gynecology* 154: 1100–1102.

Bartels, Dianne M., Bonnie S. LeRoy, and Arthur L. Caplan, eds. 1993. *Prescribing Our Future: Ethical Challenges in Genetic Counseling.* New York: Aldine de Gruyter.

Begleiter, Michael L., Debra Collins, and Karen Greendale. 1981. "Professional Status Survey." *Perspectives in Genetic Counseling* 3(4): 1–2.

Benderly, Beryl Lieff. 1984. *Thinking About Abortion*. Garden City, N.Y.: Doubleday.

Bennet, Neil G., ed. 1983. *Sex Selection of Children*. New York: Academic Press.

Berger, Peter L., and Thomas Luckmann. 1967. *The Social Construction of Reality*. Garden City, N.Y.: Anchor Books.

Bernhardt, B. A., and R. M. Bannerman. 1984. "The Influence of Obstetricians on the Utilization of Amniocentesis." *Prenatal Diagnosis* 4: 43–49.

Beutler, Ernest. 1992. "Gaucher Disease: New Molecular Approaches to Diagnosis and Treatment." *Science* 256: 794–799, May 8.

Billings, Paul R., Mel A. Kohn, and Margaret de Cuevas, et al. 1992. "Discrimination as a Consequence of Genetic Testing." *American Journal of Human Genetics* 50: 476–482.

Black, Rita Beck. 1989. "A 1 and 6 Month Follow-Up of Prenatal Diagnosis Patients Who Lost Pregnancies." *Prenatal Diagnosis* 9: 795–804.

Blatt, Robin J. R. 1988. *Prenatal Tests*. New York: Random House.

Blumberg, Bruce D. 1984. "The Emotional Implications of Prenatal Diagnosis," in Emery and Rillen, eds., *Psychological Aspects of Genetic Counseling,* Emery and Pullen: 201-218.

Blumberg, Bruce D., Mitchell S. Golbus, and Karl H. Hanson. 1975. "The Psychological Sequelae of Abortion Performed for a Genetic Indication." *American Journal of Obstetrics and Gynecology* 122: 799–808, August 1.

Bonnicksen, Andrea. 1992. "Genetic Diagnosis of Human Embryos." *Hastings Center Report: Special Supplement*: S5–S11, July/August.

Borg, Susan, and Judith Lasker. 1981. *When Pregnancy Fails*. Boston: Beacon Press.

Bosk, Charles L. 1985. "The Fieldworker as Watcher and Witness." *Hastings Center Report* 15(3): 10–14.

Bosk, Charles L. 1992. *All God's Mistakes: Genetic Counseling in a Pediatric Hospital*. Chicago: University of Chicago Press.

Brambati, Bruno, Giuseppe Simoni, and Sergio Fabro, eds. 1986. *Chorionic Villus Sampling*. New York: Marcel Dekker.

Brandenburg, Helen, Coen G. Gho, G. J. Milena Jahoda, Theo Stijnen, Hans Bakker, and Jury W. Wladimiroff. 1992. "Effect of Chorionic Villus Sampling on Utilization of Prenatal Diagnosis in Women of Advanced Maternal Age." *Clinical Genetics* 41: 239–242.

Brandenburg, Helen, L. Van-der-Zwan, G. J. Milena Jahoda, Theo Stijnen, and Jury W. Wladimiroff. 1991. "Prenatal Diagnosis in Advanced Maternal Age. Amniocentesis or CVS, A Patient's Choice or Lack of Information?" *Prenatal Diagnosis* 11(9): 685–690, September.

Breslau, Naomi. 1983. "Care of Disabled Children and Women's Time Use." *Medical Care* 21: 620–629.

Breslau, Naomi. 1987. "Abortion of Defective Fetuses: Attitudes of Mothers of Congenitally Impaired Children." *Journal of Marriage and Family* 49(4): 839–884.

Brown, Judy. 1989. "The Choice." *Journal of the American Medical Association* 262 (19): 2735.

Burke, B. Meredith, 1989. " 'Life Goes On': A Moral Burden." Letter to the Editor. *New York Times,* November 5, p. 21.

Burton, Barbara K., Charlene J. Schulz, and I. Laurence. 1992. "Limb Anomalies Associated with Chorionic Villus Sampling." *Obstetrics and Gynecology* 79: 726–730.

Canadian Collaborative CVS-Amniocentesis Clinical Trial Group, 1989. "Multicentre Randomized Clinical Trial of Chorion Villus Sampling and Amniocentesis." *The Lancet,* January 7, pp. 1–6.

Caplan, Arthur L. 1993. "Neutrality Is Not Morality: The Ethics of Genetic Counseling." In Bartels et al., eds., *Prescribing Our Future,* pp. 149–165.

Carlson, Dru E, and Lawrence D. Platt. 1992. "Ultrasound Detection of Genetic Anomalies." *Journal of Reproductive Medicine* 37(5): 419–426, May.

Chervin, Alma, et al. 1977. "Amniocentesis for Prenatal Diagnosis: Subjective Patient Response." *New York State Journal of Medicine,* August, pp. 1406–1408.

Childress, James F. 1980. "Negative and Positive Rights." *Hastings Center Report* 10: 19.

Clark, Liana R. 1985. "Sex Preselection: The Advent of the Made-to-Order Child." *The Pharos,* Fall, pp. 2–7.

Coffman, Mary A., Sharyl K. Kinney, Joyce N. Shissler, et al. 1993. "Reproductive Genetic Services in Rural Oklahoma." *Fetal Diagnosis and Therapy* 8: 128–141, April.

Cohen, Felissa L. 1984. *Clinical Genetics in Nursing Practice.* Philadelphia: J. B. Lippincott.

Comte, Auguste. 1896. *The Positive Philosophy of Auguste Comte.* Translated and condensed by Harriet Martineau. London: Bell Publishers.

Coombs, Clyde. 1977. "The Preference for Sex of Children Among U.S. Couples." *Family Planning Perspectives* 9(6): 259–265.

Corea, Genoveffa. 1985. *The Mother Machine: Reproductive Technologies from Artificial Insemination to Artificial Wombs.* New York: Harper & Row.

Cowan, Ruth Schwartz. 1992. "Genetic Technology and Reproductive Choice: An Ethics for Autonomy." In Kevles and Hood, eds., *The Code of Codes: Scientific and Social Issues in the Human Genome Project,* pp. 244–263.

Culliton, Barbara J. 1975. "Amniocentesis: HEW Backs Test for Prenatal Diagnosis of Disease." *Science* 190: 537–540, November.

Cunningham, George C., and Kenneth W. Kizer. 1990. "Maternal Serum Alpha-Fetoprotein Screening Activities of State Health Agencies: A Survey." *American Journal of Human Genetics* 47: 899–903.

Cystic Fibrosis Foundation. 1991. Bethesda, Md.: Cystic Fibrosis Registry.

D'Alton, Mary E., and Alan H. DeCherney. 1993. "Prenatal Diagnosis." *New England Journal of Medicine* 328(2): 114–120, January 14.

Dicker, Marvin, and Lois Dicker. 1978. "Genetic Counseling as an Occupational Specialty: A Sociological Perspective." *Social Biology* 25(4): 272–278.

Dixon, Richard D., and Diane E. Levy. 1985. "Sex of Children: A Community Analysis of Preferences and Predetermination Attitudes." *The Sociological Quarterly* 26(2): 251–271.

Drugan, Arie, Anne Greb, Mark Paul Johnson, et al. 1990. "Determinants of Parental Decisions to Abort for Chromosome Abnormalities." *Prenatal Diagnosis* 10: 483–490.

Duster, Troy. 1990. *Backdoor to Eugenics.* New York: Routledge.

d'Ydewalle, Gery, and Gerry Evers-Kiebooms. 1987. "Experiments on Genetic Risk

Perception and Decision Making: Explorative Studies." *Birth Defects* 23(2): 209–225.

Edwards, Janice. 1990. "Professional Status Survey Results." *Perspectives in Genetic Counseling* 12(2): 7–10. Special summer supplement.

Ekwo, Edem E., Brenda F. Seals, Jae-On Kim, Roger A. Williamson, and James W. Hanson. 1985. "Factors Influencing Maternal Estimates of Genetic Risk." *American Journal of Medical Genetics* 20: 491–504.

Elias, Sherman and George J. Annas. 1983. "Perspectives on Fetal Surgery." *American Journal of Obstetrics and Gynecology* 145: 807–812.

Elias, Sherman, and Joe L. Simpson. 1992. *Maternal Serum Screening for Genetic Disorders*. New York: Churchill Livingstone, Inc.

Elkins, Thomas E., Thomas G. Stovall, Sidney Wilroy, and John V. Dacus. 1986. "Attitudes of Mothers of Children with Down Syndrome Concerning Amniocentesis, Abortion, and Prenatal Genetic Counseling Techniques." *Obstetrics and Gynecology* 68(2): 181–184, August.

Emery, Alan and Ian Pullen, eds. 1984. *Psychological Aspects of Genetic Counseling*. San Diego, CA: Academic Press.

Evans, Mark I., S. F. Bottoms, G. C. Critchfield, Anne Greb, and J. J. LaFerla. 1990. "Parental Perceptions of Genetic Risk: Correlation with Choice of Prenatal Diagnosis Procedure." *International Journal of Obstetrics and Gynaecology* 31(1): 25–28, January.

Evans, Mark I., S. F. Bottoms, Theresa Carlucci, et al. 1988. "Determinants of Altered Anxiety After Abnormal Maternal Serum Alpha-Fetoprotein Screening." *American Journal of Obstetrics and Gynecology* 159: 1501–1504.

Evans, Mark I., John C. Fletcher, Alan O. Dixler, and Joseph D. Schulman, eds. 1989. *Fetal Diagnosis and Therapy: Science, Ethics, and the Law*. Philadelphia: J. B. Lippincott.

Ewigman, Bernard G., James P. Crane, Fredric D. Firgoletto, et al. 1993. "Effect of Prenatal Ultrasound Screening on Prenatal Outcome." *New England Journal of Medicine* 329 (12): 821–827.

Faden, R. R., A. J. Chwalow, K. Quaid, et al. 1987. "Prenatal Screening and Pregnant Women's Attitudes Toward the Abortion of Defective Fetuses." *American Journal of Public Health* 77: 288–290.

Farrant, Wendy. 1985. "Who's for Amniocentesis? The Politics of Prenatal Screening." In Homans, ed., *The Sexual Politics of Reproduction*, pp. 96–123. England: Gower.

Faulkner, William. 1935. *Absalom, Absalom!* New York: Random House.

Fava, Giovanni A., et al. 1982. "Psychological Reactions to Amniocentesis: A Controlled Study." *American Journal of Obstetrics and Gynecology* 143(5): 509–513, July 1.

Firth, H. V., P. A. Boyd, P. Chamberlain, et al. 1991. "Severe Limb Abnormalities After Chorion Villus Sampling at 56–66 Days' Gestation." *The Lancet* 337: 762–763.

Fischhoff, Baruch, Sarah Lichtenstein, Paul Slovic, Stephen Derby, and Ralph Keeney. 1981. *Acceptable Risk*. Cambridge: Cambridge University Press.

Fisher, Marc. 1992. "Germany's Fetal Position." *Washington Post,* October 29, pp. C1 and C5.

Fletcher, John C. 1980. "Ethics and Amniocentesis for Fetal Sex Identification." *Hastings Center Report* 10: 15–18.

Fletcher, John C. 1983. "Ethics and Public Policy: Should Sex Choice Be Discouraged?" In Bennet, ed., *Sex Selection of Children,* pp. 213–252.

Fletcher, John C. 1986. "Ethical Issues in Clinical Trials of First Trimester Prenatal Diagnosis." In Brambati et al., eds., *Chorionic Villus Sampling,* pp. 275–301.

Fraccaro, Marco, Giuseppe Simoni, and Bruno Brambati, eds. 1985. *First Trimester Fetal Diagnosis.* Berlin: Springer-Verlag.

Fryers, Thomas. 1984. *The Epidemiology of Severe Intellectual Impairment.* London: Academic Press.

Furhmann, W. 1989. "Impact, Logistics and Prospects of Traditional Prenatal Diagnosis." *Clinical Genetics* 36: 378–385.

Furness, M. E. 1990. "Fetal Ultrasound for Entertainment?" *The Medical Journal of Australia* 153: 371, October 1.

Gargan, Edward A. 1991. "Ultrasonic Tests Skew Ratio of Births in India." *New York Times,* June 13.

Garver, Kenneth L. 1989. "Update on MSAFP Policy Statement from the American Society of Human Genetics." *American Journal of Human Genetics* 45: 332–334.

Gegor, Carolyn L. 1992. "Obstetric Ultrasound: Who Should Perform Sonograms?" *Birth* 19(2): 92–99, June.

General Social Survey of the United States, 1972–1985: Cumulative Code Book. 1985. Chicago: National Opinion Research Center, University of Chicago.

Gilbert, Kathleen R. 1988. "Parental Grief: An Interactive Model." Paper presented at the Meetings of the Society for the Study of Social Problems, Atlanta, Georgia.

Gill, Mike, Victoria Murday, and Joan Slack. 1987. "An Economic Appraisal of Screening for Down's Syndrome in Pregnancy Using Maternal Age and Serum Alpha Fetoprotein Concentration." *Social Science and Medicine* 24(9): 725–731.

Gilligan, Carol G. 1982. *In a Different Voice.* Cambridge, Mass.: Harvard University Press.

Gilroy, Faith, and Roberta Steinbacher. 1983. "Preselection of Child's Sex: Technological Utilization and Feminism." *Psychological Reports* 53: 671–676.

Golbus, Mitchell S., William D. Loughman, Charles J. Epstein, et al. 1979. "Prenatal Diagnosis in 3000 Amniocenteses." *New England Journal of Medicine* 300(4): 157–163.

Golbus, Mitchell S. 1992. Editorial, "Prenatal Diagnosis Availability." *American Journal of Medical Genetics* 42: 800.

Goldberg, James D., Alison E. Porter, and Mitchell S. Golbus. 1990. "Current Assessment of Fetal Losses as a Direct Consequence of Chorionic Villus Sampling." *American Journal of Medical Genetics* 35: 174–177.

Goldstein, Henri, and John Philip. 1990. "A Cost-Benefit Analysis of Prenatal Diagnosis by Amniocentesis in Denmark." *Clinical Genetics* 37: 241–263.

Gorney, Cynthia. 1988. "Whose Body Is It, Anyway?" *Washington Post,* Style Section, pp. D1, D3.

Gouldner, Alvin. 1957. "Cosmopolitans and Locals." *Administrative Science Quarterly* 2: 281–306.

Green, Jeffrey E., Andrew Dorfmann, Shirley L. Jones, Samuel Bender, Laurel Patton, Patricia Robinson, and Joseph D. Schulman. 1988. "Chorionic Villus Sampling: Experience with an Initial 940 Cases." *Obstetrics and Gynecology* 71(2): 208–212.

Green, Rose. 1992. "Letter to a Genetic Counselor." *Journal of Genetic Counseling* 1(1): 55–70.

Grimes, David A. 1992. "Surgical Management of Abortion." In John D. Thompson and John A. Rock, eds., *TeLinde's Operative Gynecology,* 7th ed., pp. 317–342. Philadelphia: Lippincott.

Guillemin, Jeanne H., and Lynda L. Holmstrom. 1986. *Mixed Blessings: Intensive Care for Newborns.* New York: Oxford University Press.

Haddow, James E., Glenn E. Palomaki, George J. Knight, et. al. 1992. "Prenatal Screening for Down's Syndrome with Use of Maternal Serum Markers." *New England Journal of Medicine* 27: 588–593, August 27.

Henshaw, Stanley K., and Jane Silverman. 1988. "The Characteristics and Prior Contraceptive Use of U.S. Abortion Patients." *Family Planning Perspectives* 20(4): 158–168, July/August.

Hern, Warren M. 1984. *Abortion Practice.* Philadelphia: J. B. Lippincott.

Hern, Warren M., and Billie Corrigan. 1980. "What About Us? Staff Reactions to D & E." Advances in Planned Parenthood, Vol. 15. Report in *Excerpta Medica.*

Herz, Elisabeth. 1984. "Psychological Repercussions of Pregnancy Loss." *Psychiatric Annals* 14(6): 454–457.

Hobbins, John C., Peter A. Grannum, Roberto Romero, et al. 1985. "Percutaneous Umbilical Blood Sampling." *American Journal of Obstetrics and Gynecology* 152(1): 1–6.

Hodge, R. W., P. M. Siegel, and Peter H. Rossi. 1966. "Occupational Prestige in the United States: 1925–1963." In Rhinehart Bendix and Seymour M. Lipset, eds., *Class, Status, and Power,* 2nd ed., pp. 322–334. New York: Free Press.

Hodge, Susan E. 1989. "Waiting for the Amniocentesis." *New England Journal of Medicine* 320(1): 63–64. January 5.

Holtzman, Neil A., and Mark A. Rothstein, 1992. "Eugenics and Genetic Discrimination." *American Journal of Human Genetics* 50: 457–459.

Homans, Hilary, ed. 1985. *The Sexual Politics of Reproduction.* London, England: Gower.

Hook, Ernest B. 1981. "Rates of Chromosome Abnormalities at Different Maternal Ages." *Obstetrics and Gynecology* 58: 282–285.

Hook, Ernest B., Phillip K. Cross, and Dina M. Schreinemachers. 1983. "Chromosomal Abnormality Rates at Amniocentesis and in Live-born Babies." *Journal of the American Medical Association* 249: 2034–2038.

Horowitz, Joy, 1989. " 'Life Goes On' Stretches Reality, Within Reason." *New York Times,* October 22, Arts & Leisure Section, p. 37.

Hubbard, Ruth. 1984. "Personal Courage Is Not Enough: Some Hazards of Childbearing in the 1980s." In Rita Arditti, Renate Duelli Klein, and Shelley Minden, eds., *Test-Tube Women: What Future for Motherhood?,* pp. 331–356. London: Pandora Press (Routledge & Kegan Paul).

Hubbard, Ruth. 1988. "Eugenics: New Tools, Old Ideas." In Elaine H. Baruch, Amadeo F. D'Adamo, and Joni Seager, eds., *Embryos, Ethics, and Women's Rights: Exploring the New Reproductive Technologies,* pp. 225–235. New York: Haworth Press.

Institute of Medicine, National Academy of Sciences. 1989. *Prenatal Care.*

Jackson, Laird G. 1985. *CVS Newsletter* 32. Philadelphia: Jefferson Medical College, July 26.

Jackson, Laird G. 1985a. "First-Trimester Diagnosis of Fetal Genetic Disorders." *Hospital Practice,* March 15, pp. 39–48.

Jackson, Laird G. 1985b. "Chorion Villus Sampling." *Jefferson Alumni Bulletin,* Spring, pp. 2–7.

Jackson, Laird G., and Ronald J. Wapner. 1987. "Risks of Chorion Villus Sampling." *Bailliere's Clinical Obstetrics and Gynaecology* 1(3): 513–531, September.

Jackson, Laird G., Julia M. Zachary, Sarah E. Fowler, et al. 1992. "A Randomized Comparison of Transcervical and Transabdominal Chorionic-Villus Sampling." *New England Journal of Medicine* 327: 594–598, August 27.

Jeffery, Patricia, Roger Jeffery, and Andrew Lyon. 1988. *Labor Pains and Labor Power: Women and Childbearing in India.* London: Zed Books.

Jeffery, Roger, Patricia Jeffery, and Andrew Lyon. 1984. "Female Infanticide and Amniocentesis." *Social Science and Medicine* 19(11): 1207–1212.

Johnson, Susan R., and Thomas E. Elkins. 1988. "Ethical Issues in Prenatal Diagnosis." *Clinical Obstetrics and Gynecology* 31(2): 408–417.

Kaffe, Sara, and Lillian Y. F. Hsu. 1992. "Maternal Serum Alpha-Fetoprotein Screening and Fetal Chromosome Anomalies: Is Lowering Maternal Age for Amniocentesis Preferable?" *American Journal of Medical Genetics* 42: 801–806.

Kahneman, Daniel, and Amos Tversky. 1972. "Subjective Probability: A Judgment of Representativeness." *Cognitive Psychology* 3: 430–454.

Kahneman, Daniel, and Amos Tversky. 1979. "Prospect Theory: An Analysis of Decision Under Risk." *Econometrica* 4(2): 263–291.

Kahneman, Daniel, and Amos Tversky. 1982. "The Psychology of Preference." *Scientific American* 246: 160–171, January.

Kazazian, Haig H. 1980. "Prenatal Diagnosis for Sex Choice: A Medical Review." *Hastings Center Report* 10: 17–18.

Kazy, Zoltan., I. S. Rozovsky, and V. A. Bakahrev. 1982. "Chorion Biopsy in Early Pregnancy: A Method of Early Prenatal Diagnosis for Inherited Disorders." *Prenatal Diagnosis* 2: 39.

Keenan, Kathy L., Deborah Basso, John Goldkrand, and William Butler. 1991. "Low Level of Maternal Serum Alpha-Fetoprotein: Its Associated Anxiety and the Effects of Genetic Counseling." *American Journal of Obstetrics and Gynecology* 164: 54–56.

Kenen, Regina. 1984. "Genetic Counseling: The Development of a New Interdisciplinary Occupational Field." *Social Science and Medicine* 18: 541–549.

Kessler, Seymour. 1992. "Process Issues in Genetic Counseling." In Gerry Evers-Kieboom, Jean-Pierre Fryns, Jean-Jacques Cassiman, and Herman Van den Gerghe, eds., *Psychosocial Aspects of Genetic Counseling. Birth Defects: Original Article Series* 28, no. 1. New York: Wiley-Liss.

Kessler, Seymour, and Anna Gioia Jacopini. 1982. "Psychological Aspects of Genetic Counseling II: Qualitative Analysis of a Transcript of a Genetic Counseling Session." *American Journal of Medical Genetics* 12: 421–435.

Kevles, Daniel J., and Leroy Hood., eds. 1992. *The Code of Codes: Scientific and Social Issues in the Human Genome Project.* Cambridge, Mass.: Harvard University Press.

Klass, Perri. 1989. "The Perfect Baby?" *New York Times Magazine,* January 29, p. 45.

Kolata, Gina. 1988. "Fetal Sex Test Used As a Step to Abortion." *New York Times,* December 2, pp. 1 and 38.

Kolata, Gina. 1990. *The Baby Doctors.* New York: Doubleday.

Kolata, Gina. 1991. "Hemophiliacs, Hit Hard by H.I.V., Are Angrily Looking for Answers." *New York Times,* December 25, p. A7.

Kolata, Gina. 1993. "Miniature Scope Gives the Earliest Pictures of a Developing Embryo." *New York Times,* July 6, pp. B6.

Kolker, Aliza. 1975. "The Diffusion of Innovation in Adult Education." Unpublished Ph.D. dissertation, Columbia University Graduate School of Arts and Sciences, Department of Sociology.

Kolker, Aliza, and B. Meredith Burke. 1987. "Amniocentesis and the Social Construction of Pregnancy." *Journal of Marriage and Family Review* 11(3/4): 95–116.

Kolker, Aliza, B. Meredith Burke, and Jane U. Phillips. 1991. "Attitudes About Abortion of Women Who Undergo Prenatal Diagnosis." In *Research in the Sociology of Health Care* 9: 49–73.

Koonin, Lisa M., Jack C. Smith, Merrell Ramick, and Herschel W. Lawson. 1992. "Abortion Surveillance—United States, 1989." *Morbidity and Mortality Weekly Report 41 Special Supplement #5.*

Kristof, Nicholas D. 1993a. "China's Crackdown on Births: A Stunning, and Harsh, Success." *New York Times,* April 25, pp. 1, 12.

Kristof, Nicholas D. 1993b. "Peasants of China Discover New Way to Weed out Girls." *New York Times,* July 21, pp. A1, A4.

Larsen, John W., Jr., and Martha D. MacMillin. 1989. "Second and Third Trimester Prenatal Diagnosis." In Evans et al., *Fetal Diagnosis and Therapy,* pp. 36–43.

Lessing, Doris. 1988. *The Fifth Child.* New York: Alfred A. Knopf.

Lilford, R. J. 1990. *Prenatal Diagnosis and Prognosis.* London: Butterworths.

Lippman-Hand, A., and F. C. Fraser. 1979. "Genetic Counseling—The Post-Counseling Period: Parents' Perceptions of Uncertainty." *American Journal of Medical Genetics* 4: 51–71.

Lo, Y-M D., J. S. Wainscoat, M.D.G. Gillmer, P. Patel, M. Sampietro, and K. A. Fleming. 1989. "Prenatal Sex Determination by DNA Amplification from Maternal Peripheral Blood." *The Lancet,* December 9, pp. 1363–1365.

Luker, Kristen. 1976. *Taking Chances: Abortion and the Decision Not to Contracept.* Berkeley: University of California Press.

Luker, Kristen. 1984. *Abortion and the Politics of Motherhood.* Berkeley: University of California Press.

Manning, Frank A. 1990. "The Use of Sonography in the Evaluation of High-Risk Pregnancy." *Radiologic Clinics of North America* (281): 205–216, January.

Markle, Gerald E., and Charles B. Nam. 1971. "Sex Predetermination: Its Impact on Fertility." *Social Biology* 18(1): 73–83.

Marks, Joan H., 1989. "Foreword." In Marks, Joan H., Audrey Heimler, Elsa Reich, Nancy S. Wexler, and Susan E. Ince, eds., *Genetic Counseling Principles in Action: A Casebook. Birth Defects: Original Article Series* 25(2): v–vii. White Plains, N.Y.: March of Dimes Birth Defects Foundation.

Marteau, Theresa M., Rachel Cook, Jane Kidd, et al. 1992a. "The Psychological Effects of False-Positive Results in Prenatal Screening for Fetal Abnormality: A Prospective Study." *Prenatal Diagnosis* 12: 205–214.

Marteau, Theresa M., J. Slack, Jane Kidd, and R. W. Shaw. 1992b. "Presenting a Routine Screening Test in Antenatal Care: Practice Observed." *Public Health* 106: 131–141.

McKusick, Victor A. 1990. *Mendelian Inheritance in Man*. 9th ed. Baltimore: Johns Hopkins University Press.

Merton, Robert K. 1968. *Social Theory and Social Structure*. New York: Free Press.

Metheny, William P., Gerald B. Holzman, Jeffrey Taylor, William Young, and James V. Higgins. 1988. "Amniocentesis Use and Risk Awareness: Comparison of Knowledge and Beliefs Among Older Gravida." *Social Biology* 35(1/2): 50–61.

Milunsky, Aubrey, and Elliot Alpert. 1984. "Results and Benefits of a Maternal Serum Alpha-Fetoprotein Screening Program." *Journal of the American Medical Association* 252: 1438–1442.

Miny, P., P. Hammer, B. Gerlach, S. Tercanli, J. Horst, W. Holzgreve, and B. Eiben. 1991. "Mosaicism and Accuracy of Prenatal Cytogenetic Diagnoses After Chorionic Villus Sampling and Placental Biopsies." *Prenatal Diagnosis* 11(8): 581–589, August.

Model, Bernadette. 1986. "Some Social Implications of Early Fetal Diagnosis." In Bruno Brambati et al., *Chorionic Villus Sampling*, pp. 259–274. New York: Marcel Dekker.

Modell, Judith. 1989. "Last Chance Babies: Interpretations of Parenthood in an In Vitro Fertilization Program." *Medical Anthropology Quarterly* 3(2): 124–138.

Moore, Roscoe M., Jr., Lana L. Jeng, Ronald G. Kaczmarek, and Paul J. Placek. 1990. "Use of Diagnostic Ultrasound, X-Ray Examinations, and Electronic Fetal Monitoring in Perinatal Medicine." *Journal of Perinatology* X(4): 361–365.

Nance, Walter E. 1993. "Parables." In Bartels et al., eds., *Prescribing Our Future*, pp. 89–94.

National Institute of Child Health and Human Development (NICHD), 1984. "Diagnostic Ultrasound Imaging in Pregnancy." Washington, D.C.: U.S. Government Printing Office, NIH Publication No. 84–667.

National Institutes of Health, 1992. "NIH Workshop Statement: Reproductive Genetic Testing: Impact on Women." *American Journal of Human Genetics* 51: 1161–1163.

Natowicz, Marvin R., Jane K. Alper, and Joseph S. Alper. 1992. "Genetic Discrimination and the Law." *American Journal of Human Genetics* 50: 465–475.

Nsiah-Jefferson, Laurie. 1993. "Access to Reproductive Genetic Services for Low-Income Women and Women of Color." *Fetal Diagnosis and Therapy* 8: 107–127, April.

O'Brien, Greg D. 1989. "Limits of Ultrasound Screening for Anomalies." *Contemporary OB/GYN*, pp. 51–57, July.

Oelsner, Lesley. 1978. "Doctor Held Liable in Abnormal Births." *New York Times*, December 28, pp. A1 and B6.

Oustifine, Joan. 1990. "Abortion After Amniocentesis: Women's Lived Experiences." Paper presented at Massachusetts General Hospital, Boston, Mass., June 21.

Patel, Suha. 1991. "The Dilemma of Sex Selection: The Issue in India." *Perspectives in Genetic Counseling* 13(2): 1, 6, Summer.

Penso, Christine A., Mary M. Sandstorm, Mary-Frances Garber, et al. 1990. "Early Amniocentesis: Report of 407 Cases with Neonatal Follow-Up." *Obstetrics and Gynecology* 76(6): 1032–1036, December.

The Perfumed Garden of the Sheik Nefzaoui: a Manual of Arabian Erotology. 1964. New York: Lancer Books.

Piontelli, Alessandra. 1992. *From Fetus to Child*. London and New York: Tavistock/Routledge.

Pitz, Gordon F. 1987. "Evaluating Decision Aiding Technologies for Genetic Counseling." *Birth Defects* 23(2): 251–278.

Plauche, Warren. 1993. "Maternal-Fetal Medicine." *Journal of the American Medical
Association* 269(6): 802, February 10.

Pollitt, Katha. 1988. "Children of Choice." *New York Times Magazine,* November 20.

Powledge, Tabitha M. 1983. "Toward a Moral Policy for Sex Choice." In Neil G.
Bennet, ed., *Sex Selection of Children*, pp. 201–213. New York: Academic Press.

Powledge, Tabitha M. 1984. *The Last Taboo: Genetic Manipulation and Eugenics.* Boston: Houghton Mifflin.

President's Commission for the Study of Ethical Problems in Medicine and Biomedical
and Behavioral Research. 1983. *Deciding to Forego Life-Sustaining Treatment.*
Washington, D.C.: U.S. Government Printing Office.

Press, Nancy A., and C. H. Browner. 1993. " 'Collective Fictions': Similarities in Reasons for Accepting Maternal Serum Alpha-Fetoprotein Screening Among Women
of Diverse Ethnic and Social Class Backgrounds." *Fetal Diagnosis and Therapy*
8: 97–106.

Proctor, Robert N. 1988. *Racial Hygiene: Medicine under the Nazis.* Boston: Harvard
University Press.

Pruggmayer, M., P. Baumann, H. Schutte, R. Osmers, I. Bartels, V. Jovanovich, and R.
Rauskolb. 1991. "Incidence of Abortion After Genetic Amniocentesis in Twin
Pregnancies." *Prenatal Diagnosis* 11(8): 637–640, August.

Quindlen, Anna. 1988. "The Child I Carry is Wanted, Healthy or Not." *New York Times*,
May 12.

Rapp, Rayna. 1988a. "Chromosomes and Communication: The Discourse of Genetic
Counseling." *Medical Anthropology Quarterly* 2: 143–157.

Rapp, Rayna. 1988b. "Moral Pioneers: Women, Men and Fetuses on a Frontier of Reproductive Technology." *Women and Health* 13(1/2): 101–116.

Rhoads, George G., et al. 1989. "The Safety and Efficacy of Chorionic Villus Sampling
for Early Prenatal Diagnosis of Cytogenetic Abnormalities." *New England Journal of Medicine* 320: 609–617, March 9.

Rhoden, Nancy K. 1986. "Treating Baby Doe: The Ethics of Uncertainty." *Hastings
Center Report*, August, pp. 34–42.

Rogers, Everett M., and F. Floyd Shoemaker. 1971. *Communication of Innovation.* New
York: Free Press.

Rothman, Barbara Katz. 1983. "Prenatal Diagnosis and Genetic Counseling: New Issues
for Sociological Research." Paper presented at the annual meeting of the Eastern
Sociological Society, Baltimore, March 4–6.

Rothman, Barbara Katz. 1986. *The Tentative Pregnancy.* New York: Viking Press.

Rothman, Barbara Katz. 1989. *Recreating Motherhood.* New York: W. W. Norton.

Rothman, Barbara Katz. 1992. "Not All That Glitters Is Gold." *Hastings Center Report:
Special Supplement*, July-August, pp. S11–S15.

Rubin, Jeffrey, Frank Provenzano, and Zella Luria. 1974. "The Eye of the Beholder:
Parents' Views on Sex of Newborns." *American Journal of Orthopsychiatry* 44:
47–55.

Schwager, Edward J., and Barry D. Weiss. 1987. "Prenatal Testing for Maternal Serum
Alpha-Fetoprotein." *American Family Physician* 35(4): 169–174, April.

Seligmann, Jean, and Donna Foote. 1991. "Whose Baby is it Anyway?" *Newsweek*,
October 28, p. 73.

Simonds, Wendy, and Barbara Katz Rothman. 1992. *Centuries of Solace.* Philadelphia: Temple University Press.

Simoni, G., Bruno Brambati, C. Danesino, et al. 1984. "Diagnostic Applications of First Trimester Trophoblast Sampling in 100 Pregnancies." *Human Genetics* 66: 252.

Siraisi, Nancy G. 1990. *Medieval and Early Renaissance Medicine.* Chicago: University of Chicago Press.

Sjogren, B., and N. Uddenberg. 1989. "Prenatal Diagnosis and Psychological Distress: Amniocentesis or Chorionic Villus Biopsy?" *Prenatal Diagnosis* 9: 477–487.

Slovic, Paul. 1987. "Perception of Risk." *Science* 236: 280–285, April.

Sorenson, James R. 1973. "Counselors: A Self Portrait." *Genetic Counseling* 1(5): 29–33.

Sorenson, James R. 1993. "Genetic Counseling: Values That Have Mattered." In Bartels et al., eds., *Prescribing Our Future,* pp. 3–15.

Sorenson, James R., Judith P. Swazey, and Norman A. Scotch. 1981. "Reproductive Pasts, Reproductive Futures: Genetic Counseling and Its Effectiveness." *Birth Defects: Original Article Series* 17: 4.

Sorenson, James R., and Dorothy C. Wertz. 1986. "Couple Agreement Before and After Genetic Counseling." *American Journal of Medical Genetics* 25: 549–555.

Starr, Chauncey. 1969. "Social Benefits Versus Technological Risk." *Science* 165: 1232–1238.

Statham, Helen, and Josephine Green. 1993. "Serum Screening for Down's Syndrome: Some Women's Experiences." *British Medical Journal* 307: 174–176, July 17.

Steinbock, Bonnie. 1992. *Life Before Birth.* New York: Oxford University Press.

Steinfels, Margaret O'Brien. 1980. "The Supreme Court and Sex Choice." *Hastings Center Report* 10: 19–20.

Stenchever, Morton A. 1992. "The Lesser Tragedy." *Obstetrics and Gynecology* 80: 300, August.

Sutton, Agneta. 1990. *Prenatal Diagnosis: Confronting the Ethical Issues.* London: Linacre Centre for the Study of Ethics in Health Care.

Swinfield, Ann, Lorna Phelps, and Jean Mather. 1988. "Countertransference in the Counseling Setting." *Perspectives in Genetic Counseling* 10(3): 1, 4.

Thase, Michael E. 1982. "Longevity and Mortality in Down's Syndrome." *Journal of Mental Deficiency Research* 26: 177–192.

Thomas, William I., and Dorothy S. Thomas. 1928. *The Child in America.* New York: Alfred A. Knopf.

Thompson, Margaret W., Roderick R. McInnes, and Huntington F. Willard. 1991. *Genetics in Medicine.* 5th ed. Philadelphia: W. B. Saunders Co.

Torres, A., and Jacqueline D. Forrest. 1988. "Why Do Women Have Abortions?" *Family Planning Perspectives* 20(4): 169–176, July/August.

U.S. Bureau of the Census. 1988. *Statistical Abstracts of the United States.* Washington, D.C.

Van den Anker, J. N., E. E. van Vught, G.R.J. Zandwijken, et al. 1993. "Severe Limb Abnormalities: Analysis of a Cluster of Five Cases Born During a Period of 45 Days." *American Journal of Medical Genetics* 45: 659–667.

Verjaal, Marianne, Nico J. Leschot, and Pieter E. Treffers. 1982. "Women's Experiences with Second Trimester Prenatal Diagnosis." *Prenatal Diagnosis* 2: 195–209.

Vlek, Charles. 1987. "Risk Assessment, Risk Perception and Decision Making About Courses of Action Involving Genetic Risk: An Overview of Concepts and Methods." *Birth Defects* 23(2): 171–207.

Walker, Molly K. 1992. "Maternal Reactions to Fetal Sex." *Health Care for Women International* 13(3): 293–302, July–September.

Waller, D. Kim, Linda S. Lustig, George Cunningham, et al. 1991. "Second-Trimester Maternal Serum Alpha-Fetoprotein Levels and the Risk of Subsequent Fetal Death." *New England Journal of Medicine* 325: 6–10, July 4.

Warren, Mary Anne. 1985. *Gendercide: The Implications of Sex Selection.* Totowa, N.J.: Rowman & Allanheld.

Weaver, David D. 1988. "A Survey of Prenatally Diagnosed Disorders." *Clinical Obstetrics and Gynecology* 31(2): 253–264, June.

Weinstein, N. D., ed. 1987. *Taking Care.* Cambridge: Cambridge University Press.

Weitz, Rose. 1981. "Barriers to Acceptance of Genetic Counseling Among Primary Care Physicians." *Social Biology* 26: 189–193.

Wertz, Dorothy C., and John C. Fletcher. 1988. "Attitudes of Genetic Counselors: A Multinational Survey." *American Journal of Human Genetics* 42: 592–600.

Wertz, Dorothy C., and John C. Fletcher. 1989a. "Fatal Knowledge? Prenatal Diagnosis and Sex Selection." *Hastings Center Report* 19(3): 21–27, May/June.

Wertz, Dorothy C., and John C. Fletcher, eds. 1989b. *Ethics and Human Genetics: A Cross-Cultural Perspective.* Berlin: Springer-Verlag.

Wertz, Dorothy C., and John C. Fletcher. 1989c. "Fatal Knowledge? Prenatal Diagnosis and Sex Selection." Paper presented at the Meetings of the American Sociological Association, San Francisco, Calif., August 9–13.

Wertz, Dorothy C., Janet M. Rosenfield, Sally R. Janes, and Richard Erbe. 1991. "Attitudes Toward Abortion Among Parents of Children with Cystic Fibrosis." *American Journal of Public Health* 81(8): 992–996.

Wertz, Dorothy C., and James R. Sorenson. 1984. "Genetic Counseling and Reproductive Uncertainty." *American Journal of Medical Genetics* 18: 79–88.

Wertz, Dorothy C., James R. Sorenson, and Timothy C. Heeren. 1986. "Clients' Interpretation of Risks Provided in Genetic Counseling." *American Journal of Human Genetics* 39: 253–264.

Wertz, Dorothy C., James R. Sorenson, and Timothy C. Heeren. 1988. "Communication in Health Professional–Lay Encounters: How Often Does Each Party Know What the Other Wants to Discuss?" In Brent D. Ruben, ed., *Information and Behavior,* vol. 2, pp. 329–342. New Brunswick, N.J.: Transaction Books.

Wertz, Dorothy C., and Richard W. Wertz (1977) 1989. *Lying-In: A History of Childbirth in America.* New Haven, Conn.: Yale University Press.

Westoff, C. F., and R. R. Rindfuss. 1974. "Sex Preselection in the United States: Some Implications." *Science* 184: 633–636, May 10.

Wexler, Nancy S. 1992. "The Tiresias Complex: Huntington's Disease as a Paradigm of Testing for Late-Onset Disorders." *Federation of American Societies for Experimental Biology* 6: 2820–2825.

Wilcox, A. J., C. R. Weinberg, J. F. O'Connor, D. D. Baird, J. P. Schlatterer, R. E. Canfield, E. G. Armstrong, and B. C. Nisula. July 28, 1988. "Incidence of Early Loss of Pregnancy." *New England Journal of Medicine* 319(4): 189–194.

Wilfond, Benjamin S., and Norman Fost, 1992. "The Introduction of Cystic Fibrosis Carrier Screening into Clinical Practice: Policy Considerations." *The Milbank Quarterly* 70(4): 629–659.

Williams, Dorie Giles. 1982. "Religion, Beliefs About Human Life, and the Abortion Decision." *Review of Religious Research* 24(1): 40–48, September.

Williams, John, III, Boris B. T. Wang, Cathy H. Rubin, and Dawn Aiken-Hunting. 1992. "Chorionic Villus Sampling: Experience with 3016 Cases Performed by a Single Operator." *Obstetrics & Gynecology* 80(6): 1023–1029, December.

Williamson, Nancy. 1983. "Parental Sex Preferences and Sex Selection." In Neil G. Bennet, ed., *Sex Selection of Children,* pp. 129–151. New York: Academic Press.

Zabin, Laurie Schwab, Marilyn B. Hirsch, and Mark R. Emerson. 1989. "When Urban Adolescents Choose Abortion: Effects on Education, Psychological Status and Subsequent Pregnancy." *Family Planning Perspectives* 21 (6): 248–255, November/December.

Zare, Nancy, James R. Sorenson, and Timothy C. Heeren. 1984. "Sex of Provider as a Variable in Effective Genetic Counseling." *Social Science and Medicine* 19(7): 671–675.

Zimmerman, Mary K. 1977. *Passage Through Abortion: The Personal and Social Reality of Women's Experiences.* New York: Praeger.

Index

Abortion, 107–122; 122–140; attitudes of clients in current study, 110–117; attitudes of counselors, 120–122; attitudes of the American public, 110–113; availability, 7, 175; conflict between "pro-choice" and "pro-life" views, 109–110, 157, 174; counseling the decision, 41, 54–56, 128, 138; decisions, 72–74, 108–110; euphemisms in counseling materials, 24; following amniocentesis, 129–131; following CVS, 131–134, 138; frequency among clients in current study, 88; frequency in U.S. population, 89; and motherhood, 118–120; and parents of handicapped children, 125, 127; psychological implications, 7, 107–108, 127; psychological reactions to "genetic" or "therapeutic," 127; reactions of friends and community, 135, 138; religious objections to, 56–59; 84, 113, 174; risks associated with, 129, 169; for sex selection, 145, 155–158, 159–162;

socioeconomic status and attitudes toward, 83, 113–117; specifics of procedures, 41; support groups for parents, 135–136, 139; and women's roles, 108–110, 145. *See also* Clients; Genetic counseling; Genetic counselors; Grief and bereavement

Absalom, Absalom (Faulkner), and sex preference, 143

Adler, Bernard, 74, 127

AFP (Alpha-fetoprotein) screening: cost-benefit analyses, 22; counseling the client, 40–41; description and history, 3, 21–25; false positives, 22, 23, 51; problems with informed consent, 40, 89 n; psychological costs, 23; socioeconomic background of referred clients, 84. *See also* Clients; Genetic counseling

Alzheimer's disease, 165

American Board of Genetic Counseling, 32

American Board of Medical Genetics, 32

American College of Obstetricians and

About the Authors and Contributor

ALIZA KOLKER is Associate Professor of Sociology and Anthropology at George Mason University. She is the author or editor of three previous books on health and policy issues.

B. MEREDITH BURKE has taught health and demographic policy courses at a number of universities (most recently at San Jose State University). She has done health consultancies in the U.S. and overseas.

Both authors have published extensively in professional journals and news media about genetics and health care issues.

ARTHUR L. CAPLAN is Trustee Professor of Bioethics and Director of the Center for Biomedical Ethics at the University of Pennsylvania. He has taught at the University of Minnesota, University of Pittsburgh, and Columbia University. He is the author of numerous books and over 300 journal articles.